New Space for Women

Other Westview Titles on Women and Society

The Underside of History: A View of Women Through Time, Elise Boulding

Women and the Social Costs of Economic Development: Two Colorado Case Studies, Elizabeth Moen, Elise Boulding, Jane Lillydahl, and Risa Palm

Women and Technological Change in Developing Countries, edited by Roslyn Dauber and Melinda Cain

Working Women: A Study of Women in Paid Jobs, edited by Ann Seidman

Women in Changing Japan, edited by Joyce Lebra, Joy Paulson, and Elizabeth Powers

The Liberated Female: Life, Work and Sex in Socialist Hungary, Ivan Volgyes and Nancy Volgyes

Also of Interest

New Architecture in the World, Udo Kultermann

The City: An Introduction to Patterns and Processes in the Urban Ecosystem, Gary L. Peters and Robert P. Larkin

Westview Special Studies on Women in Contemporary Society

New Space for Women
edited by Gerda R. Wekerle,
Rebecca Peterson, and David Morley

In recent years, increasing self-awareness has led women to examine and question their environments—largely designed and structured by men—in light of their particular needs and experiences. Inevitably, these changes in consciousness have led to demands for changes in existing architectural, social, and psychological environments and for an increased role for women in their design.

This book—the first such collection of papers on women and their environments—addresses specific problems encountered in homes and office buildings, in urban and suburban areas, and in neighborhoods, and assesses the institutional barriers to change that have prevented women's needs from being adequately addressed in the decisionmaking process. Included are examples of the creative solutions and alternatives that women have proposed.

Gerda R. Wekerle (Ph.D., sociology), Rebecca Peterson (Ph.D., psychology), and David Morley (Ph.D., geography) are associate professors in the Faculty of Environmental Studies at York University.

New Space for Women

edited by Gerda R. Wekerle, Rebecca Peterson, and David Morley

Westview Press / Boulder, Colorado

Westview Special Studies on Women in Contemporary Society

Copyright © 1980 by Gerda R. Wekerle, Rebecca Peterson, and David Morley

Published in 1980 in the United States of America by
   Westview Press, Inc.
   5500 Central Avenue
   Boulder, Colorado 80301
   Frederick A. Praeger, Publisher

Library of Congress Cataloging in Publication Data
Main entry under title:
New space for women.
   (Westview special studies on women in contemporary society)
   1. Women—Social conditions—Addresses, essays, lectures. 2. Women—Political activity—Addresses, essays, lectures. 3. Architecture—Environmental aspects—Addresses, essays, lectures. 4. Architecture—Psychological aspects—Addresses, essays, lectures. 5. Architecture—Human factors—Addresses, essays, lectures. 6. Human ecology—Addresses, essays, lectures. I. Wekerle, Gerda R. II. Peterson, Rebecca. III. Morley, C. D.
HQ1154.N46   305.4   80-5047
ISBN 0-89158-775-6

Printed and bound in the United States of America

Contents

Part 1
The Domestic Workplace

Part 2
Urban Design: The Price Women Pay

**Part 3
Women in Environmental Decisionmaking:
Institutional Constraints**

**Part 4
Women as Environmental Activists**

Tables and Figures

Preface

This book was started shortly after the United Nations Conference on Human Settlements, 1976, held in Vancouver. That conference brought together an international group of women from government, voluntary organizations, the professions, and the academic community to discuss the role of women in the planning and design of urban settlements. We organized one of the eight conference sessions and were struck by the fact that women's problems with housing, transportation, urban planning, and lack of access to environmental decisions crossed national boundaries and affected women in advanced industrial countries as well as those in developing countries. For many of us, there was a great sense of excitement and joy to discover women (and some men) from other countries who also viewed urban issues as feminist issues. We felt that we were witnessing the birth of an exciting new interdisciplinary field—one that combined an interest in the urban environment with feminist analysis and consciousness.

There were not many of us and we were spread thinly across the globe. A major problem was information and support. The three of us started a newsletter to maintain and help expand our international network. We planned this book to collect the various strands of the new empirical work on women's urban experience and women's activist role in changing environments. We did not anticipate that our "simple task" would stretch into four years and would involve contacts with more than 200 persons and organizations on four continents. In the spirit of the conference where the idea for this book was born, we envisioned a book that would be international in scope, inter-disciplinary in approach, and would include contributions by academics and professionals as well as community activists. These goals were only partially met. The difficulties posed by translation forced us to focus largely on the North American experience. Nonacademics are underrepresented, since we found that women active in setting up innovative feminist alternatives were often too busy "doing" to write about their experiences. We also found that much of the current work was still in prog-ress or barely started and thus could not be included.

Inevitably, as befits a new field, the quantity of new work has outstripped even our best efforts to include it. Interest in women and environments is now at an all-time high. In Wash-ington, D.C., HUD's Women's Policy and Program's staff is sponsoring several projects on women's housing and planning needs; in England, a recent issue of the *International Journal of Urban and Regional Research* has focused on British research and action relating to women in the city; in Canada, the Na-tional Action Committee on the Status of Women is planning a special magazine issue on women and environments; in Australia, interest in the topic remains strong, and several projects are currently underway; in Paris, an international research organiza-tion has started research for policymakers on women and city life in half a dozen countries. As yet, there are no books sum-marizing and evaluating this new work.

The chapters in this book represent the output of the first generation of researchers and writers on women and environ-ments. As such, it provides an overview of the framing of some very basic questions about women's roles, attitudes, and expec-tations—and their determination to change them—as related to the nature and effects of human environments. Because the work reported here comes from many different disciplines and professional backgrounds and has largely been carried out in-dependently without recourse to established and commonly accepted frameworks, it does not provide a final or complete record of the field, but serves as a basis for further research and action. However, there is a remarkable commonality in the writers' conclusions regarding the role the environment plays in reinforcing the social forces that limit women's potential in our society. The book demonstrates the depth and underlying strength of the Women's Movement as an expression of fundamental social change capable of initiating new world views and actions necessary to implement them. It also demonstrates the value of pursuing a contextual (environmental) approach to social problems.

For us this book is the result of four years' work—discovering potential authors, assembling and editing their material, and integrating the ideas of a developing new field. The introduction to the book evolved in the process of "naming and framing" the issues that emerged through the intensive network-building that was necessary to develop a collection of this kind. We have taught one of the first courses on women and environments; we have spoken at conferences and seminars, on radio and television; and we have written papers and edited our newsletter. The book is very much the outcome of this cooperative process of interaction with many individuals and institutions.

We are indebted to a number of people for help in creating this book: to our authors who made their material available to us, accepted our editing graciously, and remained patient throughout the time it took to finally complete this volume; and to our students in the Faculty of Environmental Studies, who were fired with enthusiasm to do original work and who contributed to the development of our early ideas. Our thanks also go to those members of the expanding "women and environments" network who have listened to us, commented on our work, and shared their own ideas so generously over the past four years. We are grateful to York University, and especially to Dean Rodger Schwass, who contributed several small grants to keep the project going. And finally, we thank our families, in particular Slade Lander, Larry Peterson, and Lydia Burton, who read numerous drafts, sympathized with our troubles, and celebrated our joys. For the rest, government institutions and funding agencies have never been quite sure where "women and environments" fits or if they should support studies in such a field. It is our firm belief that our concerns should be central to those who consider the environment as a base for developing social policy, especially to those involved in improving the quality of life for all those disadvantaged by the present distribution of society's wealth.

Gerda R. Wekerle
Rebecca Peterson
David Morley

The Contributors

Stephen Barton is a research associate with the Center for Policy Research, Columbia University.

Sarah Fenstermaker Berk is assistant professor of sociology at the University of California, Santa Barbara. She is currently writing a book on the division of household labor based on a national survey of husbands and wives.

Ellen Perry Berkeley is an architect and past senior editor of *Architectural Forum* and *Architecture Plus.* She is also a founder of the Women's School of Planning and Architecture.

Richard W. Butler is associate professor of geography at the University of Western Ontario.

Mary K. Cichocki is a planner for the Central Mortgage and Housing Corporation, Oshawa, Ontario.

Anne Cools is director of the Women in Transition House, Toronto.

Sheila Levrant de Bretteville is designer and cofounder of the Los Angeles Woman's Building, where she teaches graphic design. Her work is represented in the Graphic Design Collection of the Museum of Modern Art, and she has received awards from the American Institute of Graphic Arts and the Society of Publication Directors.

Sylvia F. Fava is professor of sociology and chairperson of the Interdepartmental Program in Urban Studies, Brooklyn College, City University of New York. She has published articles on suburbs and new communities and has authored and edited books on urban society.

Dolores Hayden is associate professor of architecture at the

University of California, Los Angeles. She is the author of a book on American utopias and has also written a forthcoming book on the history of feminist approaches to housing design, from which her chapter is taken.

Jenna Weissman Joselit is a graduate student in the Department of History, Columbia University.

Ronald Lawson is associate professor of urban studies at Queens College, City University of New York. Also a senior research associate for the Center for Policy Research, Columbia University, he is currently studying the social process of building abandonment in New York City.

Jacqueline Leavitt is a planner, instructor, and doctoral candidate in urban planning at Columbia University and taught one of the first courses on women and planning.

Susan Phillips is a planner for the Government of Ontario.

David Popenoe is professor of sociology at Rutgers University. A former Fulbright Research Scholar to Sweden, he is the author and editor of books on suburbs and cities.

Cynthia Rock is an architect in New York City and teaches at the New Jersey Institute of Technology.

Susan Saegert is associate professor of psychology in the Environmental Psychology Program, City University of New York Graduate Center. She has done research on women's needs in housing and neighborhoods, sex differences in children's development of environmental competence, and the effects of high-density environments.

Mary Soper is a graduate student in the Faculty of Environmental Design, University of Calgary.

Judy Stamp is a geographer with the Coordinated Social Program, City of Toronto.

Susana Torre is an architect at the Cooper Union for the Advancement of Science and Art and the New Jersey Institute of Technology. She is also the editor of a book on women in American architecture.

Karla Werner is an ethnologist and research fellow in the Department of Architecture, Royal Institute of Technology, Stockholm. She has authored articles on Greek culture and Swedish leisure patterns and is writing a book on women in single-family houses in Sweden.

Gary Winkel is associate professor of psychology and director of the Center for Human Environments, City University of New York Graduate Center. His current work involves studies of neighborhood change and the meanings and uses associated with various housing environments.

Gwendolyn Wright is an architect/historian at the University of California, Berkeley, and is the author of two forthcoming books on housing in America.

Introduction

Gerda R. Wekerle
Rebecca Peterson
David Morley

On the basis of their common experiences, most women recognize that they occupy different social and emotional worlds from men. This sense of difference has been heightened during recent years as a result of increasing self-awareness among women, changes in their relations with men, and desires to extend their social roles. Inevitably, these changes in consciousness have led to demands by women for changes in existing environments and for an increased role for women in the design of new environments.

Indirectly, the environment has long been the concern of writers on women's issues, and it has become clear that virtually all human environments are designed, built, and managed by male-dominated professions using assumptions that tend to reinforce existing female stereotypes. This has led to the creation of many environments that discriminate against women and a design process that gives little recognition to the changing needs of women. This sense of alienation, powerlessness, and dependency felt by so many women in the settings of their everyday lives has encouraged the emergence of the study of women and their environments.

A feminist approach to women's environments is likely to lead to the reevaluation of the settings women share with men, as well as to the reconsideration of women's needs for separate and distinct environments. Focusing on "environment" provides a means of explaining from a new standpoint the nature of women's roles, a new framework for suggesting the directions of social change concerning women, and a new context for social action.

Women and Environments as a Field of Study

Three groups of feminists have been involved in the development of this new area of study: (1) design and planning professionals, (2) academic researchers, and (3) environmental activists. The first group is made up of feminist architects, designers, and planners—members of the professions responsible for the actual built forms of the environment. These women have been questioning their own roles in what are predominantly male-oriented work settings. In particular, they have begun to recognize that many of the decisions they are making as professionals are in direct opposition to their instincts and values as women, especially as those decisions concern other women who will use the environments they are helping to create. Such individual reactions were reinforced as continuing contacts between women professionals led to the creation of on-going networks.[1]

A further expression of this activity among women environmental design professionals has been the setting up of a number of architectural design firms by groups of women with the intention of developing both an alternative workplace setting and environmental designs based on a feminist viewpoint. In addition, sessions on women's environments at professional conferences and associated publications have demonstrated a distinctive feminist critique of existing architecture and design in relation to the needs of women.

The second group of people to become involved in the question of women and environments were researchers drawn from a variety of social science and humanities disciplines: sociology, psychology, geography, anthropology, political science, environmental studies, history, and others. In particular, the topic was a natural area of concern for feminists whose work was associated with multidisciplinary "environment and behavior" studies.[2] The three editors of this book have all worked within this new perspective. Researchers in this field are working on the question of the "fit" between the environments we inhabit and the behavior we are trying to carry out within those environments. Behavior is broadly defined to include "perceptual" images that influence the way we respond to and shape our environments, as well as actions taken in particular settings. Within this field, issues of user participation and user control over environments are often raised, alongside extended research into human needs in environments. Researchers often work in conjunction with planners and architects, encouraging those practitioners to modify the way in which they create environments and challenging them to pay more attention to the people who are to inhabit these spaces.

There have also been links between the researchers working in this area and the active women environmental professionals. For example, conference sessions on women and environment have been held at the annual meetings of the Environmental Design Research Association—an organization for both social scientists and architects—during the past several years. Recently a newsletter was started in hope of establishing contacts between people actively engaged in women and environments research and related activities.[3] The opportunity for the exchange of ideas and information, and for the development of contacts between the researchers and professionals working in the field, is unusually well developed for such a new and widely dispersed interdisciplinary field.

Finally, an extremely important group working in the field consists of those activist feminists who have long been intervening directly in environmental decisionmaking on behalf of women. Indeed, they have become even more active as women's issues have become more visible. The group includes originators of innovative social services for women—emergency housing, rape crisis centers, women's art centers, information and resource centers, birth centers, and so on. Also included are women who have played leadership roles in community groups or who have otherwise taken active stands on behalf of women's environmental needs at various levels of government.

This book pulls together, for the first time, the ideas and experiences of all three groups working on women and environment issues—the designers and planners, the social scientists, and the activists. The latter are somewhat underrepresented, for although they are involved in many exciting and innovative projects, these women are often too busy actively creating social change to sit down and write about their experiences. We hope that this initial compilation of the current trends in women and environment studies will act as a catalyst to others and provide the basis for further research and action.

The Meaning of Environments to Women

Human environments reflect far more than the stylistic intention of their designers or the functional uses for which they are intended. To the acute observer they display a mass of social images and symbols that suggest the character of the people who will be likely to use a particular space—their age, class, racial origins, *and* their sex. Even the general patterns of behavior in that space and their relationships to the overall life-style of the users are distinctively associated with particular settings. A bar or restaurant, a resort or campsite, one suburb rather than another, a supermarket or a boardroom—all contain distinct clues as to the kinds of people who occupy them and the activities they might be expected to carry out. This social stereotyping of people and environments also has the effect of reinforcing the social order, with all its inherent prejudices and discriminatory practices.

Similarly, to the individuals experiencing a particular environment, its "meaning" is also expressed by a myriad of clues and messages, selected and interpreted by them on the basis of their experience and expectations of that or similar settings. This combination of sociocultural and psychological expressions of reality results in both a unique individual state and a set of shared characteristics for groups with common backgrounds and experiences.

We use the term "environment" in two overlapping ways: first, it is used in a broad sense to refer to the total set of forces (sociocultural, psychological, and institutional) that define the behavior settings confronting women and reflect the habitual social roles that women are expected to perform in a given setting. This broad definition of the social environment provides a basis for the consideration of women's responses to a wide set of forces with respect to home, workplace, public institutions, and other settings by putting them within the overall social context. The second use of "environment" relates to the physical or "built" attributes of women's behavior settings—their location, design, and management—and their direct effects on the lives of the women involved in them as residents, patients, students, employees, customers, managers, and so on.

In the first approach the total social milieu is defined, and this, of course, "wraps around" the specific physical behavior settings characterized in the second approach to the environment—the actual functional settings in which women's social roles are played out, and where the pressure for change can be focused both on the limitations of women's roles and on the institutions controlling their environments.

In practical terms, women and environments studies first had to establish the nature of the distinctive behavior settings in which women operate—homes, schools, workplaces, public facilities, commercial settings, public open spaces, and so on—and to consider these "built" environments in terms of the distinctive meanings, images, and symbols with which women respond to their experiences in them. Much of the initial women and environments research also aimed at establishing the nature of the discrimination that women feel they are suffering in urban environments. This led to a focus on domestic and neighborhood environments and particularly on low density suburban residential settings. Such work was particularly important in the early problem definition phase, when it was necessary to establish without doubt that a problem existed—something widely denied!

A second aspect of women and environments studies has been the examination of women's roles (or lack of them) in the personal, communal, and institutional processes that create built environments and an investigation of the extent to which women's needs are taken into account in such decision processes. A third area of activity has been the examination of the role of past and present women environmental activists, comparing their impact with the likely future effects on human environments of an increase in women's influence. Finally, the need for an increased role by women in the creation of environments sensitive to their needs has to be examined in the light of critical issues facing Western society—economic constraints, environmental limitations, energy and resource shortages, and the demand for equal rights by other minority groups. The ultimate concern here is to determine what effects women might have on such problems through the development of innovative environmental responses in a time of general uncertainty.

The Definition of Women's Environments

Three basic distinctions help to identify the characteristics of women's environments: the *degree of segregation* between the sexes in the activities carried out in a given environment; the *intensity and nature of occupance* of a space by women users; and the *extent of control* over environments by women users.[4] These dimensions underlie the primary limitations placed on women in the environmental context: limitations on access, on the range of activities they carry out, and on the degree of autonomy they possess in different settings.

The *segregation of environments by gender* refers first to the physical separation of users of one sex as a result of the application of restrictive regulations (a women's or men's club) or as a result of biological differences (a rape center or birth environment). These formally segregated environments are, in fact, a less common cause of the concentration of users of one gender than instances of "segregation" created by social pressure or accepted practice in environments that are supposedly "mixed." Such constraints include the traditional limitations on women's mobility in remote areas or at night—their withdrawal from "environments of risk"—like inner-city streets, parks, some bars and sporting events, and from "extreme" environments like the polar regions, high mountains, outer space, and so on. Another class of "virtually" segregated environments relates to the clustering of members of one sex in spaces associated with sex-typed activities or occupations. Typing pools, nursery schools, and hospital nursing stations are examples of role-segregated environments for women; stock exchanges, boardrooms, and legislative assemblies are examples for men.

The *intensity and character of women's occupance* of certain

classes of environments relates to the significantly large proportion of their time that is spent there in comparison to men.
This distinction emphasizes the fundamental division of social
spaces in our modern culture into male-dominated public and
institutional spaces and female-occupied private or domestic
spaces. This distinction, which runs through much of the
women's studies literature, translates directly into the environmental context and lies at the heart of the major problems
associated with human environments from the women's viewpoint. As such, the environment is mirroring the nature of
women's traditional social roles of childrearing and homemaking that are performed within the realm of the localized family
space. In this respect, one of the overriding themes of this book
becomes the corollary of that status—that women have limited
access to, and a low intensity of occupance of, environments
outside the local sphere and that within those public spaces
they tend to perform subordinate or marginal roles.

The third criterion effective in the definition of women's
environments—the *degree of control that women possess in
their environments*—derives directly from the effects of segregation and the nature of female occupance of the environment. At
two different levels women lack effective control over the extent, form, and location of environments vital to their lives.
The first applies to the overall control over environments that
is in the hands of public and private institutions, which are
largely inaccessible to women at the decisionmaking level.
Institutions such as banks and finance companies, those within
the development and construction industries, the various government departments associated with human environments, and
the design, planning, and architectural professions together
command "authority" (that is, the right to make decisions)
over the form of local environments. The second level at which
women lack control over their environments is the local level in
the immediate environments of everyday contact where women
are normally assumed to have a measure of "power" (that is,
the ability to act effectively on persons or things) over the spaces
they predominantly occupy. However, control over the allocation of resources to create domestic environments and other
micro behavior settings occupied by women still resides in a

male-dominated public system that views women as "passive clients . . . accepting the spatial and social traditions which the environments they create enshrine" (Hayden and Wright, 1976).

Defined in these terms, women's environments reflect the subordinate roles allocated to women in our industrialized, urban society; furthermore, women's skills derived from the domestic setting are devalued, and women are virtually excluded from the levels of authority that control all environments—domestic as well as public. This view generates the primary themes of our book on women and their environments; it is largely supported by our contributors' conclusions and by findings in the wider field of study.

The Basic Themes of Women and Environments

The Household as Workplace

An analysis of women and environments must begin with the home environment, since we cannot understand woman's place in the city and in the public sphere without understanding her place in the home. The home remains a critical element of concern for all women because it marks the first hurdle to be crossed in any woman's attempts to expand her roles and overcome the social discrimination leveled at her. The assumption that "a woman's place is in the home" affects the way women are dealt with both in the domestic and in the public sphere (Boulding, 1977). For this reason, equal access to opportunities outside the home first requires the liberation of women from full-time responsibility for the home.

The separation of the home environment from public life and the denial of the economic contribution of domestic work are still the primary societal factors that lie behind women's problems in relation to the home. Women's traditional association with the home has been a major stumbling block to their access to the wider opportunities of the city. As a result, modern industrial cities are segregated into men's and women's spaces: women are viewed as "belonging" in the private domestic sphere of the home and neighborhood; men are dominant in the public sphere of the market workplace, public institutions, and political influence. This sexually segregated, public-private dichotomy is fundamental to modern capitalist societies and is reinforced by urban planning and design decisions.

The segregation of society into distinct male and female spheres of work and influence has not always existed. Before the Industrial Revolution women were involved in the production of goods and services and their domestic labor was integral to the productive activity of the family. As the family was the basic unit of economic production, there was no split between home and work (Zaretsky, 1976:29). Women also worked outside the home in cottage industries, agriculture, the textile industry, and as members of various guilds (Oakley, 1974:2). Houses were small and, rather than existing as a separate activity, housework was integrated with the overall work of the family (Oakley, 1974:2–23). Child care was not a separate activity but was carried on at work and often shared with other members of the family, and children were considered independent at an early age.

Industrialization fundamentally altered women's relationship to work and to the home. In the eighteenth century, men's work was shifted from the home to the factory (Bernard, 1975:231). Women gradually lost positions in those industries in which they had been accepted (Oakley, 1974:34). This gradual constriction of the women's world into the space of the home was justified by a growing ideology of women's natural domesticity and a new emphasis on the family and home as a refuge—a personal world that afforded protection from the anonymity of industrial society.

The emphasis on a separate sphere of personal life, with its new focus on childrearing and the home as a center of family activities, required a separate class of housewives and mothers whose sole responsibility was the care and maintenance of this sphere (Zaretsky, 1976:81). The term "housewife" came to signify the interconnection between women, marriage, and the dwelling place (Oakley, 1974:1). As a consequence, women's participation in the public sphere—whether in work outside the home or in public life—came to be viewed as unnatural and destructive of the social order (Bernard, 1975:356). Conversely, the home environment and women's domestic roles were seen as a private affair of concern only to each individual family and of no concern to the public interest.

The second societal factor that has defined the relationship of women to the home environment is denial of the economic contribution of domestic work. Women service male workers by providing a home environment in which emotional needs, food and shelter requirements, and personal maintenance needs are met. In addition, by shouldering the primary responsibility for these household tasks, women free other family members for job demands, for participation in public life, and for leisure activities. According to Galbraith, housework is a "service to economic interest" even though it is often justified as service to the family, since the decisive contribution of women in developed industrial societies has been to facilitate an unlimited increase in consumption. He concludes that housework is not a matter of private relationships within the family, nor does it benefit only the family. Household work is a valid societal activity that has legitimacy in its own right (Galbraith, 1973: 36–37).

Until recently, there was little empirical data on women's household roles. Housework was not considered a serious topic for study since it was outside the market economy and hence not considered "real work." Recent feminist scholarship (including the chapters in Part 1) has generated detailed empirical studies of the home as workplace (Glazer, 1976). These studies examine women's segregation in the home and evaluate the home as a "working space" by asking basic questions about women's attachment to their homes, the nature of housework, the division of labor, and how the domestic environment affects women's work in the home.

The split between the domestic and public realms and their association with men's and women's spheres of activities maintains a strong hold on our imaginations and perceptions and leads men and women to attach very different meanings to the home (see Chapter 1). These meanings seem to demonstrate the significance of a man's deep involvement in his other "world" and a woman's concept of the home as an expression of her identity, which reflects her emotional attachment to the nurturing and homemaking roles associated with being a wife and mother. It is equally clear, however, that many women also view their confinement to the domestic environment as oppressive. Access to alternative environments, for the same rewards that men derive from work and public recreational settings, is a clear objective of many women.

Another topic directly related to the consideration of domestic environments is that of the pressure on women's time and energies created by their dual role as worker outside and inside the home and the effect of this pressure on all other aspects of their lives. Women's increased participation in the work force has not changed their workload inside the home, since women continue to carry out their household duties (see Chapter 2). What many studies have found is that the dual role as worker inside and outside the home imposes enormous strain, tiredness, and lack of "free time," seriously limiting other choices regarding work, leisure, and participation in public affairs.

Because the home is not seriously regarded as a workplace by society, little attention has been paid to how good design and a concern for the needs of the user might increase efficiency, decrease the time spent in housework, or alternatively, how the work might be reorganized to minimize the traditional isolation of domestic work. Because the housewife's work is "free," there is little incentive to treat it as a scarce resource to be conserved. Our examination of this topic (represented by Chapters 3 and 4) emphasizes how the design of the home affects women and how social change in men's and women's roles might be supported by design changes.

In general, houses are not designed by women, since women constitute a mere 1 percent of all registered architects; nor have women normally been consulted by the designers of home environments. Indeed, rarely is there even a conscious recognition that women are the predominant users of the home. As a result there is frequently a poor fit between the needs of women and the design of houses. Women must often adapt their behavior to fit the environment or suffer the costs of "making do" in a space that makes their work difficult to carry out.

It can be argued that houses are designed to support traditional concepts of gender roles and domesticity. Hayden points out that houses are designed almost exclusively for nuclear families and that architects assume the need for private domestic space for each household. But houses are still not being designed for the majority of households that are not nuclear families or for households that prefer to share certain facilities.[5] In this way, the definition of domestic work as private, sex-stereotyped nonwork is perpetuated by our domestic architecture.

It is paradoxical that women's equal access to opportunities in the public sphere is so heavily dependent on fundamental changes in the private sphere of the home and nuclear family. Yet changes in this realm are hardest to effect. Because the design of the home and its contribution to women's workload have been ignored in the past, several of our authors focus on the design changes necessary to support the sharing of household tasks. Naturally, they do not suggest that changes in environments alone will provide a solution to women's dilemma; it is generally agreed that slight improvements in household technology and home design will merely make it easier for women to play dual roles—to run the home *and* handle their own careers. In order to have substantial change there will have to be a fundamental restructuring of roles and responsibilities within the home and a built home environment to support it.

The Effects of Urban Design on Women

The chapters in Part 2 outline the social costs to women of living in urban areas primarily designed by and for men. They show how the spatial structure of the city affects women's access to resources and their ability to participate in the public sphere. Basically, the argument is that the modern city derives its form from a set of assumptions about women's roles that have not changed since the Industrial Revolution, which led to women's subservient economic position and tied them to the domestic setting.

Women have, therefore, had to adapt their behavior to an urban system that has taken little account of their changing role in the economic system; the effects of later marriages and smaller families; women's more open life-styles and their increasingly more common "single" status; and their needs as working mothers, independent heads of households, or widows and elderly persons living alone on restricted or fixed incomes. All of these fundamental changes are well under way, and already the patterns of women's lives have begun to change radically; but only in isolated instances have environments of the city been adjusted to take account of women's changing needs.

The specific reasons for this environmental inertia will be considered more fully in the discussion of women's limited access to the institutions controlling environments. But, seen from the perspective of a woman struggling to assert herself in the face of restrictive zoning ordinances, difficulties in obtaining mortgage loans, inadequate public transit systems, or the absence of adequate day-care facilities, it seems very much as if men *prefer* to go on creating and maintaining environments that inhibit women's attempts to broaden their roles and activities.

Problems with the structure of the city assail all of its inhabitants, but here the focus is on the special impacts on women resulting from the predominant decentralizing trends of the metropolitan city. Five broad aspects of women's "spatial inequality" are repeated in the chapters of Part 2: (1) the impact of the decentralized city and women's low level of accessibility to the city region, (2) women's limited mobility because of inadequate public transportation systems and lack of access to automobiles, (3) inadequate and falling employment opportunities in areas accessible to most women, (4) the impact of restrictive residential ordinances and the tendency towards social and functional homogeneity of the city, and finally (5) the inadequacy and attendant inaccessibility of various public services vital to women's changing roles.

Since in many respects the quality of the metropolitan urban environment is dependent on the spatial mobility of its residents, these facts are a significant general measure of the inequality of opportunity suffered by women. Women pay the true social costs of the existing structure of cities in terms of their limited "home range" (the extent of travel outside the home) and their limited access to supportive social services. In addition, these elements are all too frequently reinforced by the relative poverty experienced especially by women who are single, divorced, widowed, or separated.

One of the major changes in the form of American cities has been the trend to suburbanization and decentralization of jobs, housing, and urban services. In his book *Social Justice and the*

City (1973) David Harvey suggests that in order to understand inequalities in the city we must pay attention not only to *what services* are provided, but also to *where* they are located, *who* benefits from this access, and *who* loses. Thus, public decisions about the spatial allocation of goods, services, and employment in the city act as hidden mechanisms for redistributing income among various groups in the urban population.

In the North American city, women are one of the groups most limited in their choice of residential location and least able to overcome the "friction of distance." Increasingly, women rank among the poorest groups in the urban population. The huge increase in families headed by women are of special concern. In 1977 they numbered 7.7 million (nearly one out of seven families); one out of three of these families lives below the poverty level (Johnson, 1978). Like blacks and other minorities, families headed by women are often forced to live in public housing or in cheap rental housing in inner-city neighborhoods. A recent study carried out by the National Council of Negro Women (1976) found that women experience discrimination on several fronts: in marketing, lending, shelter-related services, and in lack of equal rental opportunities. Often women are discriminated against simultaneously on economic, racial, gender, and marital-status grounds. Because of this, women are disproportionately represented among renters even when they can afford to own a house; they are also disproportionately represented among residents of the central city, where houses are cheaper.

Women's limited choice of housing locations means that they and their families suffer most from the impoverishment of inner-city neighborhoods—substandard housing, inadequate schools, and erosion of public services. The abandonment of cities to the poor and the process of urban decentralization leads to fewer jobs in the central city, to a falling tax base and fewer social services, and to threatening environments in which to raise children. However, since suburban zoning restrictions limit moderately priced multifamily housing to central-city sites, women find it hard to move to other areas in the metropolitan city where jobs are available and schools are better.

Even for the privileged suburban women who are part of an

intact nuclear family, the costs of suburban residence are great. The form of the typical North American low-density suburb almost requires that people have access to an automobile and that they spend additional time commuting to work and obtaining essential services. For women, inequalities within the household create pressures on time and energies that men do not experience.

Considerations of time and distance affect women's decisions about job location, where to shop, and how to use leisure time. Yet studies of women's transportation patterns in several North American cities (Madden and White, 1978; Kaniss and Robins, 1974; Palm and Pred, 1974) show that women have considerably less access to automobiles than men and are heavily dependent on public transportation. Public transportation in many smaller cities is almost nonexistent and even in the best systems it caters largely to commuters travelling at peak hours from the suburbs to center-city locations. The many women who live in the city and work in the suburbs are ill served, as are part-time workers travelling during the day and workers requiring transportation not just for journeys to work but also for taking children to day care, for shopping, and for visits to public services. Few cities provide the kind of multipurpose transportation system that women require for getting around the city. The outcome of women's dependence on public transportation is that they spend a great deal more time in travelling than men do. Yet women are least able to absorb this extra time cost precisely because their responsibilities in the home already place a high demand on their time and resources. The combination of an increasingly decentralized city (which requires access to a private automobile), women's poverty (which often limits them to housing in the city and frequently precludes ownership of a car), and women's dual role as worker outside and inside the home means that women in the urban environment operate under severe constraints.

Because a single-family home in the suburbs is still the ideal of most American families, there is some irony in the findings that women often *prefer* this kind of environment despite paying the highest cost of any member of the family for living there. North American suburbs are not planned for the working woman. The planners' image of women users (when they think of them at all) is still limited to the traditional house-bound wife and mother; the discrepancy between this image and the reality of the suburban family is striking. The suburban population is increasingly diverse; one of the most significant trends is demonstrated by the fact that women are employed in almost 50 percent of all families where the husband is also employed (Hayghe, 1975), and the fastest growing group of workers is mothers with young children.

These changing demographic trends lie behind much of the criticism of existing suburban environments presented in this volume. A theme of current writing about women and the urban environment is the elaboration of alternatives to the way suburbs, neighborhoods, and cities are currently designed (Hapgood and Getzels, 1974; Popenoe, 1977). All of these proposals recognize the necessity of enriching the local environment, decentralizing services and jobs, increasing densities, and providing better public transportation links to all parts of the urban system.

While women critically need employment if they are to escape the dependency and dominance of their domestic environments, they also need assistance in establishing themselves in the public environment. This is why the provision of social services aimed at women is so important. Lack of access to, and information on, existing job training programs, advisory and counselling services, health and welfare services, resource centers, recreational facilities, and day-care centers inhibits women's likelihood of "escape." This reinforces the tension and stress that come from women's attempts to make do with already inadequate services—especially in suburban areas.

A new trend is the increasing attractiveness of older city neighborhoods that provide a mix of public services, access to public transportation and jobs, rental housing, and a tolerance for households headed by women. Judy Stamp's chapter in this book describes such a neighborhood in Toronto; Brown (1978) described a similar neighborhood in Boston that was supportive of the life-styles of divorced mothers. There has been some speculation (Ginzberg, 1978; Wekerle, 1979) that the influx of families headed by women will contribute to the revitalization of inner-city neighborhoods (Gerard and McCormick, 1978; Michelson, 1973), but if jobs and revenue continue to move out of cities, or if inner-city crime continues to increase, the long-term advantages for women in the city will be uncertain and difficult to predict.

When it comes to decisions about the form and structure of cities and the location of jobs and essential goods and services, the impacts on women and other disadvantaged groups are not considered. It is the male corporate structure that benefits from a city segregated by zoning into the male world of business and profits and the female world of the residential neighborhood. The chapters on women in the urban environment suggest that men are most comfortable with the physical segregation of the private and public spheres, and conclude that women are often the "environmental victims" of the decentralized North American city.

Women in Environmental Decisionmaking

Discussion of the limitations associated with women's membership in the organizations controlling public and private environments is part of a very much broader issue—the nature of the roles women play in large organizations. Since we live in a society controlled by large organizations (public as well as private), our environments are also planned, designed, and managed by them. This theme is central both as an explanation of past environmental inequality and as a fundamental element in changing women's roles and increasing environmental opportunities. Changes in environments are affected by a wide range of environment-controlling organizations, including environmental design and planning groups, government regulatory agencies, financial institutions, the development and real estate industries, the construction industry, and also corporations and other large organizations initiating environmental change (steel mills, hospitals, head-office buildings, shopping centers, universities, and so on). The structures built by such organizations reflect changes in economic conditions (especially in relation to the money market), changes in government policy and regulatory control, technological and design innovations, changes in the status accorded to particular physical structures, and changing consumer/user demands.

These organizations not only develop or control *all* environments but are also responsible for their management, upkeep, and adaptation to the changing needs of the users—whether they be residents, employees, clients, customers, visitors, members of an audience, patients, or students. Unfortunately, "users" rarely participate in the development and management of such spaces, so that many of the conclusions drawn here with regard to women users apply also to the majority of men. The circumstance that distinguishes women is their lack of representation in environmental decisionmaking processes in positions that would allow their distinctive needs to be effectively considered. This concern forms the focus of Part 3.

Recognition of the existing nature of environmental decisionmaking leads to the posing of an important question: If it is accepted that women play a marginal role in environment-controlling organizations and that they have only a marginal effect on the form of environments critical to them, what if women were equally represented in the process? Could they, and would they, have sufficient influence to change the form of environments to fit more closely the changing needs of women (and, presumably, other disadvantaged user groups)? The contributors to this book respond in the affirmative. The final impact of women's changing attitudes and expectations on human environments is as dependent on the activities and influence of women *inside* the environment-controlling institutions as it is on those pressing for change from the outside. Particular importance is laid here on the activities of women in the key environmental design professions of architecture and planning (see Chapters 10–12).

However, it has long been recognized that women "inside" environment-controlling institutions usually play subordinate roles (Kanter, 1977). Women traditionally have had limited visibility, holding mainly low-status jobs providing infrastructure support services as office workers commanding low salaries. Women as a class seem to be rewarded for routine services—men as a class are rewarded for decisionmaking and leadership. Although considerable play has been made of the rise of a few women to executive and managerial positions, and some significant organizational changes in styles of operation have been made over the past decade, "the structural bases for inequalities of participation by women . . . [have] . . . remained intact" (Boulding, 1976b:783). All too often women occupants of senior positions represent token gestures to the pressure for change, and there is a strong tendency for women professionals to be fired before obtaining tenure or to be blocked from further promotion.

Women professionals and executives have been likened to Stonequist's "marginal man" (Stonequist, 1936) in the sense of being located between two cultures (male and female), never fully affiliated with either—seeking to change their sense of identity, but unable to resolve the conflicting choices between the values of their two "worlds." Women as members of environment-controlling organizations appear to follow this general pattern very closely. Considered as elements of the public decision-making process, women in elected, appointed, or staff positions are frequently not present on key bodies concerned with the environment. When they are members of decisionmaking bodies, they often serve only in women's traditional spheres of interest—education, social services, housing, or arts and culture. They tend to have a lesser role in such vital areas as urban services, transportation, planning, and finance, in which women urgently need representation (see Chapter 14). This pattern is confirmed and explained by work on women's political activities (Githens and Prestage, 1977). Women have been found to be marginal participants in the political process, to be active mainly in civic matters affecting home and family, to be concerned with community well-being, and to be involved most often in nonpartisan voluntary organizations and women's organizations.

The importance of extending women's roles as environmental professionals has been a women and environments issue from the beginning (Hapgood and Getzels, 1974). However, the chapters in this volume suggest that the bureaucratic implementation of social change through the establishment of "women's desks," the encouragement of cooperation between women's organizations, the appointment of women to policymaking bodies, or merely through informing the community about new programs cannot take us very far unless accompanied by sufficient social pressure for a general *extension* of women's roles. Without this, such activities tend to become ends in themselves—tokens to be discarded whenever the social pressure seems to ease or when economic constraints lead to cutbacks. Also, the positions themselves cease to be attractive to women when they are seen as mere tokens. Jacqueline Leavitt (Chapter 11) shows how limited the role of the planner actually is in furthering social change and explains that for women this marginal professional status is doubly constraining.

A very similar situation occurs in the environmental design professions, as is demonstrated by Ellen Berkeley's and Leavitt's chapters. After an initial group of women entered these professions early in this century, the numbers remained static or even declined. Although the present number of women in architecture and planning degree programs suggests that there will be a significant increase in the proportion of women in these professions during the next decade, women continue to play only a marginal role in decisionmaking. There are too few of them, they do not get appointed to senior positions, their incomes are far lower than men with similar qualifications, and the income gap only becomes wider as they progress in their careers.

There is firm evidence that the design professions are male dominated and inherently sexist in their view of the world. Acceptance of the claim that this results in sexist environments depends on an overall reading of the findings presented in this book. The authors would say that women are treated unequally through the design of most environments, even when explicit discrimination is not intended. In fact, most sex discrimination is built into the system; this is particularly true of human environments and it is likely to remain so as long as so few women are directly involved in environmental design. This places a great burden on those women who do reach positions of authority: their tenure is uncertain; they are in a minority position; and often they are performing roles not central to the making of final decisions.

Finally, to return to an earlier point, the form of existing environments cannot be laid at the door of planners or architects, or even particular institutions. Our environments derive from our capitalist and corporate society with its emphasis on private ownership (especially of land), and from our images of power, control, affluence, and consumption. Women fell by the wayside long ago in the evolutionary process that has brought us to the present situation, and our institutions will have to learn entirely new ways of dealing with society if they are to effect any positive changes.

Women as Environmental Activists

There are a number of possible strategies for increasing women's roles in creating environments to meet their changing needs: (1) modification of existing design and planning decision processes to include more input and control by women users, (2) strengthening the economic base and skills of women so that they have the resources as client groups to create their own environments with the assistance of women environmental design and planning professionals, (3) starting new all-female professional and academic institutions that attempt to create responsive environments on all scales, and (4) raising environmental design and planning issues within existing women's movement groups.

Women have sometimes played a very active role in design and planning processes, identifying their needs and those of others, only to find that when the final decisions were made, economic rather than social factors were paramount. Mary Soper's chapter provides an example of the involvement of women in such an abortive participation exercise. This will continue to be the typical outcome of women's attempts to have their needs addressed more explicitly unless institutions can be pressured to redefine their priorities. There is also an obvious need for women to identify the kinds of innovations that are most likely to be funded by institutions within the existing set of priorities and economic constraints. Innovations related to women's needs will be adequately financed only if they are also in line with general economic or political trends. For example, if women's design projects also serve to conserve energy, they will be more likely to win financing in a period of declining resources. Similarly, if the home birth or neighborhood birth centers[6] women want will also reduce health-care costs, that innovation may be accepted. If the needs of women for improved public transit are coupled with the general need for improving public transportation to serve all segments of the population with a lower consumption of fossil fuels then women's demands may be met.[7]

In light of these trends, the need to strengthen women's abilities to create their own environments should be clear. Through self-help projects in many cities women have scraped together their meager resources to create new environments; the chapters by Anne Cools and Sheila de Bretteville are illustrative of such environments. Women have also founded rape crisis centers, abortion clinics, women's health clinics, and storefront legal services—all dealing with the immediate needs of women in crisis that are not being met by existing institutions.

De Bretteville's case study of the founding and development of the Los Angeles Woman's Building is illustrative of a wide range of support environments created by women for women, which include women's resource and counselling centers, bookstores, art galleries and cultural centers, restaurants and clubs, and even transit services. In many communities, these projects provide the essential services that support women in their struggle to lead independent lives in the urban environment. However, they are far more than services that cater only to women's special needs. They represent an attempt to create a new paradigm for social services and for work that starts from identifying the needs of the users rather than those of the institutions. The work is often organized collectively rather than hierarchically, and many of the projects rely on volunteer labor and a high level of participation by the user group.

Women started these services and businesses because existing institutions did not meet their needs. Because they have been created outside the regular channels, women's services tend to stay small and have to struggle to survive and be considered as legitimate recipients of public funds. As the economic situation deteriorates, these women-created spaces are threatened in two ways: women's worsening economic situations lead to cutbacks in voluntary financial contributions, and government funding cutbacks lead to the withdrawal of grants for projects such as women's transition houses, health clinics, counselling centers, and employment services.[8]

Faced with the withdrawal of services that they consider essential to their survival in the urban environment, women, who have the least time and money in our society, are required to contribute their meager resources to keep these services going, while at the same time supporting through taxes the public institutions that do not serve them well. Unless they secure independent funding or manage to establish their legitimate claim on government funds (a difficult proposition when even long-established programs are being cut), women in the 1980s may well see the dismantling of the women's services that were so laboriously built up in the 1960s and 1970s.

One response to the vulnerability of women's services based on government funding has been the establishment of all-female professional and academic institutions that are financially independent. These experiments attempt to incorporate the kinds of institutional innovation that are only possible in all-female work environments. Their emphasis on nonhierarchical structures, flexible time schedules, elimination of the profit motive, organizational development skills, the fostering of creativity in the redesign of "drudgery" tasks, and attempts to meet the specific needs of female clients are examples of the kinds of values apparent in such all-female organizations.

The Women's School of Planning and Architecture described by Berkeley is an example of an all-female learning environment begun by a collective of women architects and planners running summer sessions in 1975, 1976, and 1978. Again, there is an emphasis on the connection between the social and physical environment, on cooperation rather than competition, and an attempt to define women's needs and solutions.[9] However, the impact of this innovative group has also been limited by financial stringencies and a heavy reliance on volunteer labor.

The Women's Movement and Women's Environments

The Women's Movement, either directly or indirectly, created the general atmosphere for change that led to women and environments work being undertaken in the first place. Within the different contributions that make up this book lie a number of underlying ideals and principles, many of which derive from the attitudes and aspirations of the Women's Movement. This social-change emphasis helps explain the approaches to problem definition and the kinds of conclusions that are drawn here.

Understanding the basis of the Women's Movement is critical to understanding its effects. First, it is a *grass-roots movement* derived from changing attitudes of women in response to new perceptions of their treatment in everyday environments. Its strength comes from the fact that its adherents are to be found in almost every kitchen, bedroom, and workplace, even when many reject any explicit personal association with feminist women's organizations and might even vigorously deny that they were feminists. The second, and related, critical characteristic of the Women's Movement is that it draws on a very *broad base of support*—the educated middle class, disaffected suburban wives and mothers, women with left-wing political leanings, older women, and black and other minority women. Moreover, the substantial demands made by women for improvements in their environments (day care, jobs, greater personal mobility, more accessible welfare and other social services) would help working-class women as much as the middle class, black as much as white.

From these statements, one might expect that the women who "shared a reason to organize and fight for their collective interest" (Chafe, 1977:125) would have created formal organizations to apply sustained political pressure for their mutual benefit. However, the third fundamental characteristic of the Movement has been its *decentralized* character. There is no overall structure binding together the different elements of the Women's Movement. Activity is based on small, informal groups working mainly at the local level. Energy comes from below and is based on the immediate concerns women have for the quality of their lives and their environments. Leaders were deemed unnecessary, except at the local level. Women could make decisions collectively, and activist feminists rejected the traditional organizational structure based on a centralized, hierarchical decisionmaking structure. That was a product of male culture and part of the "problem." The personal relationships between women were what counted, along with the local networks of contacts that commanded loyalty.

This description reveals the Movement's greatest advantage—its pervasiveness. It also shows its supreme disadvantage—its lack of formal structures and its heavy reliance on individual and collective goodwill. Often the Movement lacked political effectiveness, even at the local level. Its growth was based on a sense of the personal needs of individual women, and to some extent this diverted attention from wider public-policy changes.

It is worth pointing out that national and even regional feminist organizations generate as much antagonism as support among women; that despite their sharing of common experiences, women do not necessarily share social causes; and that the feminists' apparent threat to marriage and the family offend deeply many women who have already devoted their lives to the roles of homemaker, helpmate, and nurturer for a man. In these respects, the pervasive decentralized process (which is less vulnerable to symbolic defeats and can embrace an extremely wide range of opinions) may in the long run be the most effective social change mechanism for a movement that strikes at the heart of an existing way of life.

Since the Women's Movement is characteristically a dispersed and pluralistic social change process rather than a formal reform movement, it is not surprising that quite different views exist regarding the nature of the most critical environmental issues affecting women. In the broadest terms this leads, for example, to an emphasis by Marxist feminists on existing human environments as reinforcers of class distinctions among women and on women's access to the environments of production as the key to their liberation. Black feminists are most concerned with the effects of racial discrimination on women in public environments, on women's access to workplace environments, and with the social equity issues associated with black women's access to basic human needs. These examples emphasize the relationship between working-class women and their environments; active lesbian feminists who view heterosexuality as the source of female oppression are more concerned with the rights of access to separate environments, free from the pressures of the wider society.

Each of these feminist factions can be regarded as radical arms of the Women's Movement for whom changing environments is part of the process of fundamental change in existing society. The majority of the contributors to this volume represent the larger segment of the Women's Movement aiming for change in the context of the existing social structure. In general terms, the vocal constituents of this group are middle class, white, and educated. Their concerns can be divided into three broad categories: personal consciousness raising through the closer association between women; relief from the oppression of domestic roles; and greater access to the professions and other career opportunities. Each of these concerns points toward women playing wider social roles and acquiring equal access to the means of improving their social status within our existing institutional and political framework.

There are both idealistic and pragmatic elements in this approach to the Women's Movement. At one end of the spectrum women envisage a process leading to the gradual introduction of a distinctive women's style of handling social problems that will gradually pervade male as well as female society—an androgynous solution—while other women are calling for equal rights to compete with men on their own terms, in the certainty that they are at least as able to perform the political and institutional roles at present denied them.

This has considerable significance in the women and environments debate, for whichever route is taken, significant shifts in present societal attitudes will have to occur, and they will inevitably be reflected in changing environments. Since the writers in this volume predominantly argue that women's ideals *will* affect society and its environments if women are given equal access to decisionmaking, it is necessary to deal with the nature of feminist ideals and their implications for women's environments.

The argument that women would influence the planning and design of human environments can be attributed to the existence of a distinctive women's institutional metaphor. This implies that women's distinctive "underside" experience provides the basis for a different institutional style that would lead to the development of environments based on a new set of principles (Boulding, 1976). The differences between these models can be characterized in the following way:

Male Institutional Metaphor	*Female Institutional Metaphor*
Individualist	Communal
Centralized	Decentralized
Stratified, hierarchical organization	Informal network organization
A "center-periphery" relationship with environments	Localist/participatory relationship with environments
Change viewed in terms of technological innovation	Change viewed in terms of social innovation
Productivity/growth models of change	Conserver models of change
Rational decisionmaking process	Decisionmaking process involving sentiment, emotions, and instinct
Individual rewarded for leadership	Individual rewarded for service

The argument goes on to suggest that the kind of "adaptive learning institutions" (Schon, 1971:65) defined by the women's metaphor provides a useful model in the face of the scale of changes now facing our institutions (threats to the economic system, the energy crisis, an aging population, environmental/ resource issues, minority demands for equity). This model emphasizes communication between local communities, providing a strong grass-roots base for change that could be initiated through the operation of self-help networks. There is a belief that "hidden community resources" are available to be tapped, and particularly that every aware woman is a "practicing futurist" (Boulding, 1976b:781). It is suggested that women should have confidence to act on the basis of their own metaphors, which can be applied with special effect in the development of transitional strategies in an era of rapid social change.

These conclusions are based primarily on the assumption that there are inherent strengths to be derived from women's experience in performing their traditional roles and in particular that there are important creative qualities to be gained from "marginality." In a general sense it is argued that because of women's marginal roles in social institutions, they are free from the constraints that automatic membership brings and are more willing to move from traditional patterns of behavior. Added to this are the particular skills women gain from the domestic sphere, like skills in "environmental scanning and . . . taking feedback from the immediate environment . . . in family and neighborhood settings" (Boulding, 1976b:786). Such skills could easily be applied to wider environmental systems. Evidence of the application of these attributes of the female metaphor are shown by women's roles in volunteer work and in community organizing.

Finally, it is argued that the women's metaphor can act as a model for a society where women and men must join together to handle the impending breakdown of our existing social system. In such an "androgynous society," incorporating elements of both women's and men's worlds, women's wide experience at the local level will become "increasingly important in the development of 'self-help' systems that must replace poorly functioning centralized systems" (Boulding, 1977:234).

It is necessary to assess the potential contribution of these hopes and ideals to environmental design. A marked increase in the number of women occupying decisionmaking positions in the environment-controlling institutions would be expected to put greater emphasis on the needs of users of particular environments and less emphasis on centralized hierarchical organizations. Women users and community level organizations would perhaps be the major initial beneficiaries of an increase in women's professional influence. Specifically, low-cost housing facilities for single-parent mothers and aged women, child care, halfway houses, welfare services, educational programs, and more flexible working settings (flex-time, part-time employment, etc.) could become the focus for innovation. Naturally, the assumption is that such new approaches would bring with them many related changes affecting women and men alike that would be aimed at producing more humane and equitable environments in general.

Preferred Environmental Solutions for Women

The contributors to this book provide a clear and consistent view of the kind of environments that women would like to see emerge. First the home should become a symbol of changing human relations, a setting for collective familial responsibility—a shared workplace. The design of the home should be in tune with changing family needs—adaptable and capable of absorbing the multiple roles played by all members of the modern family. Some feminist designers suggest that there should be a greater emphasis on communal housing, and especially communal domestic workplaces, and a concern with efficiency rather than with consumption in the home. Above all the environment should help separate women's status from her role in the domestic setting. The home is only *one* environment that women identify with, although few believe that she should abandon the capacity to express her identity in that setting. There is no easy environmental solution to women's ambivalence in this context.

Extending the environmental scale to the local community, the emphasis of feminist design objectives is on the creation of environments that increase women's access to wider urban functions and services, both through locational changes and by increasing women's mobility. Neighborhoods should encourage the expansion of women's activities by providing additional local services (day care, educational facilities, information and resource centers), by diversifying functions at the neighborhood level (including the provision of employment opportunities, commercial facilities, and cultural activities), and by making neighborhoods more compact to encourage greater use of such facilities. The overall goal is to "enrich" neighborhoods to provide a more balanced setting for the home environment, while encouraging the widening of women's roles and therefore the range of environments in which women operate. This all implies a direct challenge to many of the established planning precepts on which the form of the city is based. For suburban and central-city dwellers alike these objectives imply that women have the right to economic security, adequate housing, and safe local environments.

There is no doubt that this first stage of solution formulation has dwelt more heavily on what should be done than on how to achieve those objectives. There are many problems inherent in a process that focuses on the way in which women's marginality can become an asset in the development of new social roles. Chafe has pointed out that, as with other equal rights move-

ments, the Women's Movement runs up against a basic characteristic of American democracy: individual opportunity. The
rights of the individual to advance her or his status through
competitive enterprise underlies the maintenance of the existing
power structure, and conflicts with the demands for social
equality inherent in the Women's Movement. This is compounded by the fact that feminist demands must inevitably
affect the entire economic system since the economic advance
of women adversely affects the existing protected status of men.

Tension over the prospect of greater competition for scarce
jobs probably underlies the powerful political and institutional
blocking of women's rights. There has been virtually no break
in the male dominance of the institutions controlling the rate
and direction of social change, and without women's involvement in those settings it seems very unlikely that the "gentle
society" will advance beyond the very limited local scale. Nowhere is this more clearly demonstrated in the environmental
context than in the rigid adherence to traditional housing, land
use, and zoning formulas in the development of suburbs. The
blocking by suburban municipalities of higher density development, housing for lower income residents, and mixed residential-
commercial land use has been maintained. Since the success of
the black civil rights movement is only now beginning to be
reflected in an increase in the racial mix of middle-class suburbs,
it seems unlikely that residential environments taking account
of women's needs will follow immediately from the efforts of
the Women's Movement.

This brings the discussion back to the social and political
milieu in which women are attempting to transform their environments. The changes women are working towards all have
to be implemented by institutions that see their futures threatened. "The more central a social pattern is to the perpetuation
of a way of life, the more difficult will be the process of altering
that pattern" (Chafe, 1977:171). The Women's Movement,
therefore, needs a public environment hospitable to change for
any fundamental success in achieving its ideals to be possible.
But this suggests a profound contradiction that may not have
been present in the past. On the one hand there is a gradual
process of social change emerging from individual women's

assertion of their rights, which is leading to increasingly independent lives and broadening roles. On the other hand there are the counteracting social and economic forces leading to such events as the rejection of abortion legislation, the failure to ratify the ERA, and movements leading to controls on government spending, such as California's Proposition 13—all of which reinforce the existing institutional barriers to the translation of the changes in women's behavior into long-term changes in the environment.

This inherent clash between primary opposing forces leads to an uncertain situation that may produce either radical change reflecting women's needs or a strong opposing movement that could block women's objectives. From the discussion in this book it appears that the issue of the quality of women's environments stands at the center of this conflict and could act as a unifying concern within the Women's Movement, joining the energies of the numerous groups of active women at present involved in the process of change.

Notes

1. The edited book by Susana Torre, *Women in Architecture: A Historic and Contemporary Perspective* (1977) provides a comprehensive overview of women's contributions in the field of architecture.

2. Textbooks that use the environment and behavior perspective include Altman (1974), Michelson (1977), and Porteous (1977).

3. This is the *Women and Environments International Newsletter*, edited by Rebecca Peterson, Gerda R. Wekerle, and David Morley of the Faculty of Environmental Studies, York University, Toronto.

4. For further discussion of these points see the paper by Peterson, Wekerle, and Morley (1978).

5. According to an article "Who is the Real American Family?" (*Ms.*, August 1978), the 1977 U.S. Statistical Abstract reports that only 15.9 percent of all households include a father as sole wage earner, a mother as full-time homemaker, and at least one child. In at least 18.5 percent of households with at least one child, both the father and mother are wage earners; 30.5 percent of households are married couples with no children or no children living at home; 6.2 percent are headed by women who are single parents; and 20.6 percent are single-person households.

7. Rebecca Dreis has documented the operations of women's transit services throughout the United States in "Innovations in Transportation for Women" (1978).

8. Galper and Washburne (1976) discuss some of the personal and organizational reasons for the demise of one women-in-transition facility.

9. For further information concerning the Women's School of Planning and Architecture, see Weisman (1979) and Marcus (1978).

References

Altman, Irvine. *The Environment and Social Behavior.* Monterey: Brooks/Cole, 1974.

Bernard, Jessie. *The Future of Motherhood.* Baltimore: Penguin, 1975.

Boulding, Elise. "Familial Constraints on Women's Work Roles." Signs 1, no. 3 (1976a):95–117.

_____. *The Underside of History: A View of Women Through Time.* Boulder: Westview Press, 1976b.

_____. *Women in the Twentieth Century World.* New York: Sage, 1977.

Brown, Carol A. "Spatial Inequalities and Divorced Mothers." Paper presented at the American Sociological Association, San Francisco, 1978.

Chafe, William H. *Women and Equality: Changing Patterns in American Culture.* New York: Oxford University Press, 1977.

Dreis, Rebecca. "Innovations in Transportation for Women." Masters Research Paper, Department of Sociology, University of California, Santa Barbara, June 1978.

Galbraith, John Kenneth. *Economics and the Public Purpose.* New York: New American Library, 1973.

Galper, Miriam, and Carolyn Kott Washburne. "A Women's Self-Help Program in Action." *Social Policy* (March/April 1976):46–52.

Gerard, Karen, and Mary McCormick. *The Impact of Women on the Economy of New York City.* New York: Economics Group, Chase Manhattan Bank, 1978. Also excerpted in *Across the Board* 15 (April 1978):27–29.

Ginzberg, Eli. "Who Can Save the City?" *Across the Board—The Conference Board Magazine* 15 (April 1978):24–26.

Githens, Marianne, and Jewel Prestage (eds.). *A Portrait of Marginality: The Political Behavior of the American Woman.* New York: MacKay, 1977.

Glazer, Nona. "Housework." *Signs* 1, no. 4 (summer 1976):905–922.

_____ and Helen Youngelson Waehrer (eds.). *Women in a Man-Made World.* 2nd ed. Chicago: Rand McNally, 1977.

Hapgood, Karen, and Judith Getzels. *Planning, Women, and Change.* Chicago: American Society of Planning Officials, 1974.

Harvey, David. *Social Justice and the City.* Baltimore: Johns Hopkins University Press, 1973.

Hayden, Dolores, and Gwendolyn Wright. "Architecture and Urban Planning." *Signs* 1 (summer 1976):923–933.

Hayghe, Howard. "Marital and Family Characteristics of the Labor Force." *Special Labor Force Report 183.* Washington, D.C.: U.S. Department of Labor, March 1975.

Johnson, Beverly L. "Women Who Head Families 1970–77: Their Numbers Rose, Income Lagged." *Monthly Labor Review* (February 1978): 32–37.

Kaniss, Phyllis, and Barbara Robins. "The Transportation Needs of Women." In Karen Hapgood and Judith Getzels (eds.), *Planning, Women and Change.* Chicago: American Society of Planning Officials, 1974.

Kanter, Rosabeth Moss. *Men and Women of the Corporation.* New York: Basic Books, 1977.

Madden, Janice Fanning, and Michele J. White. "Women's Work Trips: An Empirical and Theoretical Overview." Paper prepared for a conference on Women's Travel Issues: Research Needs and Priorities sponsored by U.S. Department of Transportation and National Research Council, Washington, D.C., September 17–20, 1978.

Marcus, Elizabeth Roper. "WSPA Theme is Social Change." *Progressive Architecture* 59, no. 10 (October 1978):22, 26.

Michelson, William. *The Place of Time in the Longitudinal Evaluation of Spatial Structures by Women.* Toronto: University of Toronto Center for Urban and Community Studies, 1973.

_____. *Environmental Choice, Human Behavior and Residential Satisfaction.* New York: Oxford University Press, 1977.

Ms. Editors. "Who is the Real American Family?" *Ms.* 7, no. 2 (August 1978):43.

National Council of Negro Women. *Women and Housing: A Report on Sex Discrimination in Five American Cities.* Washington, D.C.: U.S. Department of Housing and Urban Development, Office of the Assistant Secretary for Fair Housing and Equal Opportunity, 1976.

Oakley, Ann. *Woman's Work: The Housewife, Past and Present.* New York: Vintage Books, 1974.

Palm, Risa, and Allan Pred. "A Time-Geographic Perspective on Problems of Inequality for Women." Working paper no. 236. Berkeley: Institute of Urban and Regional Development, University of California, 1974.

Peterson, Rebecca; Gerda R. Wekerle; and David Morley. "Women and

Environments: An Overview of an Emerging Field." *Environment and Behavior* 10 (December 1978):511–534.

Popenoe, David. *The Suburban Environment: Sweden and the United States.* Chicago: University of Chicago Press, 1977.

Porteous, J. Douglas. *Environment and Behavior.* New York: Addison-Wesley, 1977.

_____. "Prime Time for Paradigm." In Walter E. Rogers and William Ittelson (eds.), *New Directions in Environmental Design Research,* EDRA 9. Tucson: Environmental Design Research Association, 1978.

Schon, Donald. *Beyond the Stable State.* New York: Norton, 1971.

Stonequist, Everett. *A Theory of Marginal Man.* 1936.

Torre, Susana. *Women in American Architecture: A Historic and Contemporary Perspective.* New York: Watson and Guptill, 1977.

Weisman, Leslie Kanes. "The Women's School of Planning and Architecture." In Charlotte Bunch (ed.), *Not By Degrees: Essays on Feminist Education.* New York: Daughters Inc., 1979.

_____ and Susana Torre. "Birth Centers: Restoring Women's Birth Rights." Unpublished paper, New Jersey Institute of Technology, Birth Studio, School of Architecture, 1977.

Wekerle, Gerda R. "A Woman's Place is in the City." Land Policy Roundtable, Basic Concept Series no. 102. Cambridge, Mass.: Lincoln Institute of Land Policy, 1979.

Zaretsky, Eli. *Capitalism, The Family, and Personal Life.* New York: Harper & Row, 1976.

Part 1

The Domestic Workplace

Introduction

Rebecca Peterson

Until now, the home as an environment has not been a significant topic for study. This may be partially attributable to the extreme segregation of public and private realms within our culture, with the subsequent devaluation of the home as an important economic or societal sphere. The five chapters in Part 1, written by psychologists, sociologists, planners, and architects, rely on scientific research, exploratory interviews, observation of behavior, and historical analysis to pose questions about women's needs within the home. Part 1 includes chapters on defining the problem as well as solving it. The authors suggest that if we fail to deal with the complexity of social and design problems within the home environment we will block women's attempts to change their life patterns outside the home.

Susan Saegert and Gary Winkel's chapter explores the relationship between sex roles and the meaning and use of the home. Their research explored the possibility that men and women with sharply segregated sex roles would hold widely different home-related attitudes and values and that the degree of physical segregation of the home from the broader world (urbanites vs. suburbanites) would be related to differences in use and meaning of the home. Saegert and Winkel found that women invested more labor in the home and placed more value on the home expressing their personalities than did men. Parallel with this is the finding that women gain more satisfaction from the home. Women in the city and men in the suburbs both tend to value home and work equally whereas urban men emphasize work and suburban women focus primarily on the home. This chapter explicitly addresses the ambivalence of the home as "woman's place" *and* the source of her oppression. The authors propose higher density mixed-use residential environments as partial solutions to the dilemmas faced by men and women who must choose small urban apartments in social and physical settings that are not suitable for childrearing (due to crime, pollution, lack of contact with nature, unsatisfactory schools) or accept the loss of social and cultural opportunities, especially for the wife, within the suburban environment.

Findings from studies by Sarah F. Berk suggest that alterations in the physical characteristics of the household, either through design or mechanical variations, will not necessarily lead to alterations in social relations. Berk reports on research she conducted on the distribution of responsibilities within the home. Her findings demonstrate that women continue to carry the primary responsibility for the accomplishment of roughly 80 to 90 percent of the household tasks investigated. This chapter has relevance to the definition of the home as a workplace and to the social definition of the division of labor between husbands, children, and wives.

Proposals for change in home design come from a number of sources. The chapters by Cynthia Rock, Susana Torre and Gwendolyn Wright, and Dolores Hayden focus on single-family dwelling and collective solutions, respectively. The chapter by Rock, Torre, and Wright presents an historical overview of the way in which women's magazines have portrayed the conflicts in the definition of the home environment as embodied by designers and users since the 1830s. The authors contend that the home as it presently exists reinforces traditional sex roles. They give illustrations of ways in which individuals can redefine the use of spaces within existing housing types in order to facilitate shared domestic work.

In contrast to the single-family housing solutions proposed by Rock, Torre, and Wright, Hayden reviews plans of improved domestic architecture proposed by the utopian socialists and cooperative housekeepers. These groups challenged the separation of work and home, production and reproduction, that they felt was brought about by industrial capitalism. Hayden chronicles their attempts to end the isolation of the housewife, increase efficiency through division of labor, provide better design and equipment in kitchens and spaces for child care, and increase the amount of leisure time available to the women in their groups. This chapter demonstrates that collective domestic architecture has existed in workable and complex forms even though these experiments have been isolated and limited in scope to groups outside the cultural mainstream.

In summary, these chapters illustrate the way in which a combination of psychological, social, and design factors interact to pose problems for women within the home environment. Economic factors limiting women's access to options for both initial choice and modification of housing were not explored here, but must be assumed to be part of the problem definition. Some alternatives for single-family and collective solutions are suggested. Mary Soper's chapter in Part 4 will explore an example of a present-day attempt by women to influence the design of housing for single-parent families.

1
The Home:
A Critical Problem
for Changing Sex Roles[1]

Susan Saegert
Gary Winkel

The home is both a physical space where certain activities are performed and a value-laden symbol. Both meanings of the word "home" are closely linked to definitions of the female sex role in our culture. Physically and symbolically the home is a private place, away from the public world of work. It is a place for being with one's family and for sharing feelings, a place to retreat to, both alone and for close relationships. The activities that go on in the home differ from those outside in many ways. Work in the home is generally not conducted on a wage basis and most of it is done by women. In fact we would suggest that it is almost impossible to imagine a "home" in both senses of the word without imagining a caretaking woman in the setting.

Clearly the idea of a home evokes many positive associations, yet as the research to be discussed will suggest, it is also the nexus of considerable ambivalence. It is a place where the cultural values of individualism and achievement can be laid aside for a time. The family and personal relationships become the focus rather than the individual. Simply maintaining life takes the place of achieving goals and striving for money and success. And in all this there is a woman on the scene, providing food, care, and nurturance. To the extent that the household runs smoothly or roughly, she is usually held responsible.

The home is so intimately tied to the definition of men's and women's roles that one might even say it exists as a cultural symbol primarily through these roles. Evidence for this assertion can be drawn from the images of women presented in the various media as well as from behavioral and interview studies concerning the home-related attitudes and activities of women and men.

From childhood, girls are presented with the role of housewife as most desirable and probable future for themselves. For example, an analysis of 134 elementary school readers (Women on Words and Images, 1972) showed that the girls portrayed in these books were constantly rehearsing domestic activities (166 instances as compared to 50 for boys). Adult women were usually presented as full-time, apron-wearing housewives. Only three mothers working outside the home appeared at all. Of the potential occupational roles presented by adults, men were shown doing 147 different jobs, while women had only 26 different jobs, most of them domestic or service work. The mass media overwhelmingly depict girls and women as domestic creatures, found primarily in the home or in supermarkets buying products to keep their homes clean and attractive (Tuchman, Kaplan, and Benet, 1978). Many fewer women than men are portrayed at all on television. When women do appear they are usually in the home as housewives, unless they are the victims of violence or are "evil women."

These images do not accurately reflect either the increasing prevalence of women who are working outside the home (c.f. Kreps, 1976; Hoffman and Nye, 1974) or the rising incidence of women who are not "house*wives*" but rather heads of households (c.f. Ross and Sawhill, 1975). However, they are correct in implying that women do most of the homemaking. A UNESCO Time Budget Series (Szalai, 1972) done in twelve countries shows that women in all countries, even the socialist ones, spent much more time on housework than did men. Only in one Soviet city was child care equally divided. Not only do women spend more time in caring for the home, they also overwhelmingly spend more time in it than men (Hole and Attenborough, 1966).

Numerous sociological investigations continue to document the identification of women's roles with the making of a home, even when other activities are pursued. In 1951, Rose found that college women's expectations for themselves were to work full time, to volunteer for church and community work, to entertain, and to raise a large family. Wilensky's 1968 data and the time-use studies described previously reveal that women who work outside the home simply add it on to other tasks.

While this taking on of additional roles may be physically tiring, it could be taken as representative of women's progress in achieving fuller lives. However, studies of very different sample populations (c.f. Komarovsky, 1973; Lopata, 1971; Oakley, 1974) reveal two sources of conflict in this identification of women with the making of homes. One arises from the assumption that for women the home must come first, regardless of what else they are involved in. The second involves cultural ambivalence toward, and at times devaluation of, homemaking activities and the homemaker role (Burnett, n.d.; Komarovsky, 1973; Lopata, 1971; Oakley, 1974). Thus women are on the one hand committing themselves to and taking responsibility for the home and on the other being denigrated when they are "nothing but a housewife." They may be providing an alternative to the pressures of the individualistic, achievement-oriented public world, but they are being judged negatively by the criteria of that world while being expected by all to continue to manage the home.

On the basis of this research we feel that it is important then to ask what part the home, as a physical locale and a symbolic space, does play in the struggles of women and men toward liberation from the constraint of sex roles in our society. Are men assuming more responsibility for household work? Are the sexes becoming more equally associated with the nurturing private world of the home? In short, are the kinds of investments, both psychological and behavioral, that men and women make in the home becoming more similar?

Most of the information presented thus far indicates little movement in the direction of greater equality either in activity or in symbolic involvement. Rather it appears that women are generally attempting to add to their repertoire of activities and social roles outside the home while continuing to bear major responsibility for the making of a home. This is a very demanding endeavor. In these circumstances the options and constraints presented by the sociophysical environment are likely to have a very significant effect on the feasibility of being involved in the private world of the home and the world beyond. Three particular aspects of the context of women's lives are expected to importantly affect their ability to combine home-related activities and values with pursuits and fulfillments in other domains.

The first of these involves the degree of sharing of household tasks with their partners. Even though, overall, men may not be taking on much of the work of homemaking, individual variation in this domain would be expected to affect a woman's opportunities to become invested in goals outside the home and the equality of the psychological investment of the man and woman in the home.

Secondly, the accessibility of other pursuits in the physical environment is expected to influence a woman's potential involvement outside the home. This hypothesis is suggested by data from several sources. Looking at couples in northern California over a forty-year time span, Maas and Kuypers (1974) found that the adult life-styles of women were more affected by the accessibility to sources of satisfaction in the sociophysical environment than were those of men. Further, women who in older age were described as least well adjusted and happy were likely to live in remote suburban or rural locations and to have focused most of their activities around home and family. The balance of interests evidenced by most of the men in the sample was apparently little influenced by the location of their homes.

We can perhaps understand women's dependency on the environment more clearly when we look at the concrete opportunities women have for pursuits outside the home. Palm and Pred have taken this approach in their thought-provoking paper entitled "A Time-Geographic Perspective on Problems of Inequality for Women" (1974). On the basis of information about the required daily activities of women and the accessibility of transportation and services in the San Francisco Bay area of northern California, they concluded that for many women the distances to activities outside the home, the unavailability of transportation, and the time schedules imposed by household duties and child care made the possibility of involvement in pursuits outside the home very remote. These data plus our own preliminary interviews led us to expect that the location of the home with respect to other activity spaces would be related to the use and meaning of the home for women.

Finally, perhaps the most important aspect of the relationship between the world inside and outside the home concerns the symbolic attachments represented by the home environment. Even though it is true that women have been associated with the home and home-related activities, it seems to us a mistake to assume that there are no rewards attached to home life for both men and women. It is perhaps in this realm of symbolism that the future changes in sex roles become most problematic.

The home is a major locale within which most people spend large amounts of time. A very great number of significant human activities take place within the home. It is a setting that provides the boundary between public on-stage activities and private interpersonal as well as solitary pursuits. But beyond that the home affords opportunities for some measure of control over how one's time is spent, what activities are pursued, and the types and qualities of interpersonal relationships that may be developed, as well as being a place in which personal fulfillment may be sought. That the home has been periodically subjected to derision and home-related activities considered somehow as second-class pursuits reflects the values of a society in which occupational achievement and success is considered to be the summum bonum. It is not at all clear, however, that the pursuit of occupational success is necessarily accepted by most people as the value to be pursued to the exclusion of all others. To the extent that people place value on other types of activities as contributors to a satisfactory life experience, it seems reasonable to inquire about the nature of these alternatives.

Since most North Americans spend their so-called discretionary time within the home it can be expected that the home will be characterized as having a set of advantages and disadvantages that serve as important components in the assessment of overall life satisfaction or dissatisfaction. Because of the close association between the home and women it may therefore be expected that the symbolic meaning of the home is associated with some measure of ambivalence regarding its place in a person's total life experience.

Thus the research to be described follows two main courses.

One is to look at the relationship between sex roles and the meaning and use of the home. Where possible, variations in role sharing are examined to see what impact less traditional definitions of roles have on the meaning and use of the home. On the other hand we feel it would be a mistake to emphasize only the social causality of role segregation. Taking a more ecological approach we also attempt to look at the interdependence of role definition and the environmental context of the home. Just as home-related activities and values are expected to be most different between men and women with sharply segregated sex-role definitions, we also expect that the degree of physical segregation of the home from the broader world will be related to differences in the use and meaning of the home. To help us to begin to understand some of the ecological constraints of sex roles as they related to the home, we will be comparing home-related activities and attitudes of urbanites, whose homes are proximal to many other activities, and suburbanites, who live in more homogeneous residential environments. Finally we shall try to explore more systematically the meaning of the home as a source of possible rewards for activities that are not conventionally defined as "work-related." We feel that it is in this area that many of the promises and obstacles to the reduction of sex-stereotyped activities will ultimately be found.

Sex Roles and the Meaning of the Home

One of the first studies conducted in this research program concerned the meaning of the home to young married couples (Hayward, 1977). While this study was not primarily focused on sex-role differences in the meaning of the home, such differences did emerge. They were in keeping with what were seen as the implications of previous research on the identification of women with the home in that the significance of the home to women tended to be greater and the meanings related to the home were more closely linked to their identities.[2] Women were more likely to think of the home as an expression or component of their own identity. They also tended to see the meaning of the home as involving important relationships with other people and to feel that the home was a personalized place. Men responded to the meaning of the home more as simply a physical place and associated the meaning of the home more with their own childhood than did women. These findings may suggest that emotional attachment to the home is more difficult for men as they grow into their adult roles, away from the home-centered life of a child.

The data from this study also confirmed our expectation that less segregated role definitions would be related to greater similarity of the sexes in the meaning of the home. Men and women were categorized according to whether or not economic responsibility and household activities were shared. Comparisons were then made between sharing and nonsharing men, sharing and nonsharing women, sharing men and women, and non-sharing men and women. The largest sex differences in the importance of different aspects of the meaning of home occurred between men who were away from home at work and did not share housework and women who were primarily homemakers. For these couples, home was most important as a place for relationships with others and as an aspect of identity for women. In contrast men found it more related to their childhood home. These differences were not found between sharing men and women. However, in both sharing and nonsharing couples, men were more likely than women to describe the home as just a physical place. In the within-sex comparisons, only one difference occurred: women who were mainly homemakers assigned more identity-related meaning to the home than women in sharing couples.

If we look at the individual concepts related to the meaning of home, the following differences between men and women emerge. Women feel that the meaning of the home involves a sense of belonging, a part of "me," refuge, a place to care about, where I am safe and secure, the center of my world, sharing of emotions, warmth and security, a core of my existence, and ability to change a place. Men are more likely to relate the meaning of the home to its being a place where things belong to me, feels like its mine, architectural design, a room, a street, where I spent my childhood, where one's parents live, where you learn attitudes, some place for a long time, leisure, a bed, and an extra space. The differences in the items women and men choose to express and meaning of the home once again emphasize the relatively greater current personal investment in the home by women. Ownership, physical descriptions, and childhood home are more salient for men.

In summary, this study of the meaning of the home indicates that positive affective associations make up most of the meanings of home to people. However, women tend to view their homes as a more emotionally significant aspect of their adult lives. Men give more neutral physical meanings and associations related to childhood. Further, the analysis in which role sharing was taken into account suggests that this difference is greatest between men and women with more traditional sex-typed patterns of responsibility. Since the main purpose of this study was not to explore sex-role difference, the data on role sharing were minimal. They suggest the importance of this in the symbolic meaning of the home but do not allow us to go much further in answering the questions posed.

Sex Roles, Home-related Behaviors, and
Home Satisfactions

The Hayward study found differences in the meaning of the home as a function of sex role, even though the explicit purpose of the study was not the study of sex roles. We have just completed a much larger and more comprehensive investigation in which we have tried to explore more fully the relationships among sex roles and home-related attitudes and behaviors. In doing so we identified a wide range of issues including the actual distribution of household labor, priorities for the satisfaction with physical aspects of the house and neighborhood, attitudes toward the home, attitudes toward sex roles, personal values and characteristics, and satisfaction with self and other family members.[3] Data were gathered by questionnaires administered by respondents.[4]

The sample chosen represented an urban neighborhood and a nearby suburban area that had been matched on the variables of average income, household composition, occupation, and racial composition. The urban neighborhood is an upper middle-class residential area in New York City known for its physical attractiveness and urban village quality. The suburban area is a Connecticut town also considered upper middle class and distinguished by large, graceful older homes with lawns. Both areas, however, do have a range of income represented and a variety of building types and sites of dwelling units.[5]

We chose both an urban and a suburban sample because the work of Michelson (1973) in Toronto and our own preliminary interviews in the New York City area suggested that the urban location eased some of the role strain women experienced by providing options, but in many cases, failed to fulfill their images of the good home and did not meet their expectations for a place to raise children. The trade-off seemed to be exactly the sort of potential conflict between different aspects of women's roles that interests us. Further, the expectations and desires for a residential environment seemed to be different for men and to favor the suburban setting more unambiguously.

Our data strongly confirm the significance of both sex and location of housing in understanding activities in the household. A few conclusions are overwhelmingly obvious.[6] First, most household tasks were extremely sex typed. Sex was not only a highly significant factor in the responses to twenty-two of the twenty-four activities questions, but it also accounted for a remarkably high proportion of the variance, in most cases about 35 to 50 percent and for some activities as much as 60 to 75 percent. The activities performed largely by women included special cooking, bed making, sewing, setting and clearing the table, laundry, vacuuming, dusting, mopping, food shopping, errands, furniture buying, and pet care. The household chores men usually reported doing were indoor and outdoor repair, taking out garbage, indoor and outdoor painting, and lawn mowing. We purposely asked about very specific behaviors rather than global ones like "housework" because we thought that some chores might be more likely to be shared, even if the bulk of the housework was still done by women. Our results suggest the opposite effect of such questions. When researchers ask more general questions, the sex differences tend to be smaller than those we obtained. We suspect that respondents asked global questions tend to present themselves as more egalitarian than might actually be the case. Our data show that most of the household tasks that must be done on a regular basis are performed by women. The only exception is taking out the garbage.

The second variable, location of home, also significantly differentiated household behavior. The suburban group reports overall greater frequency of many household tasks, as was also true in Michelson's data (except that the urbanites take out more garbage, probably due to less frequent ownership of disposals). In addition, the urban sample was significantly less sex typed than the suburban group in the performance of fourteen of the twenty-two household tasks. These included daily cooking, bed making, outdoor repairs, setting and clearing the table, washing clothes (but not ironing), vacuuming, mopping, outdoor painting, food shopping, buying furniture, and washing dishes. Window washing was more frequently done by women in the suburbs and by men in the city. Also, gardening seems to be more of a female activity in the city and a male pastime in the suburbs. We see, then, that not only are most of the household tasks sex typed but also that it would appear that females spend more time in these activities, although the sex differences are smaller in the city sample. From these data it seems quite clear that the activities people engage in at home tend to be different depending on their sex and the area they live in.

The results of the Hayward study showing sex-role differences in concepts of home would suggest that the greater involvement in home-related activities that we find for women would be reflected in a more personal identification with the home. In our own data this tendency did appear, but there was some departure from our expectation that greater activity in the home would relate to greater personal investment. While, overall, women did place greater importance on various aspects of the meaning of homes, suburban male as well as female residents were also often more "invested" in the home than were the urban groups.

Generally we found that women thought it was more important that the home express their personalities than did men (p < .001). When asked a number of questions about the importance of and satisfaction with specific aspects of meaning of the home, we found that women placed more importance on many of these aspects and were frequently more satisfied with them than were men. Women reported that they both found the following aspects of their homes more important and more satisfying than did men: home as (1) a place to see people you like, (2) the center of the family, (3) a place for intimate relationships, (4) a place to be alone, (5) a place to relax, and (6) a place to display things you own. This suggests that for women some of the social and personal functions of the home are both emphasized more and better realized. Interestingly, there were no uses of the home on which men placed more importance than women or in which they were better satisfied.

A second pattern of findings emerged that is also of particular interest to us. For a number of uses of the home, women in both locations reported feeling that they were more important than men did. Those uses included home as a place to raise children, a place to do work you enjoy, a place to have fun, a space you can use any way you want, and a setting for the kind of life you want to live. However, the female and male suburbanites reported being better satisfied with their home on these dimensions. Suburbanites rated these aspects of the home as more important than did urbanites: home as a place for intimate relationships, a place to have fun, a place to be alone, and a space you can use any way you want. Their satisfaction with these aspects of their homes was, again, greater than that of urbanites.

Thus our data on household tasks and attitudes toward the home reveal certain commonalities and significant differences. As we expected, women invest more labor in the home and seem to view the home as more an expression of themselves. Further it is important to them for a broader range of purposes and often is more satisfying to them for those uses. Further analyses of our data were done to see if those men and women who shared household tasks in a less sex-stereotyped way also were more similar in their attitudes toward the home. This did not prove to be the case. This finding does not support the Hayward data and suggests caution in generalizing such results to different samples and when different attitudes toward the home are examined.[7]

While our data did not fully bear out the implications of the earlier research that role sharing leads to more similar attitudes

to the home among men and women, we did find two interesting relationships with our measure of role sharing.[8] Those people
who divided household tasks in less sex-stereotyped ways also
tended to report enjoying their time at home more, although
this finding did not quite reach statistical significance. In addition, those people with more traditional sex-typed divisions of
household tasks were more likely to say that they wished they
were freer to leave their homes more often.

The data we have presented have a number of implications
for our interest in the home as a critical problem in changing
sex roles. The first, of course, is to once more point out that
women bear the responsibility for the overwhelming majority
of household chores. Secondly, women seem to care more
about the home and to gain more satisfactions from it. Thus
even if the home is a burden on women's time, it is seen as a
rewarding one.

The conclusions to be drawn from the differences among
urban and suburban men and women are more complex. Thus
far it would appear that while urban couples report less sex
stereotyping of household tasks, differences in attitudes toward
the home are greater for them than for the suburbanites. However, it would be too simple to conclude that, despite potentially
greater responsibility for housework, urban women might be
happier in a suburban setting. Our findings indicate that the
urban environment is used and valued by women for activities
outside the home. Our data also show that urban women place
a much higher value on working outside the home (whether or
not they are currently employed) and in this are similar to their
urban male counterparts. Suburban men also value their work
highly, but suburban women do not. (The number of women
working in the two areas is about equal.) Throughout our data,
it is clear that, as one might expect, the urban sample is more
involved in work-related and cultural pursuits, while the suburban group is primarily family centered. However, it appears
that women in the city and men in the suburbs tend to value
both areas more equally, whereas, urban men emphasize work
and suburban females focus primarily on the home.

There is also one area of activity that is more important to
females in our sample and characterizes urban life more than

suburban. This is neighboring. Women in the city have more friends within walking distance whereas men in the suburbs are more likely to be close to their friends (Sex X Area, p < .10). Females talk to neighbors more often and city dwellers talk to neighbors more often. In looking at the interaction one sees that urban women engage in neighboring very much more frequently than all other groups (p < .001). Further questions related to talking to neighbors in the streets, in shops, and in the home, as well as talking with shopkeepers, all show the same pattern of main effects and interactions. This is interesting in our upper middle-class sample, since such neighboring has chiefly been considered a working-class urban phenomenon. Data from open-ended interviews (Mackintosh, Olsen, and Wentworth, 1977) have led us to believe that this pattern of socializing is highly valued by urban women.

In this way the urban women appear to have a wider range of satisfactions outside the home and to give more importance to them. However, both urban and suburban women find and wish to find important satisfactions in the home. Here, the suburbanite is likely to be in a better position to realize these goals. Even though the area studied is considered one of the best residential neighborhoods in New York City, both urban men and women report significantly more times that they are dissatisfied with their homes (p < .01). Factors such as the smaller average size of dwelling units in the city and a lesser sense of safety, especially among women, in the urban home and urban neighborhood are probably at least partially responsible for the differences in satisfaction. Measures related to actual size and perceived adequacy of size and to safety show city dwellers to be relatively disadvantaged in these ways. One might speculate that these inadequacies of the residential environment affect women more since they spend significantly more time at home and seem to see the home as a more important place for many aspects of life. Satisfaction with home on the dimensions described was significantly correlated with perceived adequacy of the size of the home for the urban sample but was unrelated for the suburban group.

Given the different contexts in which urban and suburban women and men view their homes, we felt that the patterns of values and assessments of the home might be different, as well as the degree to which certain aspects of home were seen as important and satisfying. Rather than seeing the evaluation of the home for each purpose as independent of other evaluations, we were interested in looking for evaluations that grouped together and asking whether these relationships among evaluations were similar in the different groups. To accomplish this we performed separate factor analyses on the urban men, urban women, suburban men, and suburban women on those items in our questionnaire that asked the respondent to rate the importance of and satisfaction with various aspects of the home. Our results indicated that while there were a number of similarities in the assessments made of the home environment, some interesting differences emerged as well. We shall try to summarize the major points that could be obtained from these analyses.

If we relate those patterns of evaluation that characterize the different groups to differences in importance of and satisfaction with particular uses of the home, some interesting implications become apparent. For three of the four groups we have looked at, the very uses of the home that are most related to their enjoyment of the home are ones with which they are less satisfied. Urban men were less satisfied than urban women with the home as a retreat, yet such satisfaction was positively related to the men's enjoyment of home and negatively to women's. Urban women placed more importance on the home as a place to raise children than did their spouses, while both reported less satisfaction with the home for this purpose than did suburban couples. This may not matter too much to urban men since it was not strongly related to their overall enjoyment of home, but for urban women it is part of a complex of child- and family-centered uses of home that were very significant to their overall satisfaction. The case is less clear for suburban women, yet generally it appears that their overall enjoyment of the home is most related to adult activities and the satisfactory definition of a life-style in the home setting. Here the suburban woman must depend greatly on the resources of her own family and self, being somewhat cut off from activities outside the home. Only the suburban man seems well situated to achieve his home values most successfully. His two environments, plus perhaps the commitment of his wife to household tasks, provide both options for adult activities and a satisfying family-centered environment.

Certainly our data are not unequivocal enough to make this argument strongly. However, Michelson's previous findings (1973) and Sylvia F. Fava's chapter in this volume further support the idea. In addition, the research by Elizabeth Mackintosh and her colleagues carried out as another part of our research program on housing and life-style also indicates that urban environments offer more options for women but expose them to many difficulties in terms of childrearing, safety, and inadequate space in the dwelling unit. In her study both urban and suburban men also seem to favor suburban living.

Sex Roles and the Relative Merits of Urban and Suburban Homes

The research carried out by Mackintosh, Olsen, and Wentworth (1977) began, like that of Hayward, by asking a question that was not focused on sex roles. In this case, the investigators were interested in the experience of raising children in an urban high-rise development. Since such environments were usually thought of as bad for raising children, a development was chosen for study that has a reputation as an unusually good family environment in New York City. In preliminary interviews, many respondents indicated their intentions to move to the suburbs in the near future. Therefore the investigators decided to add a comparison group of respondents who had moved from the development to suburban housing.

Fifteen urban and fifteen suburban couples participated in an open-ended, in-depth interview in which each partner was interviewed separately by a same-sex interviewer. Of these couples, 48 percent reported a greater desire on the part of the husband to move to the suburbs while the wife was more positive in only 14 percent of the cases. When the move to the suburbs was agreed on, or anticipated as probable, women expressed more worry about the move. Typical remarks included statements like, "I was afraid of isolation, intellectual stagnation, and boredom." Husbands expressed no such fears; instead, they looked forward to a more relaxed life and more outdoor activities. Women also placed less value on owning a detached, single-family home. A conflict seemed to exist between the wife's attachment to the social and cultural opportunities of the city and the desire of many husbands for the relaxation and status of a suburban home.

After moving to the suburbs, half of the suburban women felt they suffered from lack of stimulation. They often stated that they themselves had become more boring as a result of the move. In contrast, one third of the suburban men (and no suburban women) said they enjoyed leaving behind the hectic pace of the city. Women in the suburbs also expressed discouragement about the possibility of getting a job. They saw few options available in the suburbs, yet commuting to the city was ruled out because of family obligations.

One of the attributes of this urban site valued most by women was the availability of friendships with other young mothers. Over half of these urban women listed other residents of the development as their closest friends. Only two husbands did so. Urban women commented on their enjoyment of casual socializing and indeed time-use diaries showed them spending almost two hours less alone per weekday than suburban women. Of those women who had moved to the suburbs, a third reported feeling lonely and missing their old patterns of socializing. Suburban women who located in more dense suburbs or near already established friends experienced less difficulty with isolation.

Fathers talked of the values of the suburban experience for their children quite frequently. They especially emphasized outdoor play and a more natural environment. In contrast, women committed to urban living saw the city as providing advantages to children by giving them more varied experiences. Overall, women seemed less positive towards suburban living whereas men tended to be most satisfied when living in the suburbs. Of all groups, suburban men reported the greatest satisfaction with their residences. However, despite women's generally more favorable attitude toward city living, the urban residence also had some negative impact on them. The small size of apartments and the necessity of supervising children closely to protect their safety were seen as problems. Urban mothers spent almost three hours a day more with their children than suburban mothers and reported very great concern about allowing their children outside alone. Urban women also spent more time in the apartment with the children than their husbands did, and may therefore have experienced more tension due to lack of privacy in the apartment.

The relations between husbands and wives were complexly affected by the different place these urban and suburban homes had in their lives. Almost half of the suburban residents thought family dynamics improved after the move. One suburban woman described the situation as follows: "My husband does not have to be as intimately involved in the children's activities and affairs. . . . I think that has lessened for us potential tensions. In the city, I very strongly felt that one day during the weekend, it was necessary for me to be totally alone. Which would mean I would have to leave the apartment and do something outside or he would go with the children. Here, there is more freedom for each of us to do what we want." Generally, suburban men seemed to find the time they spent with their families more relaxing than it had been in the city. The increase in commuting time was viewed negatively but was mentioned as decreasing time spent with the family by only three suburban respondents. Overall, however, suburban men spent significantly less time with their families and with their children alone and their wives alone according to time-budget data.

In summary, the residential choices of these couples were evaluated quite differently by husbands and wives. The retreat and recreational function of the home was more satisfying for men in the suburban setting. In addition suburban homes were seen as generally better for raising children and as providing better financial investment and more status. The wives in this situation appear to be caught in a rather difficult set of choices. On the one hand, they value their children's independence and well-being very highly, as well as their husbands' enjoyment of the home. In the city environment, women spend more time in their cramped apartment and thus experience the pressures of being with young children in such a space. Further, because of fear for children's safety, they generally choose to accompany children outside the home.

However, women seem to rely on the city to provide them with stimulation, opportunity for activities outside the home, and rewarding social relationships. While men maintain their involvement in urban life after moving to the suburbs by continuing to work in the city, women often feel a great loss of options after the move. Sometimes this loss of options, combined with loneliness, led to feelings of depression and stagnation. Once again, we see women in the suburbs being forced to choose between the private world of the home and the broader world. For men the range of home-related satisfactions is broadened in the suburbs without as great a loss of other opportunities.

Concluding Thoughts

The research reported confirms our initial feeling that the home is a significant physical and symbolic environment for both women and men. For women the home is the place where they spend much of their time and on which they focus much of their activity. Their activity patterns, and their sense of options and feelings about their identity are strongly influenced by its location. This seems particularly true for mothers of young children. Clearly the home represents both a set of significant satisfactions and a set of responsibilities that must be traded off with the pursuit of goals outside the home. If women are to expand their roles outside the home, a wide range of home-related activities and values must be changed in some way.

One implication of our data is that higher density, mixed-use residential environments give women more options. The current residential choices of the samples we studied force couples to choose either small apartments and social and physical environmental conditions they consider nonoptimal for childrearing (due to high crime, pollution, lack of contact with nature, unsatisfactory schools) or the loss of social and cultural opportunities, especially for the wife. Thus we are led to concur with Michelson (1977) on the desirability of maintaining and developing satisfactory residential environments in the city. Improved public transportation in suburban areas is also a potential way of ameliorating some of these problems.

A second implication of our data does not lead to such clearcut suggestions, and may even raise doubts about the potential success of the urban housing alternative. In Hayward's study and in our own, urban men appear to be less emotionally invested in the home than are their wives. For women in all samples, the home is closely linked to their identities and provides some very significant satisfactions. Men seem to be happier and more psychologically invested in suburban homes. Where does this leave women who both value their homes and want them to be meaningful centers of the family *and* who want to expand their roles outside the home?

Looking at the same issue from the male point of view, it appears that men prefer residential environments that militate against the possibility of changing sex roles. This may be an inadvertant consequence of the bonuses of suburban life—retreat, outdoor activities, home ownership, relief from the pace of the city—or it may be partially motivated by a perhaps unconscious desire in many men to assure that their home will be taken care of by a woman with few other options. Certainly this malevolent interpretation is not necessary but may nonetheless play a part in a system of expectations that are very common. Komarovsky's interviews reveal how strongly even well-educated, Ivy League students in the early 1970s saw a woman's first duty as being to provide a relaxing, well-run home for her husband and children, even when they believe that social roles outside the home are necessary for a woman to be interesting.

Thus far we have presented a somewhat bleak prospect for changing sex roles. However, we hope our data will not be predictive of the future, but rather be part of the dialectic processes of seeing where we are and moving on. The Women's Movement and discussion of changing sex roles for both men and women, accompanied by increased female participation in the work force puts us at a new historical point. Our data, and our own experiences, suggest that viable liberation for both men and women must include some of the values and satisfactions traditionally found in the home. At present, suburban men, and to some extent urban women, seem to be in a position to experience both these satisfactions and those of the broader world.

Several major obstacles appear to limit the availability of a diversity of roles and satisfactions, and these seem to particularly affect women. The time schedule and reward structure of most work is clearly one of the strongest pressures against the combination of physical and psychological investment in the home and outside. The geographic segregation of residential environments from public life reinforces the cultural choice of work or home, especially for women, who do not have the luxury of a wife. Women who invest energy in work outside the home cannot assume that anyone else will compensate. By the same token, women who commit themselves primarily to home-related goals do not gain a second meaningful environment through their husbands' work, whereas men working outside the home do gain this from marriage. In addition, the many women who are financially required to work, especially sole heads of households, must juggle both sets of demands and goals in a context that supports commitment to one or the other. Transportation, housing, work schedules, store hours, and much of the rest of the structure of opportunity in our society are predicated on the idea of the sexual division of household work and work outside the home, even though almost half the women in the United States do both.

We believe that a diversity of roles is a desirable option for many people and a necessity for some. A supportive environmental context would not force women to choose between involvement in making a satisfying home and involvement in work and cultural and social pursuits outside the home. Planners, designers, and policymakers must become aware of the impact of their decisions on the options women have and on home-related values as well as on economic and achievement values. Beyond this, however, men and women striving for more egalitarian and more satisfying social roles, relationships, and identities must begin to physically and symbolically redefine the place of the home in their lives.

Notes

1. Most of the research described in this chapter was supported by NIMH grant no. MH 124795-02.

2. Of the nine clusters of meaning that people seemed to apply to the home, three of them were differentially salient for men and women, and two others tended to show sex-role divergence in salience (although the difference only reached a probability level of $p < .10$).

3. Thanks go to Dwight Jewson, Carol Sullivan, and Gelina Zamdmer Dubnikov who participated in the design of the questionnaire and were largely responsible for data collection.

4. Because of the length of the questionnaire, all respondents were asked to respond to only two thirds of the questions although they were told that if they liked, they could request the omitted third. A small number of respondents did elect to complete all three parts. Otherwise, equal random samples of all combinations of sections were obtained.

5. Even though the areas were comparable, some slight demographic differences did emerge. The incomes for both area samples were equivalent with an average income in both places being somewhat more than $40,000 a year. The suburban sample was slightly older and somewhat less well educated than the urban group. The average age for suburban males was 40.5, for females 37.7; urban males averaged 38.7 and females 35.3. Most suburban males had obtained a college degree whereas urban males were likely to have a professional degree or some education beyond college. The suburban females also had somewhat less education than the urban females, the former tending to have some college but no degree. The number of children living at home was comparable for the groups: most had one or two children. Home ownership was more common in the suburbs although a substantial proportion of the urbanites owned their house or apartment. Apartment residents were primarily from the urban area. The sample consisted of 106 married couples in the urban area and 110 married couples in the suburban location. In all, then, 432 people responded to our interview.

6. The following analyses involved 2 X 2 Analysis of Variance (Sex X Area). All reported findings are statistically significant at least at the .05 level. Many were significant beyond the .001 level.

7. However, the younger age of Hayward's sample and the lower income level may account for those differences. Overall it is likely that our sample populations were more sex stereotyped in their attitudes and behaviors than his. Secondly, our questions were directed more at the importance of the home for certain purposes and satisfaction of those goals, whereas Hayward asked about the centrality of certain concepts to the meaning of the home. Both of these are interesting questions but we should keep in mind that they do not necessarily refer to the same attitudes toward the home.

8. An index of role sharing was constructed by assigning higher values to opposite sex-type activities and lower ones to same sex-typed activities.

References

Burnett, P. "Social Space in the City and Women's Cognition of Their Roles." In Burnett (ed.), *Women in Society: New Perspectives,* in manuscript.

Fava, S. F. "Women's Place in the New Suburbia." Chapter 5, this volume.

Hayward, G. "Psychological Concepts of Home Among Urban Middle Class Families with Young Children." Doctoral Dissertation, Environmental Psychology Program, City University of New York, Graduate Center, 1977.

Hoffman, L. W., and F. I. Nye. *Working Mothers.* San Francisco: Jossey-Bass, 1974.

Hole, M. V., and J. J. Attenborough. *Houses and People.* (Ministry of Technology Building Research Station.) London: Her Majesty's Stationery Office, 1966.

Komarovsky, M. "Cultural Contradictions and Sex Roles: The Masculine Case." *American Journal of Sociology* 5, no. 4 (1973):873–884.

Kreps, J. *Women and the American Economy: A Look at the 1980's.* Englewood Cliffs, N.J.: Prentice-Hall, 1976.

Lopata, N. Z. *Occupation Housewife.* London: Oxford University Press, 1971.

Maas, H. S., and J. A. Kuypers. *From Thirty to Seventy.* San Francisco: University, 1977.

Mackintosh, E.; R. Olsen; and W. Wentworth. "The Attitudes and Experiences of the Middle Income Family in an Urban High-rise Complex in the Suburbs." New York: Center for Human Environments, City University, 1977.

Michelson, W. *Environmental Change.* Research Paper no. 60. Toronto: University of Toronto, Centre for Urban and Community Studies, 1973.

_____. *Environmental Choice, Human Behavior, and Residential Satisfaction.* New York: Oxford University Press, 1977.

Oakley, A. *The Sociology of Housework.* New York: Pantheon Books, a division of Random House, 1974.

Palm, R., and A. Pred. "A Time-Geographic Perspective on Problems of Inequality for Women." Working paper no. 236. Berkeley: Institute of Urban and Regional Development, University of California, 1974.

Rose, A. "The Adequacy of Women's Expectations for Adult Roles. *Social Forms* 5 (1951):69–77.

Ross, H. L., and I. V. Sawhill. *Time of Transition: The Growth of Families Headed by Women.* Washington, D.C.: The Urban Institute, 1975.

Szalai, A. *The Use of Time.* The Hague: Mouton & Co., 1972.

Tuchman, G.; A. Kaplan; and J. Benet. *Hearth & Home: Images of Women in Media.* New York: Oxford University Press, 1978.

Wilensky, H. "Women's Work: Economic Growth, Ideology and Structure," Reprint Series, no. 7. Berkeley: Institute of Industrial Relations, University of California, 1968.

Women on Words and Images Task Force. *Dick and Jane as Victims: Sex Stereotyping in Children's Readers.* Princeton, N.J.: New Jersey Chapter, National Organization for Women, 1972.

2

The Household as Workplace: Wives, Husbands, and Children

Sarah Fenstermaker Berk

Interest in the impact of physical environments on the lives of women might well begin with scrutiny of the household. Whether an arena for interpersonal relations or a critical "starting point" for a wide range of extra-household endeavors, the household may be viewed as a significant "working space" for those whose labor it absorbs.

It should be no surprise to find that the household is a traditional repository for enormous amounts of productive labor. Past research into women's roles (Lopata, 1971; Glazer-Malbin, 1976) and women's work (Myrdal and Klein, 1956; Smuts, 1959; Holmstrom, 1972; Oakley, 1974) has underscored the fact that the household continues to be a significant productive environment for women. Further, despite women's growing attachments to other settings (school, employment, volunteer work), the data consistently show that they do not treat the household as a "neutral" environment, but include household activities as factors in their decisionmaking about extra-household commitments (Mahoney, 1961; Becker, 1965, 1974).

Increasingly, observers of the family, women, and social life in general have offered sweeping predictions of the relaxation of sex-typed expectations in all social settings. With the influx of women into the labor force, heightened consciousness of sex discrimination, and a general movement away from traditionally

The research reported in this chapter is part of a larger project undertaken by the author, Catherine White Berheide, and Richard A. Berk in 1976. Partial support for this research was provided through a grant from the National Institute of Mental Health (no. MH27340-01).

defined role distinctions, many have heralded a fundamental reordering of household and family relations (Young and Wilmott, 1973).

In the face of such pronouncements, it is important to examine the evidence. More specifically, research into the division of household labor will enable students of women and environments to understand how and under what conditions the household as *workplace* remains a unique encounter for women or is being generalized into a *collective* familial experience. It is the purpose of this chapter to explore some data on the division of household work, with a specific focus on the conditions under which wives, husbands, and children interact with the household as "workplace."

The discussion that follows is based on research undertaken in the context of a larger project on the characteristics of household labor (see Berheide et al., 1976, for review). The data were gathered in and around an affluent suburb of about 80,000 persons near a large Midwest metropolitan area. Three types of procedures were employed: participant observation in over forty households, a forty-minute telephone survey of a simple random sample of 309 married women from intact households, and a twenty-four-hour self-administered diary from a self-selected subset of 158 survey respondents. While all three data sets inform the questions raised in this chapter, primary emphasis is placed on those data generated by the survey instrument.[1]

The Survey Sample

The household environment and division of household labor described will be that of predominantly white, upper-income families.[2] Despite the middle-class character of this sample, sufficient variation does exist on several critical variables and some closely resemble national estimates. For example, 43 percent of the respondents are employed full time. Forty-six percent of those women employed work at professional-level jobs, such as teaching or nursing.

While formally representative of only a certain segment of the general population, this sample of suburban residents is in many ways ideal for addressing current assumptions about

changing household divisions of labor. Despite a wide range of
methodological approaches, previous research efforts have con-
verged on the identification of the central features of a more
"equitable" division of household labor among members. First,
those who have studied family life via ethnographic methods
generally agree that more highly educated, higher-income families are more likely to exhibit patterns of household labor
management that suggest a sharing of the household environment and its work imperatives (Bott, 1957; Rainwater et al.,
1959; Komarovsky, 1962). Second, a great many who are firmly
situated in the "conjugal power" school of family research
point to the heightened "resources" of wives through outside
employment as a factor in reaching more equitable "balances of
power" for family decisionmaking and household labor contributions (Herbst, 1952; Blood and Wolfe, 1960; Heer, 1962).[3]
Third, a related though somewhat nonempirical tradition in
microeconomics posits that full-time employment on the part
of household members will be accompanied by shifts in others'
household labor contributions. That is, if a wife is employed
full time (especially in a "high-energy" occupation), then
husbands will increase their contributions to the household
environment. Likewise, strong commitment to household labor
on the part of wives may be explained in part by the time
investments of their husbands in market labor spheres (Becker,
1965, 1974; Gronau, 1974, 1977).

There is necessarily a great deal that must be left unsaid concerning the empirical evidence for and theoretical foundations
of the conclusions cited above. A more complete critique may
be found elsewhere (Berk, 1976; Berk and Berk, 1978). Suffice
it to say that a major shortcoming of most of these works has
been a lack of reliable and direct evidence for the *behavior* of
household members in the everyday division of labor. Primarily,
normative expectations, extraordinary household contributions,
or hypothetical decisionmaking have been taken to represent an
accurate picture of "who does what" in the household environment. Through measurement of actual reported behavior at the
level of routine household work accomplishment, the results
summarized here seek to clarify current notions about the
"modern" family's encounter with the household as workplace.

Measuring the Division of Household Labor

Prior to the development of strategies for accurately assessing the division of household labor, it was necessary to establish a "list" of tasks that would both be meaningful to respondents and address the everyday realities of household work. Without such enumeration, it would have been very difficult to specify precisely *what* was being divided. This process seemed especially salient in light of previous studies of the division of household labor in which the *content* of work had been assumed in an uncritical fashion (Blood and Wolfe, 1960).

Since past schemes for studying household work seemed to have few behavioral referents we resorted initially to data gained through direct observation. From detailed observation in over forty households, lists of household work tasks were extracted, and any household activities even remotely linked to household members' notions of household work were consciously included (for details see: Berk, 1976; and Berk and Berheide, 1977). Lists of tasks observed in the field formed the basis for survey items on the content and division of household labor.

In order to empirically establish household work content, each respondent was asked to indicate if items in a list of particular household tasks were routinely accomplished in her household (regardless of who actually did each one). The result of these specific content lists for each household was a base-line understanding of what work was potentially divisible. These lists formed the foundation for the next step in which the reported division of such labor was examined. Efforts were made to limit the measurement of household work apportionment to routine or "everyday" tasks. In contrast to previous studies, what one might call "extraordinary" household tasks were not included. While such tasks may be critically important to the ultimate maintenance of the household environment, we wanted to be sure that we were not measuring either hypothetical divisions of labor (e.g., *"Would* your husband help with the dishes?"*) or marking some normative outer boundaries beyond which husbands or children may not venture (e.g., "Does your husband *ever* change diapers?"). In addition, even though the ideal would have been to ask all members of the household about their own and others' contributions, a relatively high degree of confidence can be placed on the accuracy of reported household behavior (as opposed to attitudes) by a single household member (for a critical review of this issue see: Sudman and Bradburn, 1974; and Berk and Shih, 1980).

Once a task was cited by respondents as "part of" household work, they were asked "who generally does" the specific job in question. "Generally" was defined as equal to or greater than 50 percent frequency of accomplishment, thus insuring a more accurate reflection of routine and everyday contributions to this work site. Of course, since household members sometimes share in the accomplishment of a task, more than one person could be recorded as "generally" doing the task, and respondents were reminded of this.

The total number of tasks actually undertaken in each household was used as a base from which the proportions done by wives, husbands, and children were calculated. For example, if a woman said that ten of the meal preparation tasks were routinely done in her household and that she actually did five of them, she was credited with doing 50 percent of the meal preparation in her household.

The mean proportion of tasks done by all household members under the six task areas of meal preparation, cleaning the kitchen, laundry, straightening, outside errands, and "other household work" are reported in Table 2.1 (see Table 2.2 for task listings).[4] Remember that since multiple designations of family contributors were allowed when divisions of tasks were explored in the survey, the mean proportions in Table 2.1 do not sum to 1.0.[5]

This chapter will focus first on a general comparison of the contributions of wives, husbands, and children to household labor. Secondly, given the specific goal of charting some determinants of the "work" lives of household members in this environment, the results of a nonrecursive multivariate regression analysis will be briefly summarized.

Household Divisions of Labor: Description

Comparing the differences among family members (Table 2.1), one is immediately struck by the salience of the household as

TABLE 2.1 Proportions of Household Tasks Done by Wives,
Husbands and Children

Household Tasks		Mean Proportions	S.D.
Meal Preparation	– Wife	.88	.18
	– Husband	.16	.24
	– Children	.12	.22
Kitchen Cleaning	– Wife	.86	.20
	– Husband	.18	.27
	– Children	.11	.24
Laundry	– Wife	.92	.21
	– Husband	.12	.23
	– Children	.10	.22
Straightening	– Wife	.89	.19
	– Husband	.23	.29
	– Children	.13	.23
Outside Errands	– Wife	.74	.22
	– Husband	.54	.29
	– Children	.07	.16
Other Household Work	– Wife	.76	.19
	– Husband	.26	.19
	– Children	.10	.16

N = 309

a workplace for wives, but not for their husbands or children. Wives are shown to do 88 percent of the meal preparation tasks, 86 percent of the tasks associated with cleaning the kitchen, 92 percent of laundry tasks, 89 percent of the straightening, 74 percent of the outside errands, and 76 percent of "other household work." A significant contribution seems to fall to husbands in the area of outside errands (going to drug store, cleaners, gas station, chauffering children, etc.).

It is interesting to note that while the mean proportions represent *summary* indications of family members' contributions, results of the division of household labor in other, more disaggregated forms lead to identical conclusions. Here, one may talk about the percentage of wives, husbands, and children who "generally" accomplish a *particular* task. These disaggre-

TABLE 2.2 Listing of Household Tasks Reported in Table 2.1

Meal Preparation

planning menus
straightening kitchen
  before starting
setting table
cooking
serving meal
clearing food or dishes
washing dishes or
  loading dishwasher
drying dishes
putting food away
cleaning counters
  or stove top
wiping table
sweeping kitchen
  or eating area

Cleaning Kitchen

wiping counters
washing dishes or
  running dishwasher
drying dishes
running disposal or
  emptying garbage
putting away dishes
  or utensils
sweeping or washing
  kitchen floor
putting away food in
  cabinets or refrigerator
cleaning sink

Laundry

stripping beds
sorting clothes
using presoak or spray
putting in bleach/softener
removing some clothes from
  washer to hang and dry
after drying, sorting/
  folding clothes
putting clothes away
making beds with clean sheets
putting out clean towels

Straightening

going from room to room
  collecting dishes/glasses
collecting trash/old newspapers
putting food away
picking up toys/books/magazines
dusting
emptying ashtrays
making beds
sorting through mail/papers

Ironing

gathering clothes for ironing
dampening clothes
using spray starch
folding clothes/hanging clothes
putting clothes away

Outside Errands

gas station
grocery stores
clothing stores
cleaners
drug store/dime store
beauty shop/barber shop
bank
babysitter--pick up/drop off

"Other" Household Work

vacuuming
laundry
washing windows
cleaning oven
arranging for babysitter
household repair
dusting
washing or waxing floors
cleaning bathroom
sewing/mending
burning/carrying out trash
pet care
plant care
paying bills/handling finances
defrosting/cleaning refrigerator
baking
cleaning/rearranging kitchen
  cabinets

gated results challenge a number of popular stereotypes associated with the contributions of husbands and children. For those tasks popularly assumed to be in the "husband" categories of domestic labor, the results are quite startling. For example, 66 percent of the wives reported that they emptied the garbage at least half the time. Fifty-five percent of the wives reported that they went to the gas station as frequently as their husbands. Sixty-two percent of the wives were found to have primary responsibility for household financial matters, including bill paying. Judging from these results, the sole "male" bastion of household work contribution is "household repair," with only 28 percent of the wives participating at the level of husbands.

Turning to those specific household jobs that are ordinarily assumed to be "children's chores," similar results are shown. Setting the table (a classic children's task) was accomplished by 74 percent of the mothers on a regular basis. Eighty-eight percent of the mothers picked up toys as often as their children. Caring for family pets also proved to be a mother's responsibility, with 70 percent of the women reporting regular accomplishment.

Returning to Table 2.1, one will notice that there is some indication of *joint* participation by household members. Within any given household task area, the sum of proportions is approximately 1.20, thus suggesting that about one fifth of the household work is shared. However, critical to any interpretation of "sharing" is the distinction between "help" and "responsibility." This distinction, identified by Ann Oakley (1974), proved striking during our initial interviewing and field observation. "Responsibility" requires a very different kind of investment from "help," and respondents articulated this difference in a variety of ways. Below are two examples, portrayed in part through the language used by respondents in describing household divisions of labor with their husbands (italics added).

He (husband) tries to be *helpful*. He tries. He's a brilliant and successful lawyer. It's incredible how he smiles after he sponges off the table and there are still crumbs all over.

What about taking care of the children?

> He doesn't help them get dressed. He takes them hiking sometimes when I visit my mother. He reads to them and goes into their rooms to talk to them. *It's not actual work,* like helping them lay out their clothes. I would call it occasional *help.*

Thus, contributions by husbands were often described as *help* (children's contributions were invariably described this way), constituting efforts in which the wife is generally present in a *supervisory* role. Further, the "work" accomplished by husbands (e.g., entertaining children) was described by wives as not being the "real work" of the task at hand.

In short, it seems that any analysis of the household must begin with the observation that it is still women who routinely encounter it as a work environment. Not only do women take responsibility for the accomplishment of roughly 80 to 95 percent of the approximately sixty household tasks investigated, but there is some indication that contributions from husbands and children are perceived as "aid," thus leaving many of the vital managerial and planning responsibilities to women. However, given that we may still view the household environment as a woman's *workplace,* there remains the question of under what conditions this general picture varies. There is clearly enough variation in the level of all members' contributions to suggest that certain identifiable factors may contribute to a shifting of household work accomplishment from solely a feature of women's lives to a more shared quality of family living.

In the following section those factors that proved salient in explaining variation in the contributions of wives, husbands, and children will be reviewed. Special attention will be given to the relationships among members surrounding the division of household labor in this unique work environment.

Determinants of Household Divisions of Labor

The process of explaining variation in the contributions of family members to household labor was simplified by the fact that none of the variables tapping "preference" or "feelings" about certain tasks proved important to predicting variation in the division of labor proportions for the six areas in question.

When respondents were asked whether any of the following adjectives described their feelings about each of the original broad task areas—"enjoyable, frustrating, fulfilling, physically tiring, tedious or boring, unpleasant, difficult, neutral"—their responses showed near zero correlations with those variables measuring the division of labor among household members. This leads one to think that the division of household labor, specifically those conditions fostering contributions from husbands and children, is influenced by factors other than those of "preference." Any given affective orientation to household work on the part of women may be largely irrelevant to day-to-day household realities.

Secondly, the variety of human and material resources available to some households also proved to have negligible effects on the *division* of labor. Only 22 percent of respondents said that they were frequently aided by friends and neighbors with tasks such as babysitting and errands. Further, only 19 percent of the respondents employed domestic labor in their homes on a regular basis, and about half of that labor was utilized only once a week. Similarly, only 24 percent of the mothers employed regular child-care or babysitting arrangements (either inside or outside the home). In short, the employment of outside human resources to support the wife's labor in this environment was only important for a few households. In any case, such resources were never salient predictors of variation in family labor apportionment.

Thirdly, given the popular view that mechanical devices are important not only to household work content but also to its division, it was expected that the number of household appliances might have a real impact on the apportionment of household labor. Sample households had an average of five "major" appliances. Ninety-eight percent of the households had a vacuum cleaner, 78 percent a clothes washer, 72 percent a clothes dryer, 63 percent a nonfrost refrigerator-freezer, and 59 percent a dishwasher. There is some suggestion that the presence of appliances actually *increases* the time devoted to household work on the part of respondents ($r = .20$), but there is no indication that such material resources fundamentally alter the division of labor. Such findings are wholly consistent with

Vanek's (1974) conclusions from her longitudinal study of time spent on household work. As appliances are introduced into the household environment, standards of work change, and certainly the content of work may be transformed. However, this is not always accompanied by a diminished investment of work time or by a change in the apportionment of tasks.

These "null" findings seem all the more striking given the current publicity for "changing" life-styles and "open" marriages. In fact, data strongly suggest that in day-to-day maintenance of the household environment and its members, women are to an important degree routinely tied to each task and have little chance to contemplate the equity of household labor arrangements.

In prior analysis of these data (Berk and Berk, 1978) it was found that wives' wages from outside employment had a negative, but not significant, effect on labor contributed by those women. Those wives employed in high status occupations (e.g., professional/technical) contributed a significantly smaller proportion of household labor than did other women. Thus, for example, women employed in professional or technical occupations were found to contribute approximately 10 percent less household labor than other wives, with businesswomen contributing about 4 percent less.

Factors outside the home that explain the contribution of husbands produced more perplexing findings. Husbands with higher incomes do less household labor. In contrast, husbands in high-status occupations (holding income constant) were found to do more household labor. The latter finding is consistent with a great deal of past literature (Blood and Wolfe, 1960; Oakley, 1974; Farkas, 1976; Robinson, 1977).

Despite the fact that the occupational commitments of wives and husbands showed some impact on the division of household labor tasks, it is important to point out that for neither husbands nor wives did employment per se have any real impact on the reduction of wives' household labor contributions or on an increase in husbands' contributions. That is, some specific occupational categories proved important in explaining variation, but simply whether wives or husbands were employed did not.

For purposes of this discussion, perhaps more interesting are those findings describing relationships among family members and revealing how the contributions of each affect the contribution of others.[6] Only the efforts of children have direct effects on the proportion contribution of wives. Changes in the contribution of husbands have no effect on the contribution of wives. In contrast, the contribution of husbands are most affected by the efforts of other members. When either wives or children (or both) heighten their own contributions, husbands will contribute less. Finally, children are least affected by shifts in the contributions of others. Their contributions seem determined by factors other than those internal to the household environment and the contribution of other members. Earlier in the present discussion, qualitative evidence suggested that the contribution of husbands may be viewed by wives as peripheral, as effort demanding supervision, and ultimately not substitutable for the contribution of wives. Thus, the proportion contributed by husbands (unlike that of wives) may have only trivial effects on the overall division of labor, since husbands' efforts often represent joint participation rather than sole responsibility. While children's efforts may have an impact on the contribution of their parents, shifts in the contribution of parents do not seem to result in a corresponding increase or decrease in children's efforts. In prior work (Berk and Berk, 1978), the lack of substitutability between the household contributions of children and those of their parents was thought to result from the fact that their household labor is fixed, commensurate with parent's ideology about "discipline," "proper upbringing," and the external constraints on children's time produced by schooling, play, etc. Thus, while children's efforts can exert an impact on the contributions of their parents, significant shifts in the labor provided by parents does not result in alterations in the level at which children contribute.

Both the qualitative and quantitative findings reported here serve to refine our notions of this work environment as one which may be characterized by the unequal distribution of labor power, but which is affected systematically by the firmly fixed (and asymmetric) relations between workers. One may describe the environment in which household labor is allocated as one in which a single member takes primary responsibility for it as a work site. However, two other parties may respond in potentially significant ways to fluctuations in the contributions of others. Yet the age and gender of members are not incidental factors toward understanding how this environment is experienced as a workplace. In short, the division of work in the household environment depends much more on *who you are* than on what you are able to contribute.

Conclusions

In analyzing household work apportionment and understanding the household as a multidimensional social environment, one must not ignore the pervasive ideology that the household as "workplace" is singularly suited to the energies of women. The behavioral outcomes of this ideology should be obvious. Women are the major contributors to the maintenance of this environment, with "help" supplied by other members. But, as the primary participants in the "production" system, change in wives' investments to it may be accompanied by changes in the ways this work environment is apprehended by other household members. The apportionment of household labor responds to a variety of social exigencies stemming from within and without the household environment. Yet women continue to stand in a unique relationship to the household work environment by providing most of the accomplishment and responsibility for the day-to-day work demanded by shared living space.

What also becomes clear from the examination of the behavioral outcomes within the household as "workplace" is that small incremental increases in the contributions of husbands and children are dependent upon household members' relationships to each other and to *external* environments. That is, fluctuations in household work investments by all members first depend upon the gender-determined roles that order their everyday lives and secondarily upon the relations that all members have to the outside world of work. It is thus important to remember that alterations in the *physical* characteristics of the household, centering either on material or mechanical variations, do not necessarily mean that alterations in *social* relations will be forthcoming. This is likewise true for seemingly significant changes in household members' attitudes and ideologies concerning family responsibility, sharing, and the ultimate equity of household work apportionment. There is no doubt that the *content* of household work has and will continue to undergo great changes as the physical features of the household environment are altered. Similarly, family life itself will be reordered and redefined within new social and ideological contexts. Despite these changes, the division of household labor and the place of women in the household work environment seem steadfastly embedded in a complex configuration of social roles, normative pressures, and sexual inequalities.

Notes

1. For a more detailed discussion and specification of a nonrecursive model for the division of household labor, see Berk and Berk, 1978. In that paper, application of these data is made to recent work in the "new home economics." The findings from that paper can be only briefly summarized here.

2. Over half the respondents' husbands hold high status jobs: professional, technical, or managerial (65.7 percent), with nearly 40 percent of the husbands earning over $20,000 per year. In addition, 65 percent of the sample own their own homes or condominiums. Over half of the respondents have at least one child living at home, while a little less than 10 percent had an infant in the household.

3. It should be remembered that most, if not all, of these studies have completely ignored the potential and actual contributions of children to household labor. Children usually become important in some theoretical schemes as "objects" of labor which must be included in the time-cost calculations of adult family members. (For exceptions, see: Schnaiberg, 1974; Schnaiberg and Reed, 1974; and Schnaiberg and Goldenberg, 1975.)

4. The task area of "ironing" was dropped from all division of labor analyses, since there was little variation in contribution across family members. Few households did much ironing at all. When ironing did represent a routine household chore, women did it almost exclusively. Only one husband and one child were reported as contributing to the task of ironing on a regular basis in their households.

Child care has been deleted from the summary of results solely for purposes of the discussion. In the larger study, child care and its division was necessarily treated separately from other household labor activities. It was found to be the most complex configuration of tasks in the household and responded to somewhat different determining factors in its division among adult members. Its consideration requires much more space than is provided here. (For a discussion of child care, see: Berheide, 1976; Berk, 1976, 1979.)

5. Some readers may see the "mean proportion" method as a partial obfuscation of the realities of household work apportionment. For those who feel that the list of tasks encourage bias in the wife's "favor," I would direct them to scores of studies, using a variety of measurement techniques and undertaken in a number of cultural settings. Researchers whose concern is with the use of household time (e.g., Cowles and Dietz, 1956; Morgan et al., 1966; Walker, 1973; Young and Wilmott, 1973; Chapin, 1974; and Robinson, 1977) find that husbands invest roughly one fifth to one tenth of the time of their wives in household work. Further, comparable results are reported by investigators concerned with the "dollar value" of household work (Gauger, 1973; Walker and Gauger, 1973). Finally, the many studies centering on simple ordinal measures of household work investment (e.g., "high" participation vs. "low" participation) come to similar conclusions (Komarovsky, 1962; Lopata, 1971; Oakley, 1974; Vanek, 1974).

6. The substantive findings discussed from the nonrecursive regression analysis are based on three dependent variable proportions: (a) proportion contribution of wife (.84); (b) proportion contribution of husband (.21); (c) proportion contribution of children (.16). These proportions represent the aggregated dependent variables based on the disaggregated mean proportions found in Table 2.1.

References

Becker, G. S. "A Theory on the Allocation of Time." *Economic Journal* (September 1965):493–517.

_____. "A Theory of Marriage." In T. W. Schultz (ed.), *Economics of the Family.* Chicago: University of Chicago, 1974.

Berheide, C. W. "An Empirical Consideration of the Meaning of Work and Leisure: The Case of Household Work." Unpublished Ph.D. dissertation, Northwestern University, 1976.

_____; S. F. Berk; and R. A. Berk. "Household Work in the Suburbs: The Job and Its Participants." *Pacific Sociological Review* 19, no. 4 (October 1976):491–518.

Berk, S. F. "The Division of Household Labor: Patterns and Determinants."

Unpublished Ph.D. dissertation, Northwestern University, 1976.

_____. "Husbands at Home: The Organization of the Husband's Household Day." In K. W. Feinstein (ed.), *Working Women and Families.* Beverly Hills, Calif.: Sage Publications, 1979.

_____, and C. W. Berheide. "Going Backstage: Gaining Access to Observe Household Work." *The Sociology of Work and Occupations: An International Journal* 4, no. 1 (February 1977):27–48.

_____, and R. A. Berk. "A Simultaneous Equation Model for the Division of Household Labor." *Sociological Methods and Research* 6 (May 1978):431–468.

_____, and A. Shih. "Contributions to Household Labor: Wives' and Husbands' Accounts." In S. F. Berk (ed.), *Women and Household Labor.* Beverly Hills, Calif.: Sage Publications, 1980.

Blood, R. O., Jr., and D. M. Wolfe. *Husbands and Wives: The Dynamics of Married Living.* Glencoe: The Free Press, 1960.

Bott, E. *Family and Social Network.* London: Tavistock, 1957.

Chapin, F. S. *Human Activity Patterns in the City.* New York: John Wiley, 1974.

Cowles, M. L., and R. P. Dietz. "Time Spent in Homemaking Activities by a Selected Group of Wisconsin Farm Homemakers." *Journal of Home Economics* 48 (January 1956):29–35.

Farkas, G. "Education, Wage Rates and the Division of Labor between Husband and Wife." *Journal of Marriage and the Family* 38 (1976): 473–484.

Gauger, W. "Household Work: Can We Add It to the GNP?" *Journal of Home Economics* (October 1973):12–15.

Glazer-Malbin, N. "Housework." *Signs* 1, no. 4 (summer 1976):905–922.

Gronau, R. "The Effect of Children on the Housewife's Value of Time." In T. W. Schultz (ed.), *Economics of the Family.* Chicago: University of Chicago Press, 1974.

_____. "Leisure, Home Production and Work: The Theory of the Allocation of Time Revisited." *Journal of Political Economy* 85, no. 4 (1977): 1099–1124.

Heer, D. "Husband and Wife Perceptions of Family Power Structure." *Marriage and Family Living* 24 (1962):65–67.

Herbst, P. G. "The Measurement of Family Relationships." *Human Relations* 5 (1952):3–35.

Holmstrom, L. *The Two-Career Family.* Cambridge: Schenkman, 1972.

Komarovsky, M. *Blue-Collar Marriage.* New York: Random House, 1962.

Lopata, H. *Occupation: Housewife.* London: Oxford University Press, 1971.

Mahoney, T. A. "Influences on Labor-force Participation of Married

Women." In N. N. Foote (ed.), *Household Decision-Making.* New York: New York University Press, 1961.

Morgan, J. N.; I. A. Sirageldin; and N. Baerwalkt. *Productive Americans.* Ann Arbor: University of Michigan, Institute for Social Research, 1966.

Myrdal, A., and V. Klein. *Women's Two Roles: Home and Work.* London: Routledge, 1956.

Oakley, A. *The Sociology of Housework.* New York: Pantheon, 1974.

Rainwater, L.; R. P. Coleman; and G. Handel. *Workingman's Wife.* New York: Oceana, 1959.

Robinson, J. *How Americans Use Time: A Social-Psychological Analysis.* New York: Praeger, 1977.

Schnaiberg, A. "The Utility of Marginal Utility Models of Fertility: Innovation or Translation?" Paper presented at the annual meeting of the American Sociological Association, Montreal, Canada, 1974.

_____, and D. Reed. "Risk, Uncertainty and Family Formation: The Social Context of Poverty Groups." *Population Studies* 28 (November 1974):513–533.

_____, and S. Goldenberg. "Closing the Circle: The Impact of Children on Parental Status." *Journal of Marriage and the Family* (November 1975):937–953.

Smuts, R. W. *Women and Work in America.* New York: Schocken, 1959.

Sudman, S., and N. M. Bradburn. *Response Effects in Surveys.* Chicago: Aldine, 1974.

Vanek, J. "Time Spent in Housework." *Scientific American* (November 1974):116–120.

Walker, K. "Household Work Time: Its Implication for Family Decisions." *Journal of Home Economics* (October 1973):7–11.

_____, and W. Gauger. "The Dollar Value of Household Work." *Information Bulletin 60,* Consumer Economics and Public Policy, no. 5. Ithaca, N.Y.: New York State College of Human Ecology, Cornell University, 1973.

Young, M., and P. Wilmott. *The Symmetrical Family.* New York: Pantheon, 1973.

3

The Appropriation of the House: Changes in House Design and Concepts of Domesticity

Cynthia Rock
Susana Torre
Gwendolyn Wright

The houses or apartments most of us live in can seem to be traps, forcing us into a mold, jeopardizing possibilities for exploring new ways of living at home and beyond. The standard spatial layout of houses, kitchens, and even of closets does indeed reflect the dominant, long-standing roles for women, men, and children in our society. Yet the city apartment and even the suburban house need not be places of rigid stereotypes and sex roles. The uses and psychological associations and the architectural details themselves are not necessarily immutable. Forms, whether they are political, cultural, or architectural, are difficult to restructure; slight changes, nonetheless, do have an effect. It is crucial that pressure be put on architects and builders to offer us a much greater variety of living alternatives, but we can ourselves—working with the housing models on the market—appropriate the spaces, redefine their meanings, and create settings that reinforce the roles and self-definitions we have chosen.

The first step is to realize how the spaces and the roles we link with them came to seem so inevitable. American women learned about potential models for their houses through two often opposing traditions of architectural advice.[1] There have been many examples of women taking control of their own home settings, and teaching other women various possibilities that might help their home lives. Some wanted to improve health conditions, others to facilitate women working outside the home or to make the home a more cooperative and supportive place. They all emphasized the need for involvement from the women who used houses, who worked in them and lived in them, who had different needs and ideas to offer. In opposition to such participation has been the legacy of the expert, the people who have dictated the way homes were to be decorated, kept up, and used. Theirs have been the voices of absolutism, insisting that only one basic model of the home could solve all needs equally well. Even as it changed, this model was presented as God-given, the eternal, universal home, every woman's dream.

In the past, as today, women who read magazines have often been treated as if they knew nothing about their homes, how to use them and vary them. Their role was not to designate spaces, but to personalize the spaces they were given by adding frills and handmade ornament.

Women's magazines have, since the 1830s, been one of the prime forces for creating popular images about housing types. The *Ladies Home Journal,* founded in 1883, first edited by the publisher's wife, Louisa Knapp Curtis, owed its great success to Edward Bok, the magazine's evangelical editor from 1889 to 1919.[2] Bok had a clearly formulated mission: to reform and simplify the American home and to keep women in it. He enlisted architects, suffrage leaders, reformers, novelists, statesmen, and even presidents to assure his readers that the right kind of home environment could preserve the family, strengthen the nation, and thereby give women more than enough meaningful work to do. For him, women belonged in these homes, and each one was to be separate from the others. Bok, a clever editor, commissioned articles from writers who opposed his ideas, and even housing models designed by and for working women, to give his journal the enticing air of controversy.[3] His policy was an effective one and by 1903 circulation had jumped to 1,000,000—the first magazine (except for a few cheap mail-order journals) to reach that pinnacle.

One of Bok's most popular series was called "In Other Women's Homes."[4] Here, and throughout the journal, he promoted competitive feelings between women, who would vie for the latest upholstery, the shiniest sink, the most up-to-date living room. He then promised to mediate that competition, so that women would not even have to compare notes in person. They could find out about the most modern home information from his magazine, learning to avoid the "Bad Taste" of parlor bric-a-brac and overstuffed chairs.[5] They read not only for fashion, but for their family's health and status—and for their own sense of choosing correctly.

Prominent architects provided models of ideal homes. Beginning in 1895, the *Journal* offered a model home in each issue, costing from one to five thousand dollars, with the complete plans and specifications available for only five dollars. Thousands of these homes were built around the country. Even the individualistic Frank Lloyd Wright contributed three designs for prairie houses as well as numerous interior designs.[6] His were truly protected, simplified environments: high walls and leaded glass windows cut off the outside. Within, the space was open and continuous, centering on the family hearth, the symbolic focus for harmony and togetherness. His was a beatific image of the family with no problems, no difficulties, with everything open to everyone else.

Earlier magazines and books had also published models for middle-class dwellings. *Godey's Ladies' Magazine,* edited by Sarah Hale, was a popular journal throughout the nineteenth century.[7] It featured illustrations of women's domestic handiwork, or "household elegancies" (see Figure 3.1), and diminutive wooden cottages with decorated trim, set in private gardens. These homes were the perfect retreats for the husband at the end of the day. His "stirring career away from home renders home to him so necessary a place of repose, where he may take off his armor, relax his strained attention, and surrender himself to perfect rest," wrote one Victorian journal. The description went on to show that home had another meaning for women: "It is not her retreat, but her battleground . . . her arena, her boundary, her sphere; to a man, it is life in repose; to a woman, the house is life militant."[8] And even the architecturally advanced houses in Catharine Beecher's best-selling *The American Woman's Home* emphasized a life of total domestic commitment. Each improvement reaffirmed the woman's duty to keep a perfect home.[9]

Victorian-period builders filled "pattern books" with illus-

FIGURE 3.1 Domestic guides for the Victorian woman, including Julia McNair Wright's popular treatise, *The Complete Home* (1879), suggested numerous ways in which the middle-class housewife could decorate and personalize her surroundings. These "household elegancies" varied from finicky patterns one would copy exactly to creative handicrafts.

trations of houses for carpenters to copy. Each was supposed to be unique, fitted exactly to the special interests and hobbies and aspirations of the family within. This mark of individuality was accomplished through symbolic ornament. Porches, bay windows, and gingerbread mouldings were tacked on the facade; spaces for entertaining company were cunningly decorated with expensive furniture and knickknacks. These designers dealt with an ideal family, allowing some variation according to wealth or size. The ornament, inside and out, was supposed to evoke the "natural" aspects of the home, expressing the timeless quality of the nuclear family. There was no accepted role for women outside this model, and consequently there was no dwelling type based on other roles. Even historians and social scientists of the time insisted that the nuclear family had always existed, everywhere the God-given state for human beings.[10] And since women, being closer to nature and responsible for the family, were also totally responsible for the home, it was they who were to stay put, to personalize their parlors, stoke their coal stoves, and care for their children.

Turn-of-the-century home magazines updated the Victorian home, with its profuse decoration and dark fussy corners, by promoting houses with sunlight and open space, with modern appliances and mass-produced furniture. They also helped spread a new concept of the woman's role in the home: she was now being taught to buy and attend to all the new technology. Her presence made all the new gadgets seem "homey," and not so conspicuously industrialized.

Even in the women's magazines, some voices discounted the universality of the "natural" family, and the assumption that women should stay in the home. *The House Beautiful* began a series, edited by Marion Talbot, an ardent feminist who was dean of women and head of domestic science at the University of Chicago. Talbot believed that houses had to be changed to allow women to reconsider how they spent their time and used their talents. And she insisted that all women should become involved in deciding upon these changes.[11] She published the findings of social scientists who showed that the nuclear family was, in fact, a recent development. It derived from middle-class notions of privacy and removal from the city's tumult. The romantic idealization of the home and the family as the refuge for the fragile individual had appeared, as Philippe Aries has shown, in eighteenth-century Europe; but it was in the nineteenth-century American suburbs that the appropriate environment was perfected.[12]

Talbot published accounts of cooperative housekeeping projects, the sharing of kitchens and dining rooms by several families.[13] Her colleagues, progressive reformers like Jane Addams and Sophonisba Breckinridge, discussed the need for mass housing and protested the enforced isolation of the middle classes. Other women in the domestic science movement—especially Isabel Bevier, head of the household science department at the University of Illinois, and Virginia Robie, assistant editor of *The House Beautiful*—published new examples of alternative housing types: owner-designed efficiency cottages, kitchenettes and dinettes, bungalows for single working women to share, and bungalow courts with communal facilities. These were housing options planned by women—as active clients and responsive professionals. These professionals—architects, decorators, authors and editors, and domestic science leaders—demanded radical changes in domestic architecture: cottages that were easy to keep up, pleasant and efficient apartments, modern farm-house complexes, and healthy, attractive low-cost housing for the poor. They were willing to accept the standardization of housing and furnishing in order to effect the highest standards of efficiency, comfort, and health. They were willing to challenge the concept of the isolated single-family house controlled by the housewife in order to help women gain some real control over their homes. (See Figures 3.2 and 3.3.) But, while critical, they did not conceive of domestic problems in a way that took full account of the larger economic and political issues underlying them.

This progressive stage of women's housing reform began to subside just before World War I as the larger feminist movement also turned from its earlier, more radical stance toward a more specific focus on gaining suffrage. The housing reformers were, in effect, replaced in popular media by women appealing directly to rising consumerism, peddling the variety of new goods for the home, and by others preaching the gospel of scientific

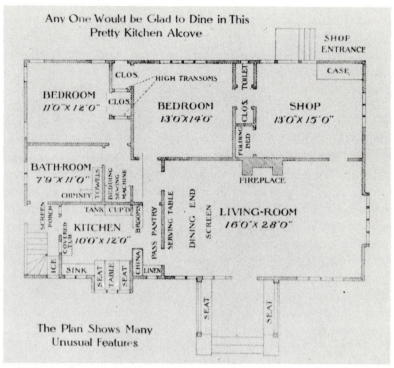

Any One Would be Glad to Dine in This
Pretty Kitchen Alcove

SHOP ENTRANCE

CASE

CLOS.

HIGH TRANSOMS

TOILET

BEDROOM
11'0"X 12'0"

CLOS.

BEDROOM
13'0"X 14'0"

CLOS.

SHOP
13'0" X 15'0"

FOLDING BED

BATH-ROOM
7'9"X 11'0"

CHIMNEY

TANK CUP'D

SCREEN PORCH

COVERED TUB

KITCHEN
10'0" X 12'0"

BROOMS

ICE

SINK

TABLE

SEAT

SEAT

CHINA

LINEN

PASS PANTRY

SERVING TABLE

DINING END

SCREEN

TOWELS

BEDDING SEWING MACHINE

FIREPLACE

LIVING-ROOM
16'0" X 28'0"

SEAT

SEAT

The Plan Shows Many
Unusual Features

FIGURE 3.2 In 1911, writing for the *Ladies' Home Journal*, architect Una Nixson Hopkins described the house she and a woman client had designed when the woman began working in her home. As this plan shows, a separate entrance at the back connected to the client's shop, which in turn could open into the living room when this was convenient.

FIGURE 3.3 The living room–dining room in Hopkins' design was extremely simple in order to cut down on housecleaning time.

management. The principles of scientific management, now applied to the home as to every other work environment, were based upon the suddenly popular industrial management policies of Frederick Winslow Taylor and Harrison Emerson.[14] They stressed the need for expert advice and absolute standards. Pseudoscientific experts in their "household experiment stations" imposed similar standards for the home. What was the single most effective way of cleaning a room? Of baking a cake? Of washing the dishes? The "one best way," that is, for the individual housewife in her own home. Christine Frederick, one of the most popular of these experts, showed exactly the course for a housewife to take in cleaning house, illustrating her point with a circulation chart that certainly promoted standardization of these separate houses, so that each one could be run more effectively; but she never suggested that the time saved was to be spent in any other way than more efficiency training.[15] The scientific management enthusiasts portrayed the housewife as a well-trained worker who followed orders and kept up on the latest guidelines in her home "office corner" of the kitchen. (See Figure 3.4.) Their reliance on expertise and rationalistic solutions eclipsed the earlier progressive emphasis on each woman questioning her own and her community's housing needs.

Tensions mounted, especially as houses became smaller and more standardized. One way in which social and architectural problems were confronted was the zoned house of the 1930s and 1940s.[16] Here were not rooms, but divisions according to functions, labelled "activity/quiet," "public/private," or "adult/children." The kitchen was the center, for the housewife was responsible for bridging the zones and bringing everyone together. Yet the real zoning was between the private house and the public space outside, the zoning off of similar types of families leading similar lives, protected from the variety of the rest of the city.

Many women, however, did not accept these models without questioning. In 1956 the U.S. Housing and Home Finance Agency announced the first Women's Congress on Housing, calling 103 housewives to Washington. The talk was heated, for the women had many complaints. Most of all they wanted more

FIGURE 3.4 Not all of the women who advocated changes in house design had the best intentions of other women in mind. Christine Frederick's *Household Engineering: Scientific Management in the Home* (1915) laid down absolute, pseudoscientific standards of cleanliness and efficiency that were to be followed to the letter.

space and more differentiation within the home, more allowances for the complexity and differences of their own families and schedules. And they wanted places of their own. "Fewer would go to our mental wards and divorce courts if they had one room, even a small one, just for themselves . . . peace and quiet without the television," one woman pleaded. But these women delegates seemed hopelessly idealistic to most of the builders who heard their suggestions. The HHFA declared that they had too much information to put out a formal report. The women had, unfortunately, expressed such differing opinions and sensed such varying needs.

Varying needs have been the focus of reform efforts by numerous women concerned about housing and about other women's lives in their homes, throughout a long history of American domestic media. These women have written for the popular press, describing alternatives that were within their culture's prevailing norms for housing prototypes and living situations. They used their architectural suggestions to encourage social changes for women in various situations, whether they worked, were single, had children, or had little money. Often their voices were overpowered by the tendency for this popular literature to put forth a single universal ideal for the woman's role and for the house: such was the stance of Edward Bok in 1900 and of the HHFA fifty years later. While becoming aware of the force of the images in women's books and magazines, we should not lose sight of the ways in which seemingly minor reformist suggestions were tied to efforts to offer alternative roles for women. These women, even if they wrote about carpetsweepers and kitchen sinks and single-family homes, were a part of a broad feminist effort of the late nineteenth century, a movement to bring women out of the home and into the larger urban world, to give them comfort and self-respect in their homes. For them, information about the house and even about housekeeping would allow women to appropriate the domestic realm, to perfect it, and thereby go beyond it.

Today, because so many of us are striving to put more energy into the development of our public selves and to break away from the restrictions of stereotyped behavior, renewed demands for the transformation of our living environments have arisen. Many demands, especially those concerning the need for a private space away from domestic demand, were articulated long ago but still remain unfulfilled.[17] Those designing and marketing houses and apartments for the majority of the population have begun to recognize that many people no longer want traditional homes and have increased the options for prospective owners. Renters, of course, do not have such luck. The replacement of all existing dwellings for less restrictive environments will be a long-term process, and we must begin to think now in which ways the house as we know it can be appropriated and transformed to be truly supportive of our changing roles. Changes in the household are reflecting trends towards shared responsibility for domestic work and the respect of each individual's autonomy. One-purpose spaces designed for traditional uses prod us back into traditional family roles and result in much wasted space and the difficult coexistence of activities that are important to each household member.

For many women, escape from restrictive roles has meant moving out to live alone and taking exclusive control of their living environments, often for the first time. The proverbial "room of one's own" can be at best the private theater of an individual's fantasies about living, allowed to emerge unencumbered by another person's presence. The transformations of the living space we are suggesting, however, imply the desirability of an existence shared with others. In this case, the use of space and the establishment of territoriality become critical issues. The question is whether coexistence and personal fulfillment have to be at odds.

Surely the solution to this problem will not depend on an adequate transformation of the living space alone. A supportive house in and of itself cannot guarantee fulfillment any more than a restrictive house should take the exclusive blame for a frustrated life. But we have seen that there is a close correlation between the way houses have been designed and socially sanctioned ideas of sex roles and domesticity. We are suggesting that it is not only possible but also urgent that women cease to adapt themselves to inadequate environments and demand publicly that changing life-styles be acknowledged in the design of homes. These changes will affect specifically the organization and relative size of spaces within the house and the redesign of all spaces directly connected with maintenance and domestic labor. The seemingly inarticulate opinions expressed by the housewives in the Women's Congress on Housing can now be given collective coherence. The articulation of demands requires introspection rather than a blind following of the models presented by today's interior decoration–cum–gastronomic and fashion magazines, where changing life-styles are never more than wallpaper deep. It also requires keen observation of what specific modifications people make in their environments that relate to and legitimize a changed self-image. The architect Elisabeth Coit proposed as early as 1938 a radical breakdown of the specific function of domestic spaces.[18] In her landmark housing studies she even suggested that the nomenclature of rooms be changed or abandoned because the name of each room had potentially restrictive connotations that would, at least mentally, stifle a more flexible use of spaces. She called for the legitimization of the kitchen as a space for dining, for study and socializing in bedrooms, and for the accommodation of such real-life needs as a bedroom or study in the living room.

Coit was not proposing that enclosed rooms be replaced by a flexible, open plan as many architects had proposed during the 1920s and 1930s; nor was she suggesting that the kitchen be completely eliminated, as advocated by feminist architects like Alice Austin and Ruth Adams during the same period.[19] In practice, when used for a shared dwelling, the open plan may aggravate conflicts due to competing uses of the space, since visual and auditory privacy are difficult to achieve. Control of the use of the single space, since it does not allow for multiplicity of use, can become an issue of power and submission or of compromise. The elimination of the kitchen, too, can be problematic if not unreasonable, especially in suburban neighborhoods, where collective cooking facilities or inexpensive take-out food services needed to replace individual kitchens may be more difficult to organize.

The two central ideas towards which changes in the design of the house are gravitating are (1) providing a private space outside the kitchen for women, and (2) facilitating the equitable sharing of domestic labor. A person's autonomous development requires, inevitably, the time to sit undisturbed and focus on one's personal undertakings, whether that involves studying, writing a journal, developing a skill, or simply taking stock of one's life and making plans for the future. The need for privacy to nurture self-identity implies limiting temporarily our interaction with others, and is usually associated with a specific location, a place of retreat. The control of such a specific space is one of the most obvious ways of asserting territoriality, and, according to environmental psychologist Susan Saegert, it is a fundamental aspect in a child's development of an autonomous, independent personality.[20] In the house, control can be asserted by claiming a room, but it can also be manifested in far more subtle ways. A few examples: The casual out-of-place position of the particularly comfortable chair where the husband reads his newspaper indicates that he can control the use of that space as well as his mate's design for the interior of the house; access to private spaces such as bedrooms through a living room into which the kitchen opens allows the wife to oversee the children's and husband's schedules and whereabouts; the male's working desk in the living area confines the female to activities in the bedroom or kitchen. More positively, the control of space can simply mean appropriating a desk or table to hold undisturbed on-going projects, homework, books, or tools. It is difficult, if not impossible, to sustain a sense of continuity with one's own work if it has to be removed from the table to make space for the family meal.

Because togetherness is often forced in the designated common spaces, we make privacy synonymous with withdrawal. But privacy is really a process involving both seeking and restricting interaction with others at different times. It is a fluid, continuous process, not a traumatic shifting of gears. Crucial to this concept of privacy is the notion that most parts of the dwelling can accommodate different kinds of activities. The dispersion of gatherings of various household members and outsiders throughout the house suggests a multiple use of spaces and is a key concept in breaking down the specialized and "efficient" use of space inherent in the traditional home. This requires the inclusion of furnishings in every space of the house or apartment that create a proper setting for socializing as well as solitude. Since each member of the household may have very different ideas about how to work or entertain, the house could be a rich kaleidoscope of options, each reflecting in organization and decor many different personalities. Perhaps with the exception of the bathroom, each room is susceptible to multiple use. But even that bastion of specificity can be modified. Because many of their important conversations take place between the bathtub and the sink, a working couple we know expanded and redesigned their bathroom to include all their plants, a wicker chair, soft lighting, and their exercise machine.

Although life-long addictions like domestic work are difficult to break, the crucial issue of an equal share for each household member can be helped by spaces that make housework seem an obvious and integral part of everyone's experience rather than a specialized, demeaning task. This means that we probably should give up once and for all the idea of the dream kitchen as

FIGURE 3.5 Kitchens are poorly designed for most users. (Diane Ellis, courtesy of the Baldwin Street Gallery of Photography)

an enclosed room lined with cabinets whose real function, besides the most obvious of storage, is to conceal objects whose correct placement only the wife knows (see Figure 3.5). High visibility and accessibility of all the tools and the means for shopping, planning, preparing, eating, cleaning up, and storing after meals promotes participation in these tasks by all members of the household. The same principle could be applied to every maintenance task, including those traditionally handled by men, like electricity and plumbing repairs, and perhaps even to storage. A "stock room" where personal and household paraphenalia is centralized and visible could replace many inadequate closets, freeing that extra space for a work counter or two chairs.

Many women have already effected changes like these in their homes, but many others who are committed to change would rather allow themselves to be held back by the house than transform it. To challenge or disturb an order made material by objects and walls is indeed very difficult. To convince those responsible for providing housing that the emerging transformations should be included in their designs may be even harder. If a new Women's Congress on Housing were called, would the recommendations made by women be dismissed as "hopelessly idealistic"?

Notes

1. For a more extensive discussion of this dichotomy, see Gwendolyn Wright, "Model Housewives and Model Houses, 1870–1910," paper presented at the American Studies Association meetings, Boston, 1977.

2. On Bok and the *Journal*, see Bok's autobiography, *The Americanization of Edward Bok* (New York: Charles Scribner's Sons, 1924) and Frank Luther Mott, *A History of American Magazines*, vol. 4 (Cambridge: Harvard University Press, 1957):537–555. Theodore Roosevelt was the president who wrote for the *Journal.*

3. See, for example, "If a Woman Must Earn Her Living at Home," by Una Nixson Hopkins (vol. 28, February 15, 1911); "Three Minimal Cottages," by Charles Elmer White, Jr. (vol. 29, April 1912, p. 95); "A Picturesque Court of 30 Bungalows: A Community Idea for Women," by Una N. Hopkins (vol. 30, April 1913, p. 99).

4. *Ladies Home Journal* 28 (February 15, 1911): cover.

5. A series, "How Shall We Furnish Our Homes," juxtaposing examples of "Good Taste" and "Bad Taste," by Max West and Mary Mills West, ran from January to March in 1907.

6. Wright's houses included "A Home in a Prairie Town" (vol. 18, February 1901), "A Small House with 'Lots of Room in It'" (vol. 18, June 1901), "A Fireproof House for $5000" (vol. 24, April 1907). The interior of Wright's Bradley House in Kankakee, Illinois, for instance, is featured in "Inside of One Hundred Suburban Homes" (vol. 19, November 1902, p. 8). On these houses, see Robert C. Twombley, " 'Saving the Family': Middle Class Attraction to Wright's Prairie House, 1901-1909," *American Quarterly* 27 (March 1975):57-72.

7. Ruth E. Finley, *The Lady of Godey's: Sarah Josepha Hale* (Philadelphia: J. B. Lippincott, 1931), and George L. Hersey, "Godey's Choice," *Journal of the Society of Architectural Historians* 18 (October 1959):104–111, describe the some 450 house designs, especially the innovative dwellings of the 1840s and 1850s.

8. "A Further Notion or Two about Domestic Bliss," *Appleton's Journal of Popular Literature, Science and Art* 3 (March 1870):329.

9. Catharine E. Beecher and Harriet Beecher Stowe, *The American Woman's Home* (1869). On Beecher, see Katherine Kish Sklar, *A Study in American Domesticity* (New Haven: Yale University Press, 1973) and, for a perceptive analysis of her architecture, Dolores Hayden, "Catharine Beecher and the Politics of Housework," in *Women in American Architecture: A Historic and Contemporary Perspective,* ed. by Susana Torre (New York: Whitney Library of Design, 1977):40-49.

10. In particular, Edward A. Westermarch, *The History of Human Marriage,* 3 vols. (New York: Macmillan, 1889) posed the monogamous patriarchial family as the natural universal state for humanity. His work and that of C. S. Wake were polemics directed in part against the theories of Lewis Henry Morgan in *Ancient Society* (1878), where monogamy was seen as secured by property rights.

11. One of the tenets shared by all of the early pioneers of domestic science in America was that women should participate actively in domestic architecture. Helen Campbell, in a series of lectures organized in 1895 by Richard Ely of the economics department of the University of Wisconsin, insisted that everyone should learn to draw floor plans. Isabel Bevier, head of the department of household science at the University of Illinois, took over courses on the history of architecture, construction, heating, and plumbing from the College of Engineering. She taught all her students to draw plans, using graph paper to facilitate their drawing to scale. See her textbook, *The House: Its Plan, Decoration, and Care* (Chicago: The

American School of Home Economics, which went through six editions between 1904 and 1912).

12. Talbot, an editor of the *Journal of Sociology,* shared with students and readers the work of Charles Henderson, Edward A. Ross, Scott and Mary Nearing, Thorstein Veblen, Charles Cooley, and William Graham Sumner. See her autobiography, *More Than Lore* (Chicago: University of Chicago Press, 1934). For Aries, see *Centuries of Childhood* (New York: Knopf, 1962).

13. See Mary Hinman Abel's series on cooperative housekeeping, "Recent Phases of Co-operation among Women," *The House Beautiful* 13 (March–November 1903). Abel was a student and protégée of Talbot.

14. Taylor's most important work was *Principles of Scientific Management* (1911). On the scientific management movement, see Samuel T. Haber, *Efficiency and Uplift: Scientific Management in the Progressive Era, 1890–1920* (Chicago: University of Chicago Press, 1964); David Handlin, "Efficiency and the American Home," *Architectural Association Quarterly* 4 (Winter 1973):50–54; Barbara Ehrenreich and Deirdre English, "The Manufacture of Housework," *Socialist Revolution* 26 (October–December 1975):5–40.

15. Christine Frederick, *The New Housekeeping: Efficiency Studies in Home Management* (New York: Doubleday, 1912; based upon her 1911 series for the *Ladies' Home Journal*); *Household Engineering: Scientific Management in the Home* (Chicago: The New School of Home Economics, 1915); "Putting the American Woman and Her Home on a Business Basis," *The Review of Reviews* 49 (February 1914):199–208; *Selling Mrs. Consumer* (New York: The Business Bourse, 1929). See also Mary Pattison, *The Principles of Domestic Engineering* (New York: The Trow Press, 1915), which included an introduction by Taylor.

16. See, for instance, Dorothy Field, *The Human House* (Boston: Houghton-Mifflin, 1939).

17. Some of the so-called "shelter magazines," such as *Apartment Life,* occasionally publish stories about women living alone or sharing a dwelling with another person in an unconventional relationship. These stories, however, present these "options" as part of an urban and young life-style, the underlying assumption being the temporary nature of such arrangements.

18. Elisabeth Coit, "Notes on the Design and Construction of the Dwelling Units for the Lower-Income Family," *The Octagon* 13 (October 1941):10–30; (November 1941):7–22. Mary Otis Stevens discusses Elisabeth Coit's work in "Struggle for Place: Women in Architecture, 1920–1960," in Torre (ed.), *Women in American Architecture,* pp. 100–102.

19. Dolores Hayden, "Challenging the American Domestic Ideal," in Torre (ed.), *Women in American Architecture.*

20. Susan Saegert and Roger Hart, "The Development of Sex Differences in the Environmental Competence of Children," in Pat Burnett (ed.), *Women in Society: New Perspectives,* in manuscript.

4

Redesigning the Domestic Workplace

Dolores Hayden

*By what art, what charm, what
miracle, has the twentieth century
preserved alive the prehistoric squaw!*
—Charlotte Perkins Gilman, 1903

*I'm not your little woman
Your sweetheart or your dear,
I'm a wage slave without wages,
I'm a maintenance engineer!*
—Combine, London, England,
folk song, 1974

The Private Home

A rosy glow suffuses the portrayal of domestic life in much American and European visionary architecture of the past century. Economic and technological developments have subjected offices, factories, and transportation systems to cycles of design and redesign while the plans of dwelling units have remained much the same. Whether the private home is a freestanding house in Frank Lloyd Wright's Broadacre City or a high tower flat in Le Corbusier's Radiant City, domestic work has been treated as a private, sex-stereotyped activity, and most architects continue to design domestic work spaces for isolated female workers. Political revolutions have not shaken the home either. In most socialist countries housekeeping remains private, "women's" work. Although extensive child-care facilities allow women workers to extend their hours in the factory, nothing has changed their jobs at home.

The feminist economist Charlotte Perkins Gilman satirized home worship in a short poem:

> *Oh! the Home is utterly perfect!*
>   *And all its works within.*
> *To say a word about it—*
> *To criticise or doubt it—*
> *To seek to mend or move it—*
> *To venture to improve it—*
>   *Is the unpardonable sin!*[1]

Gilman was perhaps reviewing her own unpardonable sins. Between 1898 and 1903 she laid out the lines of an attack on the home which is still valid today: "The two main errors in the right adjustment of the home to our present life are these: the maintenance of primitive industries in a modern industrial community, and the confinement of women to those industries and their limited area of expression.[2] A good number of nineteenth-century feminists had anticipated Gilman in these views; many contemporary feminists are still working along these two lines. Unwaged female labor in primitive domestic industries is the subject of Mariarosa Dalla Costa's "Women and the Subversion of the Community" and Selma James' "A Woman's Place"; the sex stereotyping of domestic work is the subject of Patricia Mainardi's "The Politics of Housework."[3] These contemporary manifestos have been translated into political campaigns—some groups demand wages for housework, while others encourage men to assume an equal share of housework and child care. Ultimately these two political movements must converge, calling for drastic changes in traditional "women's" work and drastic redesign of the environments in which domestic work is conducted.

This chapter surveys some social and architectural aspects of feminist agitation for domestic reform in the United States and Europe between 1800 and 1915. The designs and buildings are aimed at restructuring domestic work. They are not presented as solutions to the problems of "women's" work, but as critiques of the traditional home developed in architectural form rather than in words. In many respects they suggest more significant social options than the ideal family housing of the same period. Promoters of company towns often constructed "ideal" factories along with "ideal" workers' housing, demonstrating the role of the housewife and the house in keeping workers happy on the job. Tenement house designers played a similar role in late nineteenth-century cities. In contrast to those reformers who promoted domestic stability through improved family housing, the utopian socialists and cooperative housekeepers discussed in this chapter challenged the traditional single-family home. They questioned the appropriateness of isolated domestic work and criticized the separation of work and home, production and reproduction, brought about by the development of industrial capitalism.

Utopian Socialist Alternatives

The earliest campaigns against private domestic work in the United States and Europe were launched by utopian socialists committed to building model communities as a strategy for achieving social reform. Both Robert Owen (1771–1858) and Charles Fourier (1772–1837) supported collective housework and child care to assist in the development of equality between men and women, and each of them inspired some twenty to thirty American experiments in model community building as well as a few European experiments. As Fourier put it, the Associationist movement would introduce communal facilities which would make the most elegant conventional private home appear "a place of exile, a residence worthy of fools, who after three thousand years of architectural studies, have not yet learned to build themselves healthy and comfortable lodgings."[4]

Fourier's followers and other advocates of cooperative housekeeping criticized private houses as isolated, wasteful, and

oppressive. John Humphrey Noyes, founder of the Oneida Community (1847–1881), complained of the "gloom and dullness
of excessive family isolation," or the "little man-and-wife
circle," where one suffered "the discomfort and waste attendant
on the domestic economy of our separate households."[5] Alice
Constance Austin, architect of the Llano del Rio Community
(1914–1938), described the traditional home as a "Procrustean
bed" which maimed women, and an "inconceivably stupid"
arrangement which confiscated their labors.[6] Other domestic
reformers who were not themselves utopian socialists echoed
these sentiments. Melusina Fay Peirce, founder of the Cambridge
Cooperative Housekeeping Society (1869–1872), claimed that
all the best years of her life were sacrificed to the "dusty drudgery of house-ordering"—"a sacrifice so costly and unnatural"
that she started organizing.[7]

In contrast to the private houses which these domestic reformers denounced as isolated, wasteful, and oppressive, they
hoped to build communal or cooperative facilities for domestic
work—tangible, architectural demonstrations of the workings
of a more egalitarian society. The architectural form which
various arrangements took was determined by the economic and
social structure of the communities they served, so that the
problems of mechanizing and measuring domestic work were
met with a great variety of ingenious solutions in urban, suburban, and rural situations. To begin with, at least three types
of economic and social organizations must be distinguished: the
rural utopian socialist community functioning as a large family;
the rural utopian socialist community containing nuclear
families within it; and the urban or suburban cooperative housekeeping society whose members included both nuclear families
and individuals.

The Communal Family

Utopian socialist communities organized as large families
often wished to abolish the nuclear family in order to promote
greater attachment to a shared communal ideology. Total
economic communism and a commitment to free love (viewed

as the sexual counterpart of economic communism) were often required by such groups. They often preferred large communal dwellings where members were housed in rooms or dormitories connected to a communal kitchen, dining room, and nursery.

Some communal families and their architecture are well known. The Oneida Perfectionists, led by John Humphrey Noyes and Erastus Hamilton, the community's architect, built a very substantial communal home for 200 members, beginning in 1846 in central New York State. The masthead of their paper, *The American Socialist,* dedicated it to "the enlargement and improvement of home," and in 1862, with the dedication of their Second Mansion House, they claimed that "Communism in our society has built itself a house."[8] Views of Perfectionist communal housekeeping facilities were widely published in popular illustrated magazines between 1850 and 1875 (see Figures 4.1 and 4.2).

Compared with the eclectic Victorian mansion of the Oneidans the housekeeping arrangements of *A Cityless and Countryless World* seem rather diagrammatic. Based on free love and non-sectarian utopian socialism, these plans for "big houses" were published in 1893 in Holstein, Iowa, by Henry Olerich, who argued that "a family of husband, wife and their children living alone in a country home, are largely wasting their lives, socially and economically."[9] Single bedrooms for every individual line broad corridors leading to communal service areas. The "big houses" are surrounded by mills and factories. Olerich described his later designs as "modern paradise" and predicted they would form the living arrangements of "the world a thousand years hence."[10]

Another plan for a "Social Palace" for a spiritualist community, headed by Thomas Lake Harris at Fountaingrove, California, in 1894, suggested the possible whimseys of collective housekeeping in a communal family practicing free love. Facilities for "special household arts and crafts" are balanced by those for "light industry"; one has a view of a menagerie, another a view of an aviary. A section through the communal kitchen and dining facilities shows curtained banquettes in tiers, labelled "A Hundred Bowers of Love's Repose."

FIGURE 4.1 Domestic work in a communal family: Oneida Perfectionists' dining room, 1870. (*Frank Leslie's Illustrated Weekly Newspaper*, April 9, 1870)

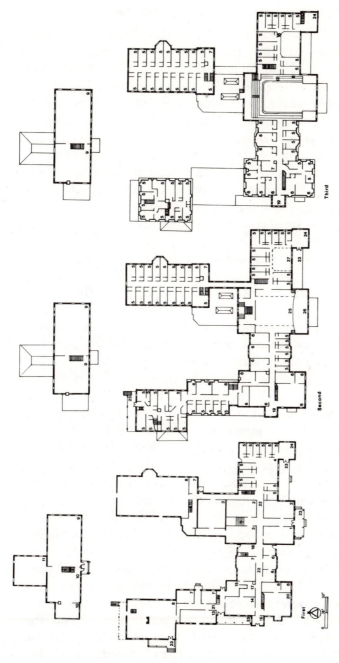

FIGURE 4.2 Plans of communal dwelling for 200 Perfectionists at Oneida, New York, 1861–1881: 1. office, cloak-room; 2. reception room; 3. library; 4. lower sitting room; 5. single bedroom; 6. shared bedroom; 7. bathroom; 8. lounge or workshop (?); 9. workshop; 10. dining room; 11. dining room addition; 12. balcony of hall; 13. west sitting room; 14. home parlor; 15. nursery kitchen; 16. balcony of upper sitting room; 17. nursery; 18. "hub"; 19. south tower; 20. children's parlor; 21. west avenue; 22. ground corridor; 23. porch; 24. north tower; 25. hall; 26. stage. 27. upper sitting room. (Hayden, *Seven American Utopias*)

The Communal Organization, Including Families

In contrast to those utopian socialist communities where specific social, religious, or sexual practices were enforced among members of the communal family living under the communal roof, the utopian socialist communities which contained nuclear families within them offered more diverse housekeeping and child-care arrangements. Usually nuclear families had some private territory to themselves as well as access to communal kitchens, dining rooms, and nurseries. Some organizations wished their housing to take the form of a "unitary dwelling," which contained all of these disparate communal and private facilities; others developed networks of related buildings, including private family houses or small apartment houses and various communal housekeeping facilities.

Fourierists, or Associationists, favored the Phalanstery, a single building containing both communal housekeeping facilities and private apartments for resident families. The Familistère at Guise, France, built by Jean-Baptiste-André Godin, beginning in 1859, provided innovative housing for several hundred iron foundry workers and their families (see Figure 4.3). Apartments included private kitchens, but the Guise complex contained a large dining hall and cafe as well. Some earlier Fourierist communities in the United States built an even greater range of dwellings. At the North American Phalanx—a community of about 125 members established in New Jersey in 1843—a communal kitchen, laundry, and bakery were contained in the same building as private apartments (without kitchens) and dormitories, but members were also permitted to build private houses (with kitchens) on the domain.[11]

In contrast to the Fourierists' "unitary dwellings," coherent villages composed of private apartments and communal housekeeping facilities were built by other groups. The Harmony Society, led by George Rapp, built three towns in the United States between 1805 and 1824. Nine hundred members at Economy, Pennsylvania, lived in small communal houses and dormitories, each with its own kitchen, but they also had a large communal kitchen and "Feast Hall" used on special occasions. The Amana Inspirationists built fifty-two communal kitchen

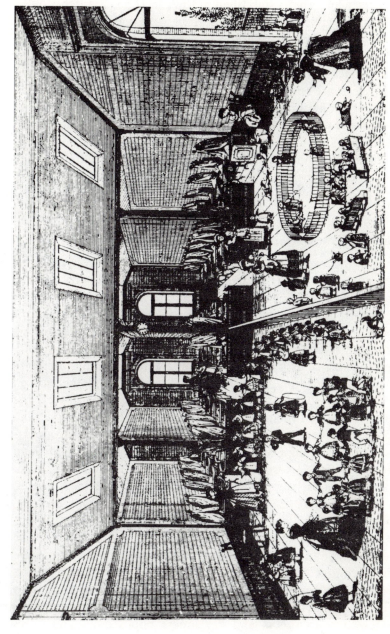

FIGURE 4.3 Nursery at the Familistère. (Godin, *Social Solutions*, 1873)

houses, each serving about fifty people, in the seven communal villages which they established in Iowa in 1855. Residents dwelt in family apartments (usually four apartments to a house) and in dormitories. Schools, kindergartens, and other work-shops were located near the residences and kitchens.[12] Similar arrangements prevail in the Bruderhof and Hutterian communities which are still active in the United States and Canada: small buildings containing several family apartments, some with minimal private kitchens, are served by communal cooking and dining facilities. This is also the arrangement most common in Israeli *kibbutzim,* although communal residences for children replace day-care facilities, giving parents even more freedom to take part in other aspects of communal life.

The Cooperative Housekeeping Service

The organizers of cooperative housekeeping services were not utopian socialists. They believed in private property and the private home. They hoped to imitate the utopian socialist housekeeping arrangements previously described and transplant them to urban or suburban neighborhoods. These organizers expected nuclear families to subscribe to a cooperative house-keeping service as a matter of rational self-interest. Of the three approaches to domestic reform, this one required the least in the way of social and economic conformity, but proved the most difficult to finance and control in practice.

Melusina Fay Peirce and members of the Cambridge Coopera-tive Housekeeping Society, middle-class women, many of them the wives of Harvard professors, organized the first such co-operative housekeeping service in Cambridge, Massachusetts, in 1869. In 1870 they established a cooperative store, laundry, and bakery for forty subscribing households, but they did not provide child care, since the scheme was intended to give women the opportunity to spend more time with their children. The members argued for the inclusion of cooperative house-keeping services in the apartment houses which were at that time being introduced for middle-class residents in the United States, but architects and developers opposed any measures which would involve the owners of multiple dwellings with the problems of domestic cooperation. In 1871 the Cambridge experiment was discontinued, but Peirce continued to lecture and write for the cause, publishing *Cooperative Housekeeping: How Not To Do It and How To Do It, A Sociological Study,* in 1884. Although Peirce herself was not an architect and never published plans of the cooperative housekeeping facilities she described, Marie Howland, a feminist and a former resident of the Familistère in Guise, France, collaborated with an engineer, Albert Kimsey Owen, and an architect, John Deery, to produce architectural plans for cooperative neighborhoods around 1885. One plan shows four single-family houses grouped around a building with kitchen, dining room, laundry, and bakery.

In *Women and Economics,* published in 1898, the economist Charlotte Perkins Gilman recommended kitchenless houses of a similar sort, suggesting that they can be linked in urban rows or connected by covered walkways in a suburban block. Like Peirce, Gilman also recommended the construction of kitchenless apartments with collective dining facilities for women with families.[13] Two later books added to this vision: *Concerning Children,* 1900, described the benefits of professional day-care arrangements; *The Home, Its Work and Influence,* 1903, provided a detailed critique of private, inconvenient domestic architecture.

Cooperative housekeeping schemes were not only supported by feminist reformers; they also became the subject of popular utopian novels at the end of the nineteenth century. In 1874, in *Papa's Own Girl,* Marie Howland described a Familistère transported to Massachusetts. Edward Bellamy's best seller of 1887, *Looking Backward,* dealt with a socialist Boston in the year 2000, when families dwell in luxurious private apartments and dine in communal halls served by communal kitchens. A slightly later novel, *The World A Department Store,* published by Bradford Peck in Lewiston, Maine, in 1900, included illustrations of such an arrangement. Private apartments were restricted to parlor, bedroom, and bath, and the city was dotted with "public restaurant buildings" looking very much like many city halls built at that time. Peck's housing was similar to that built in Amana, Iowa, described in the previous section, but he expanded a communal system to include a whole city of cooperative consumers.

English enthusiasm for cooperative housekeeping was as keen as American. Melusina Fay Peirce, Charlotte Perkins Gilman, and Edward Bellamy all had English disciples as well as American ones. Raymond Unwin advocated cooperative housekeeping arrangements in his influential treatise written in 1901, *The Art of Building a Home,* and he seems to have interested Ebenezer Howard in cooperative housekeeping as well; Howard organized extensive experiments in cooperative housekeeping at the Garden Cities of Letchworth and Welwyn, England. "Homesgarth" included thirty-two kitchenless units built in 1909, while "Meadow Way Green" included twenty-three kitchenless units built in Letchworth between 1915 and 1924. Residents shared a common dining room and kitchen, where they ate one co-operative meal a day, prepared at first by the women tenants on a two-week rotation and later by a hired cook. The experiments (see Figures 4.4 and 4.5) lasted at least thirty years. Guessens Court at Welwyn was a similar venture including forty kitchenless units served by cooperative housekeeping facilities which functioned until the time of World War II.

This brief review of housing arrangements designed by utopian socialist communities and cooperative housekeeping societies can only begin to suggest the variety of plans for domestic reform devised in hundreds of utopian socialist experiments and dozens of cooperative housekeeping societies. It is difficult to assess the effect of such unorthodox domestic architecture on the female and male domestic workers who participated in these innovative projects. Nevertheless, one can examine evidence from various experiments relevant to Gilman's two demands: an end to primitive domestic industries and an end to women's confinement within domestic industries.

Most experiments in utopian socialism hoped to seize economic initiative in three areas: agricultural, industrial, and domestic work. By combining the labor of many workers, male and female, they proposed to end the isolation of the individual farmer, industrial worker, and housewife, improving efficiency through some division of labor while keeping all individuals involved with these three areas of work. Improved work environments and equal wages were often advertised to make such communities attractive to both men and women, farmers and indus-

FIGURE 4.4 A view of the Homesgarth project in Letchworth, England, designed by H. Clapham Lander and built in 1909. (C. B. Purdom, *The Building of Satellite Towns*, 1925)

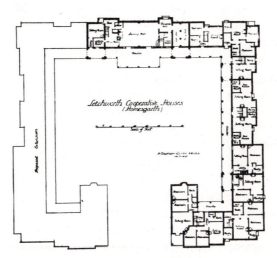

FIGURE 4.5 The ground plan of Homesgarth. (C. B. Purdom, *The Building of Satellite Towns*, 1925)

trial workers. This was the ideal: the reality for female workers often included improved work environments but rarely equal pay, and only occasionally an end to confinement in domestic industries.

More Efficient Domestic Work

The major achievement of both utopian socialist communities and cooperative housekeeping societies was ending the isolation of the housewife. Shaker women sang funny songs about cooking and cleaning while they worked; Moravian women and men working together in a communal bakery reported that "If you have pleasure and love for anything, all effort and labor are light." Workers in the fifty-two kitchen houses which were built by the Amana community claimed that they were the "dynamic centers of the villages." Besides being places for village celebrations, the Amana kitchen houses, with eight or ten women working under a *Kuchenbas,* became centers of news and information. A resident described going to the kitchen house "for the only social life we know, for snatches of gossip and legitimate news, and just ordinary companionship."[14]

Sociable work usually implied more efficient work through the division of labor. One of the difficulties of private housework which Melusina Fay Peirce and the Cambridge Cooperative Housekeepers protested was the lack of specialization. According to Peirce, a young bride with a traditional home was not setting up housekeeping, but undertaking to practice "three trades at once," cooking, laundering, and sewing.[15] Cooperative housekeepers found, however, that new approaches to the division of labor were difficult to reconcile with traditional concepts of private property, which might include both the home and the wife. "What!" exclaimed the husband of one of the Cambridge Housekeepers. *"My* wife cooperate to make other men comfortable?"[16]

Societies with some commitment to utopian socialism were able to exploit the division of domestic labor most effectively. Kitchens became shops serving the entire community, like other facilities. Gardening, preserving, cleaning, baking, cooking, ironing, gathering herbs, and caring for children were all skills required within the communal economy which could be learned. Activities aimed at reproducing the community's labor power took their place on organizational charts parallel to agricultural or industrial production. All members, male and female, were required to put in a certain number of hours per day, and all work areas were designed to a certain standard.

Economies of scale in domestic life provided an obvious justification for better design and equipment: fifty private families might need fifty kitchens and fifty stoves, but a communal family, with one large kitchen and one large stove, had the resources to invest in additional, more sophisticated labor-saving devices. Both utopian socialist communities and cooperative housekeeping societies took pride in providing themselves with the latest in heating, lighting, and sanitation devices, designed to ensure the health of their members and lighten domestic labor. And what they didn't acquire, the men and women of the group might invent.

The Harmony Society constructed floors which could be removed so that it was never necessary to carry furniture up and down stairs, and they devised special insulation and ventilation for their houses. The Oneida Perfectionists installed gas light, steam baths, and steam heat in their communal Mansion House in the 1860s. This last comfort caused almost hysterical excitement: "Good-bye wood sheds, good-bye stoves, good-bye coal scuttles, good-bye pokers, good-bye ash sifters, good-bye stove dust, and good-bye coal gas. Hail to the one fire millennium!"[17] Yet, significantly, the Oneidans retained one wood-burning stove in a small room they called their "Pocket Kitchen." The warmth of a direct heat source in a small space was appreciated as having nurturing qualities which couldn't be improved upon. Here was the community medicine chest and a place for telling one's troubles.

Charles Nordhoff, a travelling journalist who visited many American communes in the 1870s, commented that "A communist's life is full of devices for ease and comfort."[18] Lists of domestic inventions produced by members of various utopian socialist communities are equalled only by the lists of inventions in their other industries. The Shakers have to their credit an improved washing machine; the common clothespin; a conical stove to heat flatirons; the flat broom; a removable window sash, for easy washing; a window-sash balance; a round oven for more even cooking; a butter worker; a cheese press; a pea sheller; and an apple parer which quartered and cored the fruit. Members of the Oneida Community produced a lazy-susan dining-table center, an improved mop wringer, an improved washing machine, and an institutional-scale potato peeler. (Their community policy was to rotate jobs every few months, so that a technique learned in one community shop might be the source of inventions to speed another sort of task.) Members of co-operative housekeeping societies designed different types of containers to keep cooked food warm for delivery to subscribers, and sometimes their inventiveness was applied to the design of special wagons and vans for delivery as well.

Inventiveness also extended to developing equipment and spaces for child care. The Amana Inspirationists built large cradles which could hold up to six children for their kindergartens. At the Familistère in Guise, France, great care was spent on designing the perfect individual cradle—one which was finally devised was a cradle filled with bran, screened to eliminate dust. Moisture caused the bran to form pellets, which could easily be removed without the need to bathe the child or change linen. Bran was changed once a month. The same community devised a special device for teaching young children to walk, a circular structure of supports surrounding a center filled with toys and games. Other communes had specially designed furniture at child scale, a novelty not to be found in most nineteenth-century homes. One commune, the Bruderhof, still supports itself today by manufacturing "Community Playthings." Outdoor spaces might be designed with children in mind as well: the Oneida Community had an extensive landscaped playspace; the Shakers created model farms and gardens for their boys and girls; the Llano del Rio community organized their teenagers to build a clubhouse and dormitory called the "Kid Kolony."

Commercial Extensions of Domestic Work

Utopian socialist communities often found it profitable to manufacture and market their domestic inventions, such as the

Shakers' improved washing machines, their sash balance, and the Bruderhof's toys, but this was not the only commercial extension of their domestic life. Once domestic "women's" work was officially recognized, timed, and costed it might become a source of revenue to extend these domestic services to customers outside the community. Thus a communal sewing room might begin to manufacture cloaks, or a communal kitchen might also function as a restaurant. Among the Shakers, well-equipped facilities for spinning, dyeing, weaving, sewing, and ironing made it possible to fill a demand among outsiders for warm Shaker cloaks. And the Oneidans, by the 1870s, were serving hundreds of visitors meals every week. Members of the Woman's Commonwealth, a community in Belton, Texas, actually made hotel and laundry management their major source of income, taking over a hotel in their town as both a communal residence and a profit-making venture.

Women's Confinement to Domestic Industries

If the first goal of domestic reformers was efficiency in domestic industries, the second was ending the confinement of women to domestic work. This could be achieved in part by allowing women more time to themselves, but full achievement required the involvement of women in many traditionally "masculine" areas of work.

In most of the experiments described, cooking, cleaning, and child care remained "women's" work, despite some limited participation by men in these activities. But, because of the division of labor and the introduction of labor-saving devices, women's overall hours of work were limited. Rather than being on call day and night, like the average wife and mother, most utopian socialist women had leisure to develop their interests—reading, writing, participating in musical or theatrical performances, developing friendships, enjoying amorous relationships. This gave them a degree of freedom unimaginable in the larger society. Women involved in cooperative housekeeping societies enjoyed increased leisure as well, especially if their organization provided day-care facilities, but many urban and suburban societies did not develop such programs.

Although most experiments managed to limit the hours of

work for women, utopian socialists did not always grant equal pay for domestic work compared with other communal industries and they did not always encourage women to enter other areas of work. The celibate Shakers kept all areas of work restricted by sex; men and women never worked together. Other communes, like Oneida, the North American Phalanx, and the Llano del Rio community, made gestures toward encouraging women to enter administration, factory work, and other non-domestic jobs. (Llano, however, offered women only 75 percent of male wages, whatever jobs they did!) Consciousness of the problems of socialization for "women's" work was high at Oneida, where young girls were told to get rid of their dolls lest they learn to be mothers before they had learned to be persons.[19] Consciousness was not enough, however, for although some Oneida women worked in the community factory, most worked in domestic industries, apparently by choice, and the situation was the same in most other utopian socialist communities, especially those which encouraged women to perfect domestic skills. One old photograph of a sewing class at Guise showing only young women in attendance suggests the kind of community pressures which countered some groups' official proclamations on "women's" work.

If the utopian socialists had problems in ending the sex stereotyping of domestic work, the cooperative housekeepers had even greater difficulties in overcoming both sex and class divisions in urban and suburban communities. Some cooperative housekeepers like Melusina Fay Peirce attempted to restrict their experiments to women participants, arguing that domestic work was women's proper sphere, and that women must develop domestic industries without male interference. Other groups did include male participants. Many cooperative housekeeping societies, however, accepted hierarchical organizational structures which put educated, middle-class managers at the top and paid less-skilled dishwashers and laundry workers rather poorly. As a result, there was often much more conflict among the cooperative housekeepers than in the communal "families" of the utopian socialists.

What, in the end, did all these attempts to develop convincing domestic alternatives actually achieve? The typical houseworker today, in Europe or the United States, is still isolated in the home, a workplace relatively unchanged since the 1860s. A recent sociological study estimates that the housewife puts in, on an average, seventy hours of work per week, experiencing monotony, fragmentation, and speedup in her work which exceed that of assembly-line workers.[20] Yet most assembly-line workers at least have labor unions which can demand that their labor be recognized and compensated; the housewife works on an invisible assembly line, and she is expected to deliver a "labor of love."

The experiments described in this chapter did not have much influence because these plans were only suitable for a socialist, feminist society, the like of which we have not yet seen. The most convincing experiments are the utopian socialist ones; when private property gets in the way, cooperative housekeeping either falls apart or is relegated to servants, and middle-class women (and men) purchase their freedom at the expense of working-class women. Even in the most consistent experiments, there is a sense of unreality—it is all too perfect, with round ovens, clever tables, and ingenious cradles. Everyone is so busy working out the details of the new arrangements that they have no time to think about the world outside the experiment. Nevertheless, it is essential to know that a domestic architecture developed on a collective rather than a private basis has existed, in workable and complex forms as well as in fantastic and unrealistic ones.

The problem of isolated female domestic labor is not one which can be solved by architects, but architects can refuse to collaborate in idealization of the private home with the "little woman" smiling over the stove. A collage by the collective of Italian architects, Superstudio, satirizing the "Happy Island" with the woman isolated behind the ironing board, provides effective criticism of private housing. Even more pointed is "Womanhouse," an exhibition of environments designed by the Feminist Program at California Institute of the Arts in 1971. A collection of satirical domestic environments was arranged within a single house to demonstrate the fusion of women's identity with the dwelling as workplace. The linen closet was portrayed as a prison, with a woman shut behind the shelves.

The kitchen shocked visitors with surrealistic fried eggs turning into nurturing breasts, and a simple comment on the sex stereotyping of the kitchen as a place for woman's work. Every appliance, every workspace, and every tool was painted light pink, that "feminine" color.

These artists and architects are extending men's and women's consciousness of the home as a workplace where women are traditionally exploited as unpaid workers. The historic plans and experiments of previous generations of domestic reformers may not seem particularly practical now, but they are part of a long history of revolt against the single-family home. They suggest our power to imagine something better; they revive a sense of possibilities, urgencies, and priorities. We can no longer take the housewife, or the house, for granted. The angry refrain of the patronized, unpaid woman echoes through a ballad composed of workers' demands: "I'm not your little woman, your sweetheart or your dear, I'm a wage slave without wages, I'm a maintenance engineer!"

Notes

1. Charlotte Perkins Gilman, *The Living of Charlotte Perkins Gilman, An Autobiography* (1935) (New York: Harper Colophon Books, 1975), p. 286.

2. Charlotte Perkins Gilman, *The Home: Its Work and Influence* (1903) (Urbana, Ill.: University of Illinois Press, 1972), p. 10.

3. Mariarosa Dalla Costa, "Women and the Subversion of the Community," and Selma James, "A Woman's Place," *The Power of Women and the Subversion of the Community* (London: Falling Wall Press, 1972). Patricia Mainardi, "The Politics of Housework," in Robin Morgan (ed.), *Sisterhood Is Powerful* (New York: Vintage, 1970). Also see Ann Oakley, *Woman's Work: The Housewife Past and Present* (New York: Pantheon, 1974); and Michelle Zimbalist Rosaldo and Louise Lamphere (eds.), *Woman, Culture and Society* (Stanford, Calif.: Stanford University Press, 1974) for historical and cross-cultural analyses of the housewife's role. Gwendolyn Wright, "A Woman's Place Is in the Home," M.Arch. thesis, University of California, Berkeley, 1974, is an excellent critique of architectural aspects of domestic mythology.

4. Charles Fourier, *Traité d'association domestique-agricole* (1822), tr. in Jonathan Beecher and Richard Bienvenue, *The Utopian Vision of*

Charles Fourier (Boston: Beacon Press, 1971).

5. John Humphrey Noyes, *History of American Socialisms* (1870) (New York: Dover Press, 1966), p. 23.

6. Alice Constance Austin, *The Next Step* (Los Angeles: The Institute Press, 1935), p. 63.

7. Melusina Fay Peirce, *Cooperative Housekeeping: How Not To Do It and How To Do It, A Sociological Study* (Boston: James R. Osgood, 1884), p. 181.

8. John Humphrey Noyes, address on "Dedication of the New Community Mansion," *Circular,* Oneida, N.Y., February 27, 1862, p. 9. Further details of this project are discussed in Dolores Hayden, *Seven American Utopias: The Architecture of Communitarian Socialism, 1790–1975* (Cambridge, Mass.: M.I.T. Press, 1976).

9. Henry Olerich, *A Cityless and Countryless World* (Holstein, Iowa: Gilmore & Olerich, 1893).

10. Henry Olerich, *Modern Paradise* (Omaha, Neb.: Olerich Publishing Co., 1915), and *The Story of the World a Thousand Years Hence* (Omaha, Neb.: Olerich Publishing Co., 1923).

11. See "The Architecture of Passional Attraction," in Hayden, *Seven American Utopias.*

12. See "Communes Within Communes," in Hayden, *Seven American Utopias.*

13. Charlotte Perkins Gilman, *Women and Economics* (1898) (New York: Harper Torchbooks, 1966).

14. Barbara S. Yambura, with Eunice Bodine, *A Change and A Parting: My Story of Amana* (Ames, Iowa, 1960), p. 79.

15. Peirce, *Cooperative Housekeeping,* pp. 38–39.

16. Ibid, p. 108.

17. Oneida *Circular,* February 14, 1870, p. 380.

18. Charles Nordhoff, *The Communistic Societies of the United States* (1875) (New York: Dover Press, 1966), p. 401.

19. Judith Fryer, "American Eves in American Edens," *American Scholar* 43 (spring 1974).

20. Ann Oakley, *The Sociology of Housework* (London: Martin Robertson, 1974) gives average figures for hours of housework (p. 94) and develops an argument about monotony, fragmentation, and speed, based on a survey of housewives in London (p. 87).

Part 2

Urban Design:
The Price Women Pay

Introduction

Gerda R. Wekerle

The chapters in Part 2 outline the social costs to women of living in cities primarily designed by and for men. They show how the typical land-use patterns of the North American city, with separation of home, work, and services, support the traditional nuclear family and accommodate only minimally to women's changing roles.

Chapters by Sylvia Fava, David Popenoe, Mary Cichocki, and Karla Werner discuss the costs to women of living in suburban environments. Through studies in different communities in three countries, they conclude that while the life of suburban women has changed radically, the environment has not. Suburbs facilitate the housewife-and-mother role, but often foreclose other options. Fava's chapter reviews a diverse and fragmented literature on the effects of suburbia on women's lives. She argues that women are more adversely affected by low density than men because women's mobility is more restricted and hence their opportunities more limited. Women's home responsibilities mean that time and distance take on added significance and affect decisions about job location, where to shop, and how to use leisure time. The reliance on the private automobile and the poor public transportation facilities of suburban communities further limits women's mobility. Black and minority women, teenagers, and the elderly are especially penalized by suburban location.

Cichocki's case study of women's travel patterns in one community supports the findings of research on women's travel needs in other major North American cities: husbands have most access to the family car; women rely more on public transportation. The combination of limited mobility and household responsibility means that women tend to work closer to home or near public transit routes and thus their choice of jobs is more limited than men's.

Popenoe and Werner's chapters document the on-going psychological costs to women of isolation in a domestic world. Popenoe's comparison of an American and Swedish suburb highlights the deprivation of women living in low-density American communities where mothers of young children experience isolation, boredom, and incredible loneliness. It is virtually impossible for them to work outside the home given the absence of local jobs, transportation, and day care. In contrast, the Swedish suburb of Vallingby is well designed for working women with its compact clusters of low-rise apartments, many public facilities and day-care options, and good transit links with the central city. Popenoe concludes that the inadequacy of the suburban environment for women's needs is largely a design problem. Werner's chapter supports this view. Now that Sweden is building North American–style low-density suburbs of single-family homes, women are beginning to experience problems similar to those of their North American counterparts. However, Werner also warns against placing too great a reliance on planning and social welfare measures to change women's lives. For even in Sweden, where women are encouraged and supported in working outside the home and where environments are much more suited to women's needs, there are still strong social pressures for women to conform to traditional sex roles.

Several authors suggest alternatives to the way suburbs and urban neighborhoods are currently designed in order to make the environment of the city more supportive of women's changing life-styles. These proposals generally agree on the need to enrich the local environment, to decentralize services and jobs, to increase densities, and to provide better public transportation links to all parts of the urban system. Popenoe's chapter shows that these elements can exist in the suburbs, and Judy Stamp argues that city neighborhoods can also be havens for women and especially for households headed by women. Some city neighborhoods are more tolerant of nonconventional life-styles and provide the kinds of densities that make it possible to create cooperative services for child care, housing, and related functions. Their research suggests a new type of urban planning—one with an emphasis on mixed land use and the creation of environments that will satisfy the needs of a broader range of incomes, family types, and life-cycle stages.

The chapters in Part 2 document the extent of women's victimization due to current land-use practices and attempt to outline some alternatives. However, the present system evolved because it benefited powerful economic interests. Only when women gain power and influence in the professions and institutions that shape the environment will their needs be incorporated into the shape and form of cities.

5

Women's Place in the New Suburbia

Sylvia F. Fava

This chapter begins with the premise that suburbs constitute a different environment for women than for men. As geographic extensions of our male-centered society, suburban environments offer a secondary place to women, a place inhibiting the full expression of the range of women's roles, activities, and interests. Nevertheless a feminist critique of suburbia scarcely exists. We will review briefly the methodological-ideological reasons for this lack of response before proceeding to our major focus—the impact of low-density suburban sprawl on women. Recent changes both in the suburban environment (which has entered a new phase of even greater spread and more scatteration) and in the characteristics of suburban women (which have become more varied) suggest that the discrepancy between the suburban setting and the needs of women will become more acute. We will conclude with a discussion of the special implications of suburbia for subgroups of women—such as the aged, teenagers, minority women, corporate wives, the single, and the divorced—as well as with some policy recommendations.

The antifeminist nature of suburbia is well expressed in the experience of a sociologist/planner who found herself the only woman at a conference dealing with the future city:

Discussion moved to the issue of increased leisure and its implications for projected alterations in the workday and the workweek and, hence, for anticipated changes in the physical arrangements of the metropolis. Great interest and indeed great excitement began to generate, revolving around the prospect of the four-day week. This,

one after another concurred, would be an absolutely marvelous design for living. It would permit even *more complete* separation of
work from residence! 'A *man* could go into the city to work, spend
three nights there, and then *return to his family* out in the country
for the other four nights.'

The more excited they became, the more appalled and angry I
became. The vision of the future city they were so enthusiastic
about was one which maximized the interests of a very small class . . .
it was designed for the upper-middle and upper classes, since it pre-
sumed ability to maintain two dwellings, albeit perhaps only a hotel
in the city. It was designed for men only. Married females with
children presumably were to remain on rural "breeding farms."
The status of single women was indeterminate; perhaps they were to
be kept in the city for those other three nights? Sex roles were to be
totally differentiated, for, obviously, both women with children *and*
their husbands could hardly expect to desert the children in the
exurbs for four days and three nights, even given the existence of
TV dinners.

No woman I have told this story to has felt that it was a matter
to joke about. We are frightened by the handwriting on the wall.
[Abu-Lughod, 1974:37]

In the few years since Abu-Lughod made those comments we
have become aware of significant changes in suburbs, most of
them serving only to exacerbate the problems she depicted. The
essential problem pointed up by her experience remains the
same: namely, how the meaning of the same suburban environment can vary significantly for men and women.

We also find the same blindness among social science professionals to the confining character of the suburbs for women.
Recently there has been a revival of interest in and study of
suburbs, as a result of the general recognition that the United
States has entered a major new stage of suburban life. Three
major collections, reflecting the new thinking and research on
suburbs, have appeared (Masotti and Hadden, 1973; Masotti,
1975; and Schwartz, 1976a). In the total of forty-five articles,
women in suburbia are virtually ignored as a topic of special
study, concern, or planning. Often the data are not even disaggregated by sex, despite the fact that these volumes deal with
topics such as employment patterns, religious organization,
transportation, and political decisionmaking, activities in which

we cannot assume a priori that men and women behave similarly.

The recent books on suburbs include sins of commission as well as omission. Paul Davidoff, reviewing Barry Schwartz's *The Changing Face of the Suburbs* (Schwartz, 1976a), points to some "unenlightened analysis which dichotomizes metropolitan regions into masculine productive centers and peaceful and domestic, feminine suburbs" (Davidoff, 1977:98). Davidoff was referring to that portion of Schwartz's summary culminating in the statement, "The suburbs, in this sense, conform to the Freudian conception of femininity: passive, intellectually void, instinctually distractive—in short, anti-cultural" (Schwartz, 1976b:335).

In part the lack of sensitivity to and study of women in suburbia results from inadequate, "masculine," if you will, conceptualization of the city and by implication of the suburbs. Lyn Lofland has noted in a very perceptive critique that in the literature of urban sociology women "are mostly and simply, just there. They are part of the locale or neighborhood or area—described like other important parts of the setting such as income, ecology, or demography—but largely irrelevant to the analytic action" (Lofland, 1975:145). The situation in urban and suburban study reflects in turn the situation in sociology as a whole. Sociology has not yet participated in what Jessie Bernard calls the "fourth revolution," that is, the recognition that "not only do men and women view a common world from different perspectives, they view different worlds as well. The fourth revolution demands that we include the world women inhabit" (Bernard, 1973:782). The fourth revolution involves the coming together of the women's movement and the substantive aspects of sociology as a scientific discipline. Since the sociological theory and method appropriate to this revolution are only emerging, we shall find little in suburban study that focuses on the women's world in suburbia or that even presents male-female comparisons in activities. Nevertheless the outline of the special problems of women in suburbia is clear.

As we shall detail below, the chief environmental feature of suburbs that impinges differentially on women is low density. Furthermore, the demographic and labor force characteristics of suburban women are changing in ways that make low density more of a problem, yet suburbs themselves are being constructed at ever lower density levels!

Suburbia as a built environment, at least as presently built, is conducive to and facilitating of only one female role, that of housewife and mother. The low density and scatteration make other activities, such as employment or even socializing with other than immediate neighbors, difficult to attain except in a limited way without incurring high costs in time and physical and psychic energy. Significantly, Betty Friedan sets the locale for the feminine mystique—that apotheosis of housewifery and motherhood—as the post–World War II suburbs (Friedan, 1963: 240 and *passim*).

Friedan's description of the suburban housewife never included all suburban women; it now includes even significantly smaller portions of suburban women. A nationwide study of suburbs using census data concluded that "in terms of family status, suburban areas became more heterogeneous during the 1960s, with proportionately more persons in the 'singles' category, fewer married couples, more working wives and more working mothers" (Long and Glick, 1976:52). Specifically the percentage of married suburban women declined from about 68 percent in 1960 to 62 percent in 1970. On the other hand the percentage of suburban women who were single—that is, divorced, separated, or never married—increased from almost 22 percent in 1960 to nearly 28 percent in 1970. The percentage of suburban women who were widows remained at about 10 percent in both 1960 and 1970. Many of the single and widowed women were heads of households, so the percentage of female-headed households also rose in the suburbs.

In addition, related to the increasing percentage of suburban women who are "single," suburban women have become far more active in the labor force. Employment rates for women have been going up in general in the United States in city as well as suburban areas, but census data show that from 1960 to 1970 the labor force participation rates of suburban women increased faster than those of city women. Taking the case of suburban wives only, whose labor force participation we would expect to be most constrained, we find that suburban wives increased their labor force participation by one third in the

1960–1970 decade. In 1960, 29.4 percent of suburban wives worked, and by 1970 38.4 percent were working. Even among suburban mothers of children under six, labor force participation rates rose sharply. By 1970 more than a quarter (29.4 percent) of all married suburban women with children under six were in the labor force. Among suburban women not living with their husbands but having children under six, the labor force participation rate was even higher; 56 percent of these women had paid employment (Long and Glick, 1976: Table 3, p. 45).

Further changes in women's roles are underway. The marriage rate in the United States has been down since 1973: women are marrying later, often staying single until their mid-twenties; the birth rate is at or near zero population growth; the divorce rate continues to rise (Morrison, 1976; U.S. Bureau of the Census, 1974, 1975).

For our purposes it is equally important that the suburbs are also undergoing change in ways that are a poor "fit" with the increasingly varied needs of women. First, suburbanites now make up the largest share of the American population. Defining suburbs as counties within the census Standard Metropolitan Statistical Areas but outside the central-city county, suburbanites totaled 75 million in 1970, constituting 38 percent of the American population, while the central cities of metropolitan areas included 31 percent of the population; population not in metropolitan areas made up the final 31 percent. More and more women will be living out their lives, seeking their destinies if you will, in suburbs. Whatever takes place in women's liberation will increasingly take place in suburbs.[1]

Second, suburbs are no longer simply part of the metropolis, a geographically large but essentially single-center entity, a sort of enlarged version of the Park-Burgess model. Suburbs have now become part of the megalopolis—a multicentered, very complex, very geographically spread regional entity for which we have no models.[2] Decentralization of jobs, for example, has proceeded to the point where by 1970 in the very largest metropolitan areas over one million in size, 72 percent of the suburban labor force both lived and worked in suburbs (Birch, 1975:29). The increasing range of suburban jobs means also that a broad range of goods and services is now available in suburbs. For women the impact is that they are likely to carry out most of their activities within the suburban ring. The question is whether restricting one's activities to the suburbs also restricts opportunities for role expansion. The question must be considered in light of the *decreasing* density of suburbs, that is, the tendency for suburban homes, shopping malls, industrial sites, and other facilities to be spread even more thinly on the landscape. For example, between 1950 and 1970 the average density of suburban counties dropped by 20 percent (Regional Plan Association, 1975:11).

Translation of these abstractions and trends is in order. Lower densities and the thinning out of population mean, of course, that on the average there will be more distance among people and their activities. This factor, above all others, appears to be at the root of the suburban problem for women. A recent extensive review of the suburban literature indicates that distance and "its depressive effects on population potential" are greater for women than for men (Fischer and Jackson, 1976: 287; Fischer et al., 1977: Chapter 7). The review shows, for example, that while both suburban men and women are more locally oriented than their city counterparts, the increased localism is more marked among the women. One aspect of this is the "substitution by women of neighbors in place of friends and relatives," since only the neighbors are readily available in the suburbs (Fischer and Jackson, 1976:286). Fischer and Jackson's analysis notes that the effects of distance are indirect, in that distance must be translated into access "from an individual's home to the homes and gathering places of people who are his real and potential associates" (Fischer and Jackson, 1976:281). The social networks of suburbanites, especially suburban women, tend to be located closer to their homes because the "cost" (time, money) of access to the nonlocal areas is greater than for city dwellers. Fischer and Jackson indicate that women are less mobile, more committed to the home, and include subgroups with specialized needs not likely to be served among the relatively small number of people in their immediate vicinity.

The locational disadvantages of suburbia for women are brought out sharply in a study by Michelson comparing the experience of new residents upon arrival and a little more than a year after their move. The married couples were located in four different residential environments—apartments downtown, single-family homes downtown, suburban apartments, and suburban single-family homes. On a scale rating from one to ten the degree of satisfaction with how they spend their time, women in suburban houses had by far the lowest scores among all four residential groups, while the husbands in suburban homes had the highest scores (Michelson, 1973a:38).[3] The data pinpointed the source of the suburban wives' dissatisfaction: they were increasingly satisfied with the social characteristics of their neighborhood, but increasingly dissatisfied with the locational disadvantages of that neighborhood. Wives, in other words, felt increasingly burdened by the relative isolation of the suburbs while their husbands, who left the neighborhood every day to work, remained highly satisfied with both the social characteristics and the locational aspects of the suburban neighborhood.[4]

The friction of space weighs heavily on suburban women because they have less ability to overcome distance, that is, to make themselves physically mobile. Not only are they more likely to be bound to the home by child care, obligations to aged parents, and by general household duties but they simply have less access to the auto transport needed in suburbs, *when that transport would assist in their development as individuals in their own right.* Since suburban women spend large amounts of time in chauffeuring children and in shopping, auto transport is an adjunct to the wife-mother role. Indeed, projections are that the spouse's (i.e., woman's) time spent daily in auto transport will increase faster than the husband's in low density areas of urban sprawl and will eventually exceed his (*Real Estate Research Corporation, 1974:150–151*). The bulk of the wife's driving time will be devoted to shopping and recreation, not to work trips.

An analysis of the use of private auto transportation by employed suburban women shows the other face of the coin. Kaniss and Robins (1974) found that when the use of the automobile could enhance their job search, earnings, and preparation for career advancement, women are in a distinctly inferior position to men. The study, which encompassed twelve large metropolitan areas and included expanded data for Philadelphia, demonstrated that working women in suburbs more often rely on public transportation, and they more often work closer to home. The authors sum up the implications:

> Lack of mobility for the worker, according to traditional economic theory, can result in depressed wage rates because the worker is unable to migrate to locations of higher-paying employment and is forced to accept a lower-paying job. Women, as we have seen, are forced to search for work near their homes, either because the transportation system limits their access to distant job opportunities or because their domestic responsibilities require that they be near their homes. Thus women become a captive labor force in their area of residence, obliged to accept lower-paying jobs or part time employment as a substitute for full-time work . . . many firms have taken advantage of this situation by deliberately choosing locations which are accessible to this pool. [Kaniss and Robins, 1974:66].

No causal relationship to suburbs has been established but it is more than interesting that since 1955 the differential between males and females in earnings has *increased* markedly. The U.S. Labor Department reports that "the earnings of men who worked full-time and year round in 1974 were 74.8 percent higher than those of women who also worked full-time and year round. . . . In 1955 the gap was 56.4 percent" (Shanahan, 1976).

The constriction of suburban residence on women's employment occurs in all socioeconomic levels. Epstein's study of professional careers reports that "women lawyers in my study who practiced full time tended to live in the central city; those who lived in the suburbs practiced part time or not at all. This does not include those whose homes were in suburban towns having genuine business and commercial centers. This was found to be true also for women physicians, accountants, and even geographers" (Epstein, 1970:133). In his study of a blue-collar suburb Berger found that only 18 percent of the wives were employed full time, although over one third of the wives had been employed full time in the city before the suburban relocation of the large plant that employed their husbands. As Berger notes, "this reduction in the number of working wives is a mixed blessing. For some, of course, it means more time for homemaking and for 'kaffeeklatsching' and other kinds of neighborly activity. For others, it means an enforced idleless and isolation which in some cases may be quite difficult to bear. Two of our respondents lost their wives simply because of an inability on their part to survive happily in the suburb; the wives simply picked up and went back to their jobs in the city where they had lived before the suburban relocation" (Berger, 1960:70, note 31).

The sociological analysis of transportation is barely born, but the title of a perceptive article by Rose Laub Coser, "Stay Home, Little Sheba," could well be a summary of compound effects of low density and scarcity of transportation on suburban women. Coser's thesis, which is a broad one and not especially formulated with regard to suburbia, is that geographical displacement, the ability to travel for example, threatens social stability and hence is patterned or controlled to maintain existing status relations (Coser, 1975). The de facto constraints on the movement of suburban women would seem to provide an excellent example of Coser's analysis.

Coser's main point is that "the use of physical space is typically linked to the regulation of social relations" (Coser, 1975: 471). She indicates, for example, that in the American family the wife-mother role includes the supervision of geographic movements of the children and is intended to insure that children engage in associations and activities appropriate to the social-class level of their parents. However, Coser notes that the social function of physical placement also involves the wife-mother: her "place" is in the home. The wife-mother's home and locality-bound role contrasts with that of the husband-father, which includes more opportunity for travel. Significantly, Coser's analysis concludes that the male's greater opportunity for travel provides him also with opportunities for extension of his role set, that is, for meeting new people and having new activities, as direct or indirect preparation for occupational advancement. For women, "their restriction of horizontal movement means restriction of upward mobility; it means restriction of opportunities" (Coser, 1975:477).

The ability to overcome the conditions of time-cost distance imposed by suburban location varies significantly by age, race, and socioeconomic status. Women toward the two ends of the age continuum and black and other minority women are especially penalized by suburban location.

The suburbs offer aged women safety, but generally diminish their accessibility to congenial associates, to shopping, recreation, and any possible hope of employment. The specter of adult children "dumping" their mothers to spend the day in shopping malls so that the women will have something to do while the children are away at work is real. Demographic projections indicate that the older American population will be composed increasingly of females: in 1950 women made up 53 percent of the population sixty-five and over, by 1970 the percentage was 58 and it is expected to reach 60 percent by 1980 (Morrison, 1976:7–8). As a corollary, an increasing portion of aged women will be without a mate; by 1975 61 percent of the women sixty-five or over were widowed or divorced. Much of this aged female population is expected to seek housing in the "mature suburbs," suburbs in the inner ring of the metropolis that have already passed the peak of growth and have begun to decline (Morrison, 1976:9). If aged suburban women are living alone, suburbia imposes special problems: the physical labor and financing needed to maintain a single-family home and zoning restrictions that typically prevent her from renting out rooms or subdividing the house into apartments. Such restrictions, by the same token, provide little in the way of alternative, inexpensive, smaller-size homes or apartments if she wishes to rent.

Although not usually so regarded, teenage girls are a deprived group in suburbs. The transportation sequence and its link to the nonneighborhood world is revealing. The early years of reliance on the bicycle with its limited range shift in the early teens to the bus lines whose destination is typically the shopping centers where other junior high school students "hang out." At about age fifteen the girls, at least the middle- or upper-middle income girls, often "graduate" to using an available commuter railroad to a large downtown where there is a much broader range of recreation, friends, and shopping (Vecsey, 1976:31). Their real liberation comes from having a driver's license at age sixteen to eighteen, provided they have access to a car.

The teenage boy also is subjected to the limitations of suburban transportation, but there are fewer alternatives for the girls. Girls seldom hitchhike. Nor are girls as likely as boys to have odd jobs in gas stations or to tinker with cars, activities that may lead to affordable auto ownership. A study of the use of public vs. private transportation by adults in the Indianapolis metropolitan area suggests that the "data point up the centrality of the car to the American male's life style. Alternately they also suggest the lack of importance attached by females to the car" (Mamon and Marshall, 1977:20). Teenage girls are being taught to "stay home, little Sheba," and in suburbs have few alternatives, while the boys are being prepared for their lifelong love affair with the car.

Thus Popenoe describes the teenagers of Levittown, Pennsylvania:

> The car in Levittown suddenly provides, at age sixteen, the independence, *especially for boys,* that in previous years was dearly sought for and denied. The use of a car is a *big ego builder for boys* . . . in view of the fact that not all teenagers possess one, it becomes one of the most significant (and more significant because scarce) status symbols in teen culture. *The boy* who has one gains high status; *girls* find it useful to link up with such boys so as to be assured . . . that they have transportation, as well as a measure of independence from adults. Those teenagers who don't have a car feel deprived and often bitter; some of the most vicious antagonisms between teenagers and their parents arise over the use or purchase of a car. *This has become increasingly true for girls as well as boys; girls need a car as much as their brothers, but their parents show greater reluctance to grant permission.* [Popenoe, 1977:200; emphases added]

Gans' earlier study of Levittown had also noted cars are less available for girls (Gans, 1967:207).

Blacks and other minority women constitute another obvious subgroup of suburban women. Generally speaking, residential segregation of blacks within suburbs has been investigated as a crucial point of concern, which it is. However, from our point of view the question of whether suburban residence increases or diminishes the opportunity for minority women to enter the mainstream labor market is of equal importance. The scant research results are unclear. Teenage black girls clearly fare very poorly in the suburban labor market compared to their white counterparts. Black suburban girls enter the labor market at a much lower rate than white suburban teenagers and they have much higher unemployment rates, 41.9 percent of black suburban teenage girls compared to 16.6 percent of white girls (Westcott, 1976: Table 1). The same trend characterizes black and white teenage girls in urban areas, but the contrasts are not as great. The suburb seems to provide a "good" labor market for white teenage girls; in the suburbs these girls enter the labor force in larger proportion than their counterparts in the cities or in nonmetropolitan areas and have the lowest unemployment rates, but this is not true of black teenage suburban girls. Put another way, white teenage girls seem to be preferred for the kind of jobs young suburbanites are most eligible for, namely entry jobs in retailing and other consumer services (Stanback, 1974:60).

For adult black women, a complex analysis of patterns of job decentralization and commuting patterns by race and sex suggests that postwar trends may serve to upgrade *inner-city* black females to office jobs unless the growing shortage of white-collar labor in central cities serves to accelerate the relocation of office work to the suburbs where the white female labor force is now increasingly concentrated (Thompson, 1974: 20–21; see also McKay, 1973; Tirone, 1974; Stanback, 1974; and Conservation of Human Resources Project, 1977).

These data suggest not only how problematic suburban residence is for the employment and job upgrading of black women, but for white women as well. If suburban women merely repeat in suburbs their traditional concentration in low-paying secretarial, retailing, and service jobs the suburbs will, at best, merely transfer geographically the prevailing sexist patterns, well portrayed in Louise Kapp Howe's *Pink Collar Workers: Inside the World of Women's Work* (1977). Suburbs must provide for women a wide "mix" of jobs and the facilities for further education and training for career advancement. To this end, pressure must be exerted on policies governing corporate decentralization,[5] nondiscriminatory opportunities for upgrading within the firm, as well as related issues such as zoning restrictions pertaining to industrial, office, and commercial location vis-à-vis residential location in suburbs. These are broad questions and serve to underscore the deep roots of the inferior *place* of women in the suburban setting.

There are many other subgroups of suburban women who have special needs: (1) Single women, whether divorced, separated, or never married, require less housing and less expensive housing than suburbs typically provide. Changes in zoning laws and in mortgage practices are in order to make such housing available. A New York State law that took effect in 1974 prohibiting sex discrimination in the granting of credit has already been followed by an upsurge of women homebuyers for small and medium-sized houses in suburban Westchester County. According to real estate brokers and bankers, "most of these buyers are unmarried professional women seeking stability, good investments and tax savings in place of monthly rent payments that yield no equity. Smaller in numbers but still a significant part of the market are newly divorced women who cannot afford to stay with their children in the family home" (Potter, 1977:1). Prior to passage of the 1974 law, single women typically had great difficulty in securing mortgages in their own names and on the strength of their own incomes.

(2) Blue-collar women have special difficulty in adjusting to the social-class levels and associated life-styles of suburbia. Comparison of working-class wives in Minneapolis with similar wives in a metropolitan area suburb indicated that the suburban wives had a greater sense of personal isolation and discontent than their urban counterparts (Tallman, 1969; Tallman and Horgner, 1970; see also Warren, 1975). The problems of suburban wives stem from loss of the close family and friendship ties characteristic of urban working-class neighborhoods. This network of contacts, on which working-class women depend for personal support and confidence to a greater degree than white-collar women, could not be maintained or reformulated readily in suburbs.

(3) "Corporate wives" and other women who move frequently, usually from suburb to suburb, experience disruptions

of their lives that are harmful to their mental health and sense of identity. Although the research literature on the effects of moving is small and somewhat diverse in focus, the studies agree that the emotional impact is greater on women than men and sometimes produces severe depression (Seidenberg, 1973; Weissman and Paykel, 1972; McAllister, Butler, and Kaiser, 1973; Butler, McAllister, and Kaiser, 1973; Jones, 1973). For corporate executives and professional men, moving is typically associated with upward mobility; these men retain and indeed enhance their status by the move. The wife's status and connections in the local community are not similarly transferable, however, and if the wife is employed, moving in conjunction with her husband's job usually precludes her own job advancement (Seidenberg, 1973; Weissman and Paykel, 1972). The characteristics of suburban life are seen to make it especially difficult for the wife to establish contact and credentials in her own right. "The entire corporate life-style encourages her to live solely through and by her husband. . . . The mad rush to the suburbs has added to her miseries by cutting her off from the civic and cultural centers. The suburbs are like isolation wards, separated from all but the most superficial contact with fellow human beings and from the vitality of the city . . . we have created suburban social starvation" (Seidenberg, 1973: 132). A study of depressed women in New Haven found as one subgroup those who had been functioning well before moving from a city to the suburbs: "These women could not adapt even though the move was considered desirable by the family. In these cases, it seems that the depressive illness was intensified or exacerbated by the suburban life-style. For example, the low population density and the loss of natural daily social gatherings on the porch, the street, or the corner drug store made sharing experiences and ventilating problems more difficult" (Weissman and Paykel, 1972:27).

To summarize the points made in our discussion of women and the suburban environment is at the same time to compile a list of research needs. The necessarily fragmentary evidence we have presented makes it clear that the suburban environment confines women in ways it does not confine men. Low density and segregation of housing from commerce and industry provide a pleasant haven for men who leave for employment every day, but provide a facilitating setting only for women who are housewives and mothers. As more suburban women are elderly, single, or employed, the disparity between the suburban environment and the needs of women will become more marked. For these subgroups of women as well as teenage girls, blue-collar wives, minority women, and "corporate wives" the existing data are unsystematic and often tangential to other research. Research focused on women in suburbia needs to be formulated. Our review indicates at least three specific lines of inquiry: the levels and types of local contact; employment by location and type of job; and transportation patterns and their overall costs in time, money, and energy. Such research would be as much a contribution to urban and suburban sociology as to the study of women.

Research on suburban women would also enable us to plan more adequately for women, although as Joan Goldstein has pointed out, a "consciousness-raising" process is a necessary prerequisite; present suburban and "new town" planning is based on women as wives and mothers (Goldstein, 1975). Suburban planning often fails in facilitating even the wife-mother role, as indicated in Charlotte Temple's examination of the use of the neighborhood centers designed for Columbia, Maryland. "The chief weakness of the neighborhood center concept as it relates to women is its view of the women who are to use it. The stereotype of the 'woman-at-home' denies her sophistication and her need to continue her personal growth, even through a cloistered period when children are young and demanding. . . . What they [planners and developers] fail to see is the relationship of an urban style of living to the sophisticated woman within her housewife's role. Emphasis has been on easing her burden by rural simplification rather than increasing the options available given the limitations of that burden" (Temple, 1974:46). Stereotyped planning for Columbia's women contrasts markedly with the diverse range of needs, interests, and problems they expressed in a survey of a stratified random sample of Columbia's households (Stuart, 1974).

Effective planning for "opening up" the suburbs to women should include specific legislative goals. State laws prohibiting sex discrimination in the granting of credit, such as the already-noted legislation passed by New York State in 1974, are a vital need if women are to be able to purchase homes. On a less than statewide level, local zoning ordinances that restrict homes to large lots or prohibit apartment construction must also be challenged since they effectively prohibit the construction of smaller, less expensive homes or rental units that would be suitable for elderly or single women. Many communities also zone against PUDs (planned unit developments), clustered townhouses that are less expensive and easier to maintain than housing on conventional lot sizes.

Obviously some of the legislative action proposed above would benefit groups other than suburban women. Insofar as the confining impact of suburbia on women has deep social interconnections, the legislative and policy actions needed to help suburban women must include many programs of broad social change not limited to suburbs or to women. Abu-Lughod, for example, proposes shortening the workday and the work-week, using the larger number of jobs to increase labor force participation rates among teenagers, the aged, and women, while desynchronizing the daily time shifts of work (Abu-Lughod, 1974:38–39). She contends that one effect of the resulting flexibility in work roles and schedules would be the easing of transportation burdens and child-care arrangements for suburban women in a society where homes and workplaces are separated by long distances.

Strong campaigns on behalf of policy issues relevant to women can be expected as women themselves enter the arena of policymaking and as they seek to use the finding of social science to assist them. This chapter suggests that the suburban environment of women is ripe for extended sociological analysis and appropriate action.

Notes

1. There are some early signs that the changing "mix" of women in suburbs is beginning to reach popular awareness. A current magazine article notes there are four cornerstones to affluent suburbia, all of them changing. One cornerstone was "women: wives who have been willing to take on

the bulk of the parental role and, in addition, do volunteer work on which much of the community's functioning depends" (Tarrant, 1976:52). In November 1976 a conference at Adelphi University, cosponsored by their Institute for Suburban Studies, had the theme "The Long Island Woman: Moving Beyond the Myth." The conference introduction opened with the statement "The mythical Long Island woman is white, lives in a split-level house, drives a station wagon, has two children and a husband who comes home about 6. In reality, many Long Island women are nonwhite, work outside the home, can't afford a car, are single, divorced heads of households, over 65, or have employment difficulties" ("The Long Island Woman," 1976).

2. For an extended discussion of this point see Fava (1975).

3. These data mirror in a striking empirical way the experience Janet Abu-Lughod recounted at the opening of this chapter! Another phase of Michelson's study examines the extent of husbands and wives' agreement and disagreement on reasons for moving to a downtown or suburban location and for choosing a single-family or apartment residence. "The data show that the wives and husbands generally agree on reasons for choice which are related to the physical characteristics of the dwelling itself; but otherwise have somewhat different criteria for selection. This suggests that adaptation to the new environment and the changes which follow the move will not be identical for husbands and wives, and that each will be subject to different sources of stress" (Michelson, 1973b:195).

4. Gans' study of Levittown also showed that with the passage of time women became less impressed with suburban living than men: 59 percent of women sampled said they would like to live in the city "were it not for the children," almost three times as many as the 23 percent who had answered this way before coming to Levittown. For men the percentage increased from 23 percent to only 29 percent (Gans, 1967:272).

5. Examination of this issue gains special urgency in view of the findings of a recent study in 111 metropolitan areas. The data show that the greater the suburbanization of jobs the greater the labor force participation rates of suburban married women (Rubin, 1977). The rates were unaffected by such generally powerful variables as educational level, thus allowing for the interpretation that married suburban women are a pent-up labor force willing to take advantage of *locally* available jobs.

References

Abu-Lughod, Janet. "Planning a City for All." In K. Hapgood and J. Getzels (eds.), *Planning, Women and Change*. Chicago: American Society of Planning Officials, 1974.

Berger, Bennett. *Working Class Suburb.* Berkeley: University of California Press, 1960.

Bernard, Jessie. "My Four Revolutions: An Autobiographical History of the American Sociological Association." *American Journal of Sociology* 78 (January 1973).

Birch, David L. "From Suburb to Urban Place." *Annals of the American Academy of Political and Social Science* 422 (November 1975).

Butler, Edgar; Ronald McAllister; and Edward Kaiser. "The Effects of Voluntary and Involuntary Residential Mobility on Females and Males." *Journal of Marriage and the Family* 35 (May 1973).

Conservation of Human Resources Project, Columbia University. *The Corporation Headquarters Complex in New York City,* 1977.

Coser, Rose Laub. "Stay Home Little Sheba: On Placement, Displacement and Social Change." *Social Problems* 22 (April 1975).

Davidoff, Paul. "Review of Barry Schwartz (ed.), *The Changing Face of the Suburbs.*" in *Journal of the American Institute of Planners* 43 (January 1977):88–90.

Epstein, Cynthia Fuchs. *Women's Place: Options and Limits in Professional Careers.* Berkeley: University of California Press, 1970.

Fava, Sylvia F. "Beyond Suburbia." *Annals of the American Academy of Political and Social Science* 422 (November 1975):10–24.

Fischer, Claude S., and Robert Max Jackson. "Suburbs, Networks, and Attitudes." In B. Schwartz (ed.), *The Changing Face of the Suburbs.* Chicago: University of Chicago Press, 1976.

Fischer, Claude S., et al. *Networks and Places.* New York: Free Press, 1977.

Friedan, Betty. *The Feminine Mystique.* New York: W. Norton, 1963.

Gans, Herbert. *The Levittowners.* New York: Pantheon, 1967.

Ginzberg, Eli (ed.). *The Future of the Metropolis: People, Jobs, Income.* Salt Lake City: Olympus Publishing Co., 1974.

Goldstein, Joan. "Planning for Women in the New Towns: New Concepts and Dated Roles." Paper delivered at the annual meeting of the American Sociological Association, San Francisco, 1975.

Hapgood, Karen, and Judith Getzels (eds.). *Planning, Women and Change.* Proceedings of the Workshop on Planning for Women, sponsored by U.S. Department of Housing and Urban Development. Chicago: American Society of Planning Officials, 1974.

Howe, Louise Kapp. *Pink Collar Workers: Inside the World of Women's Work.* New York: Putman, 1977.

Jones, Stella B. "Geographic Mobility as Seen by the Wife and Mother." *Journal of Marriage and the Family* 35 (May 1973).

Kaniss, Phyllis, and Barbara Robins. "The Transportation Needs of Women." In Hapgood and Getzels (eds.), *Planning, Women and Change.*

Chicago: American Society of Planning Officials, 1974.

Lofland, Lyn. "The 'Thereness' of Women: A Selective Review of Urban Sociology." In Marcia Millman and Rosabeth Moss Kanter (eds.), *Another Voice: Feminist Perspectives on Social Life and Social Science.* Garden City, N.Y.: Doubleday, 1975.

Long, Larry, and Paul C. Glick. "Family Patterns in Suburban Areas: Recent Trends." In Schwartz (ed.), *The Changing Face of the Suburbs.* Chicago: University of Chicago Press, 1976.

"The Long Island Woman: Moving Beyond the Myth." A Conference at Adelphi University, cosponsored by University College and the Institute for Suburban Study, November 6, 1976 (press release).

Mamon, Joyce, and Harvey Marshall. "The Use of Public Transportation in Urban Areas: Toward a Causal Model." *Demography* 14 (February 1977).

Masotti, Louis (special issue editor). *The Suburban Seventies. Annals of the American Academy of Political Science* 422 (November 1975).

_____ and Jeffrey Hadden (eds.). *The Urbanization of the Suburbs.* Beverly Hills, Calif.: Sage, 1973.

McAllister, Ronald; Edgar Butler; and Edward Kaiser. "The Adaptation of Women to Residential Mobility." *Journal of Marriage and the Family* 35 (May 1973).

McKay, Roberta. "Commuting Patterns of Inner-City Residents." *Monthly Labor Review* (November 1973).

Michelson, William. *"Environmental Change."* Research Paper no. 60. Toronto: University of Toronto, Centre for Urban and Community Studies, 1973a.

_____. "Intentions and Expectations in Differential Residential Selection." *Journal of Marriage and the Family* 35 (May 1973b).

Morrison, Peter. *Demographic Trends that Will Shape Future Housing Demand.* Santa Monica, Calif.: The Rand Corporation Papers no. 596, 1976.

Popenoe, David. *The Suburban Environment: Sweden and the United States.* Chicago: University of Chicago Press, 1977.

Potter, Joan. "More Women Buying Homes." *The New York Times,* July 31, 1977. (*Westchester Weekly.*)

Real Estate Research Corporation. *The Costs of Sprawl: Environmental and Economic Costs of Alternative Residential Development Patterns at the Urban Fringe.* Prepared for the Council on Environmental Quality; the Office of Policy Development and Research, Department of Housing and Urban Development; and the Office of Planning and Management, Environmental Protection Agency. Washington, D.C.: U.S. Government Printing Office, 1974.

Regional Plan Association. *Growth and Settlement in the U.S.: Past Trends and Future Issues.* New York: Regional Plan Association, 1975.

Rubin, Marilyn. "The Suburbanization of Industry and Its Effects Upon Labor Force Participation Roles of Suburban Women." *Journal of the American Real Estate and Urban Economics Association* 5 (spring 1977).

Schwartz, Barry (ed.). *The Changing Face of the Suburbs.* Chicago: University of Chicago Press, 1976a.

_____. "Images of Suburbia: Some Revisionist Commentary and Conclusions," In *The Changing Face of the Suburbs.* Chicago: University of Chicago Press, 1976b.

Seidenberg, Robert. *Corporate Wives, Corporate Casualties?* Garden City, N.Y.: Doubleday, 1973.

Shanahan, Eileen. "Gap in Earnings between the Sexes Reported Up Threefold since '55." *The New York Times,* November 29, 1976.

Stanback, Thomas M., Jr. "Suburban Labor Markets." In Ginzberg (ed.), *The Future of The Metropolis.* Salt Lake City: Olympus Publishing Co., 1974.

Stuart, Mary. "A Study of Women's Needs in Columbia." Columbia, Md.: Columbia Association (April 1974). Mimeo.

Tallman, Irving. "Working-Class Wives in Suburbia: Fulfillment or Crisis? *Journal of Marriage and the Family* 31 (February 1969).

_____ and Ramona Horgner. "Life Style Differences Among Urban and Suburban Blue-Collar Families." *Social Forces* 48 (March 1970).

Tarrant, John. "The End of the Exurban Dream." *New York* 9 (December 13, 1976).

Temple, Charlotte. "Planning and the Married Woman with Children— A New Town Perspective." In Hapgood and Getzels (eds.), *Planning, Woman and Change.* Chicago: American Society of Planning Officials, 1974.

Thompson, Wilbur. "Emerging Issues in Metropolitan Economics." In Ginzberg (ed.), *The Future of The Metropolis.* Salt Lake City: Olympus Publishing Co., 1974.

Tirone, James F. "Problem-Oriented Manpower Research." In Ginzberg (ed.), *The Future of The Metropolis.* Salt Lake City: Olympus Publishing Co., 1974.

U.S. Bureau of the Census. *Population of the U.S., Trends and Prospects 1950–1990.* Current Population Reports, Series P-23 no. 49. Washington, D.C.: U.S. Government Printing Office, 1974.

_____. *Fertility Expectations of American Women.* Current Population Reports, Series P-20 no. 277. Washington, D.C.: U.S. Government Printing Office, 1975.

Vecsey, George. "On Long Island, Growing Up Means Leaving the Mall." *New York Times,* December 22, 1976, p. 31.

Warren, Rachelle Barcus. "The Work Role and Problem Coping: Sex Differentials in the Use of Helping Systems in Urban Communities." Paper presented at the annual meetings of the American Sociological Association, San Francisco, 1975.

Weissman, Myrna, and Eugene Paykel. "Moving and Depression in Women." *Society (Trans-action)* 9 (July/August 1972).

Westcott, Diane. "Youth in the Labor Force: An Area Study." *Monthly Labor Review* (July 1976).

6
Women's Travel Patterns in a Suburban Development

Mary K. Cichocki

The extent to which the physical form of the metropolis discriminates against the existing life-styles and future opportunities for women has become a major theme pervading studies of women and environments. This chapter examines the issue with reference to women residents in an outer suburban housing development in a Canadian metropolitan city.

Postwar suburbia has been studied by many social theorists in an attempt to explain the differences between the way of life in the residential neighborhoods of cities and suburbs.

> Suburbs are more likely to be dormitories—further away from the work and play facilities of the central business districts. They are newer and more modern—designed for the automobile rather than for pedestrian and mass transit forms of movement. They are built up with single-family structures and are therefore less dense. Their populations are more homogeneous—demographically, they are younger, more of them are married; they have higher incomes; and they hold proportionately more white collar jobs.[1]

The problem with such descriptions of suburbia was that they did not take account specifically of the presence of women and their potential for change in the new communities that make up the sprawling metropolis. The new suburbia is more heterogeneous in both physical and socioeconomic composition. Demographically, the population comprises both young and old, an increasing proportion of single people, female-headed households, working wives and mothers, and fewer married couples.[2] In terms of social and economic composition, the

suburban ring houses a broad spectrum of upper-, lower-, and
middle-income groups, including welfare recipients and families
in public housing projects.

The problem for women, however, lies in the traditional
practices that separate work and home, as much as in the form
of the residential neighborhoods. Although a substantial proportion of women suburban residents with outside employment
commute to the central business district, socially and politically
suburbia is still independent of the city. The decentralization of
industrial and commercial activities, along with recreational
and cultural facilities, provides employment opportunities for
many suburbanites, as well as most of the amenities of life.

The introduction of multiple dwelling units has increased
residential density in dispersed pockets of the outer suburban
ring (a peculiarity of Canadian cities), but overall densities are
still low, with a resulting increase in travel distances and the
dependence of suburbanites on the private automobile. Women
comprise a minority of licensed drivers and private car owners,
and this has serious implications for their mobility. The alternative is public transportation, but because transit systems are
designed primarily to move large numbers of workers at peak
hours, their efficiency and quality of service declines with the
increased costs of serving low-density residential neighborhoods.
The problem is compounded for lower income women who
must work away from transit routes because of the dispersed
location of many industrial activities, and the lack of direct
cross-suburban transit routes.[3] The lower-income mother also
has greater difficulty in finding an adequate day-care facility
within traveling distance from *both* her home and her place of
work. Constraints on income also limit the ability of women to
maintain or purchase a suburban home. Zoning regulations
frequently prohibit the homeowner from renting rooms to non-
family persons or taking in work to supplement the household
income.

Although social scientists and planners have become more
aware of the constraints with which women in the suburbs must
cope, few empirical studies exist to demonstrate the need for
change in social policy, planning practices, and more importantly,
in public attitudes. This chapter describes the results obtained

from a study designed to examine the extent to which women
in the suburbs are more constrained than men in their ability
to take advantage of the opportunities the location provides.
The study focuses on a recently established residential community located on the western edge of metropolitan Toronto
(approximately 17 miles from the central business district) in
the regional municipality of Mississauga. Aspen is a mixed high-
rise/stacked townhouse condominium project designed for
middle- to upper-middle-income residents, professional and
white-collar workers, and with a variety of households in mind,
including established families, young working couples, and elderly people.

A newly constructed municipal and regional shopping complex, three minutes away by car, was expected to serve most of
the shopping, personal business, and some of the entertainment needs of the Aspen residents. In addition, they were also
promised a recreational center for their personal use. In terms
of accessibility, a direct bus route to the Toronto subway system and a suburban train station 5 miles due south of Aspen
provide access to the metropolitan transit system. A major
arterial road bordering the northern boundary of Aspen provides
a link to the highway system, while the Toronto International
Airport is located a ten-minute car-ride away.

Twenty-four women and their husbands were the respondents
chosen from among the Aspen residents to take part in the
activity analysis.[4] The analysis took the form of a time and
space study that examined the movement patterns of men and
women as a means of assessing the extent to which the city and
suburbs fulfilled their needs and preferences, and the spatial
and temporal effects that physical and perceptual constraints
have on their movements. The sample was evenly split between
working and nonworking women. Only married women were
chosen for the purpose of comparing their movements against
the travel activities of their husbands and to determine the
degree of interdependence between them. For this reason, the
travel log consists of recorded data for twenty-four women
(twelve working and twelve nonworking wives), and eighteen
working husbands.[5] The interview, however, was administered
only to the women to ascertain their attitudes and perceptions

of the constraints on their movement activities.

An overview of the social and economic characteristics of the respondents reveals a range of income levels between households, differences in occupational status between husbands and wives, and variations in the age and family structures (Table 6.1). The men hold a higher proportion of jobs in managerial and professional positions, while most of the women's occupations may be classified as clerical or skilled secretarial. Household incomes for both groups are mainly in the range from $15,000 to $19,000 per year (Table 2). Some 42 percent of the working couples have a net income of $25,000 per annum or more, while only 8 percent of the working husband/housewife couples are in this income bracket.

TABLE 6.1 Occupation of Respondents

	Working Couples		Working Husbands of Housewives
	Husbands	Wives	
	%	%	%
Skilled Workers, Clerical, Sales	34.0	75.0	42.0
Managerial and Professional	66.0	25.0	58.0

TABLE 6.2 Household Income of Respondents

Annual Income ($'000)	Working Couples	Husbands & Housewives
	%	%
Over $30	25.0	8.0
25 - 29.9	17.0	0.0
20 - 24.9	17.0	42.0
15 - 19.9	33.0	25.0
10 - 14.9	8.0	25.0

In terms of family structure, both groups of women have an average of two children. Although only 42 percent of the working women are mothers as well as wives and homemakers, the implications of this dual role for their daily routine are discussed in the course of the analysis.

Travel Patterns

In terms of trip structure the nonworking women carried out mainly single-purpose trips, while the working women tended to carry out multipurpose trips, combining household errands with their journey to work (see Table 6.3). The dominance of single-purpose trips for the nonworking women apparently relates both to the demands of their homemaking role and the subsequent constraints on their mobility caused by inflexible household schedules and the lack of transportation opportunities. Similarly the prevalence of multipurpose trips for the working wives arises out of their need to fulfill family shopping needs and to meet both home and work schedules under the limitations imposed by public transit services. The husband's day trips, however, primarily involved the use of private vehicles for a

TABLE 6.3 Distribution of Single- and Multipurpose Trips

	Weekday %	Saturday %
Nonworking Women:		
Single-Purpose	28.0	32.0
Multi-Purpose	8.0	32.0
Mean Number Trips Per Day	.75	1.3
Working Women:		
Single-Purpose	15.4	34.6
Multi-Purpose	30.8	19.2
Mean Number Trips Per Day	1.0	1.2
Husbands:		
Single-Purpose	28.0	24.0
Multi-Purpose	26.0	22.0
Mean Number Trips Per Day	1.5	1.3

range of activities, split between single- and multipurpose out-ings. In the Saturday pattern, access to the family car allowed the nonworking women to increase their proportion of multi-purpose trips to one half of their total outings, while the working women appear to revert to the single-purpose trip pat-tern of the weekday housewives.

The effects of the availability of the household automobile are also reflected in the increase in the number of trips made by nonworking women during the weekend. The number of trips made by working women varies only slightly, suggesting that they also share their Saturday travel patterns with their hus-bands. The difference between the nonworking women and their husbands is reflected by the fact that their Saturday move-ments make up 64 percent of their total trips, while only 46 percent of their husbands' total trips for the two-day period occur on Saturday. The working women, however, appear to be more independent, as their Saturday movements make up 54 percent of their total trips.

Movement Activities

Movement patterns for both groups of women and their husbands were reconstructed from the respondent's travel logs on the basis of total trips made and the purpose and destination of each stop; several overall trends emerged.

The workplaces of the women were located along main arteries and in the center of downtown Toronto, suggesting the importance of proximity to public transit and access to a variety of shopping locations between work and home. The husband's workplaces were either located in the downtown core or were widely dispersed throughout the metropolitan area. The average distance traveled to employment for the women was 9 miles; for the men it was over 13 miles.

Recreation and entertainment outings were limited for all three groups, but particularly for the women, due to varying com-binations of constraints including longer work hours, household schedules, family shopping needs, and the limitations of public transit. However, working wives did show greater independence of their husbands in the selection of leisure-time activities.

Shopping activities account for the highest proportion of outings for the nonworking women, but seemingly excessive hours
were spent in this activity in single-purpose trips. This appears
to result from the need to cope with irregular public transit
schedules, and the inability to carry home sufficient quantities
to last more than a few days. Most shopping was carried out at
local shopping centers. Shopping trips for working women were
predominantly incorporated into journeys to and from work.
Men share the characteristics of the working women in carrying out shopping activities during multipurpose trips, and they
overlap in the locations of the retail activities of their nonworking wives due to their tendency to accompany them on a substantial number of weekend shopping trips.

Social visits were second in importance only to shopping trips.
The majority of social trips were shared by husbands and wives.
The independent trips were made chiefly by the nonworking
women and the men.

The husband's movement patterns were also subject to role
expectations. Husbands played an important part in fulfilling
some of their wives' transportation needs. The time spent on
"serve-passenger" trips was, however, minimal and did not
appear to impinge on their participation in other activities.

Aggregate Movement Activities

The variations in the aggregate activity patterns of the working and nonworking women cannot be accounted for by the
simple observation and comparison of their trip patterns. For
example, nonworking women would be expected to have the
greatest opportunity to take advantage of leisure-time-activity
choices, yet the twelve housewives allocated the lowest proportion of their total trips to either visiting, recreation, or entertainment activities.

Similarly, not all the differences between the working wives
and their husbands can be attributed to shopping demands or
a higher proportion of trips by public transit services. This
suggests that the women are limited by the demands they must
fulfill at home, as wife, mother, and housekeeper. Although
the potential mobility of the married woman without children

is greatly increased, insofar as she accepts prime responsibility for the preparation of daily meals, household chores, and shopping, she makes sacrifices that can limit her participation in the leisure-time activities of her choice. This is largely because of the inflexible components of her schedule which are built largely around the needs of the other members of the family and which determine that time for visiting and other leisure activities must be allotted intermittently around this set of fixed daily demands.

Access to a private automobile was one of several variables chosen to verify the assumptions made on the basis of the activity patterns concerning the interdependence of movements between husbands and wives. As a group, the nonworking women show the greatest dependence in their movement behavior, in the sense that they possess the lowest percentage of car owners and drivers (17 and 58 percent respectively), and 72 percent of their total trips were made in the company of their husbands or another adult. Working women are less dependent—42 percent of the group were car owners, and 83 percent were licensed drivers; 60 percent of their total trips are made with their husbands or another adult.

The husbands appear to have the greatest amount of independence of movement. All were licensed drivers and each had use of a private car. Half of the trips made by the men were in the company of their wives or other adult friends. Many of these trips were outings where the husband was serving his wife's transportation needs for shopping purposes or accompanying her on joint activities.

The working wife without a car is restricted in her ability to choose among potential job opportunities, and this may ultimately result in her unemployment. For the carless suburban homemaker, however, the consequences are even more frightening:

> Her daily activity prism is restricted to those opportunities available on foot or by use of the often inconvenient or even nonexistent bus service . . . routine shopping becomes a chore; socializing is limited to the very restricted neighborhood in which she lives. She spends much time alone during the average weekday . . . with

preschool children, she is virtually locked into a world of very limited physical space because of coupling constraints and societal expectations concerning her family role.[6]

The interdependency between husbands and wives is further demonstrated by breaking down the total trips for each group according to travel mode (Table 6.4). Among the entire sample, only the nonworking women recorded a small percentage of trips by foot. Similarly, public transit is not a major travel mode, even for the working women. The private car is by far the most popular mode of transportation for all three groups. The majority of car trips by both groups of women were made as passengers, while the men made most of their trips as drivers. In particular, the working women made surprisingly few trips as drivers, considering that over 80 percent of them were licensed drivers. On the basis of these observations it would seem that both groups of women are relatively matched in their choice of travel modes, as a result of their husbands' predominant use of the family car.

Table 6.5, indicating the hours spent in different activities, provides a comparison of time allocation for different activities by the respondents. In general, the men are significantly more active outside their work hours than women, especially in terms of their leisure-time activities. The combination of social visiting, recreation, and entertainment activities average 4 hours per day for the men, as opposed to averages of 3.4 hours for the working women and 3.0 hours for the nonworking women.

TABLE 6.4 Total Trips by Travel Mode

	Nonworking Women %	Working Women %	Husbands %
Foot	4.0	–	–
Public Transit	4.0	15.7	4.7
Car Passenger	72.0	60.0	2.3
Car Driver	20.0	24.3	83.0
Air Travel	–	–	10.0

TABLE 6.5   Time Spent in Recorded Activities

	Nonworking Women	Working Women	Husbands
		(Mean No. Hours/Day)	
Work	–	9.3	7.7
Shopping & Eating	3.6	1.0	1.3
Visiting	1.8	2.1	2.3
Recr/Entertainment	1.2	1.3	1.7
Personal Business	0.1	0.1	0.1
Education	0.7	–	–
Serve Passenger	–	–	0.2

A comparison of the activity schedules between men and working women reveals that the working wives spend proportionately more time at their place of employment. This difference is most likely due to the distinction in occupational status between the husbands and wives. The women hold mainly clerical and sales jobs that required longer work hours or working on Saturday. The husbands are independent businessmen or professional and white-collar workers who work a five-day week within fixed business hours, usually from 8:00 A.M. to 4:00 P.M., with extended lunch hours, paid travelling and expense accounts, and other fringe benefits. When work hours are separated from the rest of their outside activities, the average number of hours allotted by men and working women becomes identical.

More distinct differences emerge from a comparison of the activity schedules of the two groups of women. The housewives have a heavier expenditure of time in shopping and eating activities; by contrast the working women spent an average of only one hour on shopping activities, but spent more time on social visits.

Attitudes and Preferences

To discover what activities the women preferred in their leisure time, the location they would choose for it, and whether or not they perceived themselves as being able to carry out such activities, the following question was posed to each of the respondents: "If you could do one activity more often than at present, what would you do, and where would you go to do it?" The list of choices ranged from recreational and entertainment activities to increased free time to take advantage of educational opportunities and activity options such as shopping and visiting, as well as one woman's wish to do "nothing"!

The working women expressed their choices as: "love to do more swimming"; "my husband would like to go to the 'promised' recreation center which was supposed to be located across the street"; "to visit my brother-in-law"; "playing tennis and walking in the Mississauga area"; "horseback riding"; and "backpacking." Similar wishes were expressed by the nonworking women, to become involved in activities such as: "sports like volleyball and tennis at the community center"; "bowling"; "going out to dinner"; "camping"; "swimming"; "golf"; "exercise at Vic Tanny's"; "to go to a show"; "night school"; and "to take up sewing."

The nature of these responses seems to indicate that both working and nonworking women would prefer to participate in more leisure-time activities that can be classified as recreation and entertainment. This suggests that the prevalence of shopping activities in the housewife's activities is not necessarily a matter of preference. It is more likely that their shopping trips arise out of the necessity to maintain a supply of family groceries and other household goods. To fulfill these shopping needs without the use of a car, the nonworking women must choose one of two options: a trip to one of several convenience stores within moderate walking distance; or a ride to the regional shopping center on a direct bus route. Given the time involved and that of other household demands, either option would limit them to a single-purpose trip and a fixed amount of purchases that could be carried home.

The working women exhibit a greater range in the location of their first-choice preferences—the central or "median" location of these activities being 5.75 miles from Aspen. Although nonworking women show several intermediate range locations in their activity preferences, they generally tend to perceive themselves as being closer to home, with the median location of their preferred activities located 2.9 miles from Aspen.

TABLE 6.6   Constraints on Preferred Activities

	Working Women	Nonworking Women	Total
Physical Limitations*	14	18	32
Time Factors	19	3	22
Financial Limitations	12	4	16
Attitudinal Factors	4	11	15

* Transportation, distance, weather conditions, child and babysitter problems.

The women were further asked: "What stops you from doing that preferred activity as often as you like, and what difficulties do you find in carrying out activities away from Aspen?" Given the variations in the proportion of responses by each group (significant at the 1 percent level x^2 test) it seems that the working and nonworking women are limited by differently perceived constraints. The working women appear to have been more limited by time and then by physical factors, while the nonworking women tend to be limited first by physical factors and then by their own mental attitudes. The results are not surprising however, for given the physical constraints of household chores, childrearing responsibilities, a constant set of inflexible daily family demands, and their location in an isolated setting with inadequate transportation it is understandable that the suburban housewife's expectations for her leisure-time mobility would not be met. The expectations of the working women are greater, since they have experienced more independence in the range and frequency of their movements, despite time and similar physical constraints.

Conclusions

The spatial and temporal characteristics of the women's movement behavior and associated activity patterns reveal the existence of serious inequalities in the form and structure of outer suburban areas. The nature of these inequalities lies in the physical isolation of residential neighborhoods, increased distance in travel, infrequent transit scheduling, and inadequate social services in outer suburban communities. Not only does the problem require the coordination of facilities such as the provision of more day-care centers, more efficient and accessible means of transport, and better job opportunities strategically located in time and space, but also a means to alter the perceptions and attitudes of women themselves with respect to their roles in the home and as members of modern society.

Notes

1. H. J. Gans, "Urbanism and Suburbanism as Ways of Life," in R. Gutman and D. Popenoe (eds.), *Neighborhood, City and Metropolis* (New York: Random House, 1970), p. 76.

2. S. Fava, *Women's Place in The New Suburbia*, Chapter 5, this volume.

3. K. Hapgood, and J. Getzels, *Planning, Women and Change* (Chicago: American Society of Planning Officials, 1974), p. 17.

4. A body of literature on the temporal and spatial allocation of the myriad of human activities in the urban environment has emerged as a result of recent attempts in social research to better understand the complexity of "living patterns" in the city. Studies of human activities in time and space have focused in general on the ways in which people use the city, as a function of individuals attempting to fulfill needs and preferences under the physical and perceptual constraints that serve to limit human activity choices. The approaches to the study of human activities have varied, by disciplinary view, the type of activity under investigation, and the interpretation of human choice as a product of incentives or constraints. See F. Stuart Chapin, *Human Activity Patterns in the City. Things People Do in Time and Space* (New York: Wiley Series in Urban Research, 1974), p. vii.

5. Movement activities were monitored for two complete days: a weekday and a Saturday. For each trip, the respondents were asked to record the day, time out or departure by the clock, origin by street address, time in or arrival by the clock, anyone who might have accompanied them on their trip, and other remarks for any further information that they wished to provide.

6. R. Palm, and A. Pred, *A Time-Geographic Perspective on Problems of Inequality for Women* (Berkeley: University of California Institute of Urban and Regional Development, 1974), p. 36.

7

Women in the Suburban Environment: A U.S.-Sweden Comparison

David Popenoe

One of the things observed by a person returning to the United States after a stay in Northern Europe is the apparent stridency of the American Women's Movement. American Women's Movement leaders often are accused of being angry, even bitter, and taking ideological extremes. These accusations are made both when Movement leaders are promulgating their own chosen life-styles and when they are raising questions about the lives of women who remain "unliberated."

In seeking reasons for this stridency, one naturally must consider the extremism that exists in many aspects of American culture. But could it also be that the actual conditions of life for women in America are inferior to those of women in Europe, and that the heightened response of the American Women's Movement is in part environmentally determined? The comparative living conditions of European and American women have been the subject of a body of literature ranging through familial roles, employment opportunities, public child-care support, and the sexual attitudes of men. One dimension is often overlooked, however: the community environments in which women live.

A particular concern of the Women's Movement in America is women living in suburban environments (indeed many Movement leaders have been raised in such environments). One hears frequently that many American suburban women, especially those who are "just housewives," lead lives that are lonely, isolated, and cut off from action, activities, and from life itself. They are overly dependent on their husbands both socially and economically, too reliant on television as a source of culture, and excessively materialist in their attitudes and life-style. In a systematic comparison of American and Swedish suburbs (Popenoe, 1977) I found some support for these observations, and determined that characteristics of the American suburb may be in part to blame.

The North American suburban environment, so pervasive in the late twentiety-century United States that it seems normal and almost inevitable, is in fact not common outside this area of the world. Its characteristics are low-density urban development oriented almost exclusively to the automobile, with detached single-family houses on large lots. Much of the character of the suburban environment is aptly captured by the phrase "urban sprawl": a scatteration over a broad area of residences and jobs, together with shops and services often in the form of strip commercial development; a dearth of large open or green spaces; and a lack of community focus in both the physical and social senses (Council on Environmental Quality, 1974). It is as if the pieces of a balanced, self-sufficient community had been pulled apart and spread haphazardly across the landscape. The pieces still exist, but are scattered: homes in one area, jobs in another, shopping in a third, other services in a fourth. To a large extent, these characteristics apply not only to the suburbs of metropolitan areas in North America, but to all those portions of American metropolitan areas built since the age of the automobile, whether suburban or not (National Research Council, 1974).

That this built environment pattern is not "normal," much less inevitable, can be seen by a visit to almost any northern or eastern European nation (see Berry, 1973). In the case of Sweden, for example, urban development has been planned in such a way that suburbs enhance central-city areas, rather than detract from them, as do most American suburbs. Most housing units in Swedish suburban areas are in low-rise apartment buildings. The suburbanites are closely tied to the central city and to the metropolitan job market by excellent public transportation. And the suburban communities are compact, physically focused, and heavily endowed with public services. Due to the availability of public transportation and the proximity of services, reliance on the automobile is much less.

One may reasonably ask, So what? Are Europeans "better off" with their compact environments than Americans are with their urban sprawl? That is precisely the kind of question that prompted me, several years ago, to venture to Sweden for a systematic comparison of U.S. and Swedish suburbs built for the same class and type of people: lower middle-income families with young children. My findings in regard to the suburban women in the two nations are briefly summarized below.

First, let us examine more carefully the North American suburb. Unless one takes the conspiratorial view that this urban development form is the undesired result of actions by the automobile makers, the homebuilders, the energy suppliers, and the federal government (which I do not), the pervasiveness of low-density, automobile-oriented development suggests that many people desire it and want to live this way. Indeed, a majority of suburbanites answer in public opinion polls that they prefer their environment to available alternatives and are reasonably content with what they have (Gallup, 1974). These residents find low-density suburbs, especially in contrast to conditions in the denser parts of American cities, to be relatively safe, more peaceful, quiet, and offering a greater measure of privacy. They appreciate the spaciousness and privacy of a single-family house, being at ground level, having a private yard and garden, and enjoying the personal mobility that is afforded by the private automobile. Some of these advantages stem from low density; others are associated with suburban middle-class status and distance from the problems of North American cities.

The most rapid growth of low-density suburbs occurred after World War II. At the cutting edge of this growth were the families of returning GIs: a husband of middle-class standing or aspiration, a young wife looking forward to a home of her own with plenty of space to raise a family, and several young children. How this prototypical family fared when they actually reached their new suburban home became a matter of some dispute. Popular writers uncovered problems ranging from overconformism to alcoholism (Donaldson, 1969). Most sociological studies of the time, however, found conditions in the suburbs to be quite satisfactory (Berger, 1960; Gans, 1966). Moreover, public opinion polls showed the suburbs to be strongly desired, and the problems perceived by residents to be relatively minor.

One sociological way of looking at these new suburban residents—and at people in general in their environmental relationships—involves the concept of environmental fit or congruence: the match between environments and patterns of behavior (Michelson, 1976). Thus, in a particular environmental setting, some patterns of behavior are viewed as easier to develop and maintain, others as more difficult or even impossible. Residents of an environment are held to be well matched or congruent with an environment when that environment readily accommodates their needs, goals, and patterns of behavior without undue limitations and constraints, especially those that generate social and psychological stress. Most of the postwar generation of sociologists who studied the situation found, translating their views into the language of environmental fit, that these young families were congruent with the suburban environment. The environment well accommodated the residents' needs and desires for space, privacy, and informality.

Yet if the early suburbanites were once congruent, they may not be so today. Dramatic changes have taken place in the needs and behavior patterns of suburban families. The average age of the typical suburbanite has increased markedly, fewer suburban families are young and on their way up, and the children are now teenagers, or have perhaps left home entirely. Moreover, the families are smaller than they once were: the number of inhabitants in the single detached house has declined sharply (Masotti and Hadden, 1973; Masotti, 1975).

But the most dramatic change of all has been in the needs and behavior patterns of suburban women. Columbia economist Eli Ginzberg has called it the single most outstanding phenomenon of this century (Ginzberg, 1978). In the years following the war, very few suburban women worked outside the home. Now nearly half do, and the figure climbs each year. The dependent suburban wife with large family is a vanishing breed; and for those who do still exist, the familial and social role structure is coming to be strikingly different from that of their mothers.

Not only does the emerging middle-class woman want a job

outside the home, but she also prefers only one or two children, if any. Moreover, she desires a husband who is at home more to help with domestic chores, an easy-to-maintain home, and public facilities such as transportation and day-care centers to ease her path through life.

While the life of suburban women has changed radically, however, the environment in which she exists has not. One must ask, if the old middle-class suburban woman was congruent with her environment, how can the new one be?

The low degree of environmental congruence of today's suburban women in the United States was one of the major findings of my U.S.-Sweden suburban comparison (Popenoe, 1977). Both of the two suburbs I compared (Levittown, Pennsylvania, and Vallingby, a suburb of Stockholm) were built soon after the end of World War II and were intended to house similar types of people: lower middle-class families with young children. But the Swedish suburb, in contrast to the American, is moderately high density, tied to the city by public transportation, and contains relatively abundant day care and other services. Although both suburbs were designed originally for the stay-at-home housewife and mother (few suburban women in either nation worked at the time), today nearly three quarters of the Swedish women are gainfully employed, compared to less than one half of their American counterparts.

One reason so many Swedish women work is because the suburb is exceptionally well designed from the point of view of working women; it is highly congruent with their needs and behavior patterns. Swedish women have access to a large job market, easily reached by public transportation, and they have necessary public facilities, such as day-care centers, play parks, and youth centers. Moreover, they have a safe environment for their children, a low maintenance dwelling unit, and a husband who has a reasonably short journey to work and hence can be home more.

In contrast, American suburban women have a more limited job market, a virtual lack of public transportation, and an often unreliable automobile. Moreover, they have few day-care facilities (having to rely on friends, relatives, or neighbors), a hard-to-maintain home, and a husband who is away from home for a longer period each day.

One major flaw of the American suburb pointed up by the Swedish comparison, then, is the lack of facilities essential in the lives of working women, and the inaccessibility of those that are available. Public services and facilities on which women depend, such as public transportation, day-care centers, shops, and places of employment are limited, and where available, not easy to get to (see National Research Council, 1974).

It is hard to escape the conclusion that the suburban environment in North America was designed by and mainly for men. This type of built environment is most congruent with residents who have regular and direct access to automobile transportation, and the person with the greatest access is the adult man who can afford, and has regular use of, a functioning automobile. Fewer women than men are able to drive a car, and if a family has just one car, that car traditionally is used by the man. In a study of automobile access among San Francisco Bay area residents, it was found that more than twice as many women as men lacked primary access to an auto—exclusive use of an auto, or greater use than any other household member (Foley and Redwood, 1972).

In many other ways, the life of the American suburban man is relatively advantaged compared to that of his female counterpart. His job market is much larger because he does not have to be in a position to return home quickly for child care, home care, and emergencies. Moreover, he is away from the suburban community much of the time, and when home relishes the spacious house with recreation room (maintained by his wife). Is it any wonder that study after study has shown that men enjoy suburban living more than their wives? (Michelson, 1977; Campbell et al., 1976.)

The suburban environment works best as well for the large, intact family that has the resources to create within their own home the community elements that formerly encompassed people's lives. In such environments it is expected that most recreation will occur in places like the recreation room or the backyard basketball area, that most entertainment will emanate from TV in the privacy of the home, and that social life is the voluntary activity of each household. But many households are

FIGURE 7.1 Women's dependence on inadequate transportation systems affects their access to jobs, shopping, and other services. (Sheila Luck, from the collection of Gerda R. Wekerle)

unable to provide these communal elements, because they don't have the resources, the family is broken, the household is so small that it does not have enough "community" members, or the adults necessary for community guidance are all away at work. In such circumstances, the private, microcommunity breaks down. This has come to be the case in many American settings.

What is the optimum built environment for women? Of course

women have divergent needs at different stages of the life cycle and a wide choice among many different life-styles; no environment is perfectly congruent with all of their needs. The needs and desired behavior pattern of many women now combine a job or career with a small family for a large portion of their adult life, a position of equality with their husbands, and a substantial place in the community arena (see Fava, 1975). Also, as a parent, a woman wants a safe and orderly place for her children to grow up. In terms of this profile, the most congruent environment for women is probably a medium-sized town or self-contained suburb that is rich in facilities and services to which she has easy access. Many American suburbs struggle to achieve these characteristics, but very few win that struggle.

The typical woman also wants diversity in her life; she may desire a different residential environment at each stage of her life cycle. In her youthful, single days, she may want the advantages of the large city; and she may want it again in her retirement, to maximize her access to cultural and recreational opportunities. Yet another tragedy of the American suburb is that it has pulled cities apart, virtually destroying many of them by drawing off people, services, and resources.

What next in America? The rise of the Women's Movement has not yet led to much diminution in the suburbanization of life. Mainly for economic reasons (the high cost of the single-family house), there has been a growth of garden-apartment developments, accompanied by a modest increase in suburban densities. But seldom is this increase in density accompanied by a Swedish-like accumulation of public services or the development of focused communities. Indeed, some garden-apartment developments, pushed out of built-up areas by overly restrictive zoning, are more isolated than the early suburban houses ever were.

Americans continue to move to the periphery (Berry, 1976). Each year hundreds of thousands of households move farther from jobs, services, and other people. Can the need of modern women to be better integrated into the community be thus served? It is hard to see how. By all indications men still dominate the decision about where to live. The community development of America appears to be driving women further and further into the box of familial privatism, isolation, and dependence.

To achieve a new direction, American women are going to have to take a much more active hand in the planning of this nation's urban development. Perhaps the Women's Movement, at least in this respect, has not become strident enough.

References

Berger, Bennett. *Working Class Suburb*. Berkeley: University of California Press, 1960.

Berry, Brian J. L. *The Human Consequences of Urbanization*. New York: St. Martin's Press, 1973.

_____. *Urbanization and Counterurbanization*. Los Angeles: Sage Publications, 1976.

Campbell, Angus; Philip E. Converse; and Willard L. Rogers. *The Quality of American Life*. New York: Russell Sage Foundation, 1976.

Council on Environmental Quality, Environmental Protection Agency, HUD. *The Costs of Sprawl: Environmental and Economic Costs of Alternative Residential Development Patterns on the Urban Fringe*. Washington, D.C.: Government Printing Office, 1974.

Donaldson, Scott. *The Suburban Myth*. New York: Columbia University Press, 1969.

Fava, Sylvia F. "Beyond Suburbia." In Louis H. Masotti (ed.), *The Suburban Seventies. The Annals* 422 (November 1975):10-24.

Foley, D. L., and J. Redwood. "Auto Nonavailability as a Component of Transportation Disadvantage." *Working Paper* no. 168/Bart 5. Berkeley: Institute of Urban and Regional Development, University of California, 1972.

Gallup Opinion Index, no. 110. Princeton, N.J.: August 1974.

Gans, Herbert. *The Levittowners*. New York: Vintage, 1966.

Ginzberg, Eli. "Who Can Save the City?" *Across the Board—The Conference Board Magazine* 15 (April 1978):24-26.

Maslotti, Louis H. *Suburbia in Transition*. New York: Franklin Watts, 1974.

_____ (ed.). *The Suburban Seventies. The Annals* 422 (November 1975).

_____, and J. K. Hadden (eds.). *The Urbanization of the Suburbs*. Beverly Hills: Sage, 1973.

Michelson, William. *Man and His Urban Environment*. Reading, Mass.: Addison Wesley, 1976.

_____. *Environmental Choice, Human Behavior and Residential Satisfac-*

tion. New York: Oxford University Press, 1977.

National Research Council. *Toward an Understanding of Metropolitan America.* San Francisco: Canfield Press, 1974.

Popenoe, David. *The Suburban Environment.* Chicago: University of Chicago Press, 1977.

8

Swedish Women in Single-Family Housing

Karla Werner

The phenomenon known as "urban sprawl" did not develop in Sweden until the 1970s. The typical North American suburb with its single-family homes and its dependence on the automobile for transportation to work, stores, and so forth—described by Whyte (1956) and Gans (1967)—has its counterpart in a completely different type of suburban development in Sweden. While there were also single-family home developments during the postwar period in Sweden, the term "suburb" means an area of multifamily housing. Every suburb typically has its own business center and also houses public institutions within walking distance of all community inhabitants. In addition, suburbs have relatively good public transportation links to the city center. The social implication of these differences between the typical American and the typical Swedish suburb have recently been analyzed by Popenoe in the book, *The Suburban Environment* (1977).[1]

It is symptomatic that Swedish sociological research has come to deal almost solely with life patterns and social structure in areas of multifamily housing (Dahlstrom, 1951; Daun, 1974). By contrast, this chapter deals with the housing market as it developed during the 1970s. In 1977, single-family homes were almost the only housing being built in Sweden; even in the large cities multifamily housing construction was negligible.[2]

The preliminary results of a recent anthropological research project presented here are intended to throw light on the conditions and lives of women in this new type of Swedish suburban housing (cf. Liljestrom, 1975). The crucial question is:

How does the present trend in Sweden towards single-family housing allow for the Swedish woman's self-realizing work outside the home? In the eyes of the rest of the world the Swedish woman is, after all, regarded as being relatively emancipated and comparatively free from the responsibility of caring for the children. Official Swedish policies are intended to ease women's participation in working life through the creation of generally available day-care facilities. It would seem that such social services would favor a truly equal relationship between the sexes, i.e., a situation in which both parents work for a living, share the responsibility for the children at the end of the workday, and also share the remaining household duties. Since Sweden is presented in other connections as a particularly modern and progressive society, such an expectation does not seem farfetched.

A study was made of two areas outside Stockholm. They were chosen because they seem to fulfill all demands for giving women an equal chance with men. Both areas are situated about 35 kilometers from the city center; one to the north, the other south of Stockholm; both are easily reached by well-functioning public transportation in the form of commuter trains and buses from the train station directly to the housing area. In both cases total travel time is about thirty-five minutes. Furthermore there are highway connections to Stockholm. Both areas have schools for all levels, day-care institutions, and so-called neighborhood stores for daily needs all within walking distance from the home. In addition, both areas have a shopping center with post office, banks, pharmacies, etc. at about five to eight minutes' driving distance.

The choice of an area was also determined by the date of construction, the purpose being to gain a time perspective of the conditions for the younger women with children who lived in the newer area built four years ago and for the middle-aged women with teenagers in the older suburb which was twelve to fifteen years old. The newer area is located south of Stockholm in Botkyrka commune and also includes, apart from single-family houses, some multifamily high rises and garden apartments. Of the single-family houses, which had been built in several stages, the newest part was selected for study; it consisted of sixty separate houses planned in two parallel rows. Every second household was interviewed, with the main focus on the women.

The older area is located north of Stockholm in Sollentuna commune. In addition to garden apartments located close to the railroad station and the shopping center, the detached houses are placed in rows of five or ten at right angles to each other. Here I interviewed only families who had lived in the area since the time of the houses' construction.

Focused interviews lasting from two to four hours were conducted with residents; in some cases I stayed at the home the entire day. I also participated in various activities outside the home, for example, attending a course for day-care personnel, a parents' meeting at school, women's jogging sessions, coffee parties, private meals in other homes, local meetings on common matters, dinner parties, and dances.

The Women's Backgrounds and Employment

Of the thirty women interviewed in Botkyrka, eighteen were gainfully employed. Only two had university degrees and comparable professions, while the rest were mainly employed in typical women's low-paid jobs such as office clerks and nurses. Five of the twelve housewives had received professional job training, one was studying at the time of the interview, and six worked at home as day mothers. Three of these day mothers had made private agreements with other parents; the others were employed by the community and could receive paid sick leave and retirement benefits, and were to that extent integrated into the more regular working life. Of the twelve housewives, ten reported plans to eventually get a job outside the home.

This area can also be generally characterized as an area inhabited by families with a working-class background. Let us take a closer look at a housewife in Botkyrka:

Ingrid, 30, with two sons, 10 and 7 respectively. Occupation: housewife and day mother. When Ingrid finished school at 16 she began working immediately. Her first job was in the stockroom of a store, and a year later her position was improved when she became a clerk at an insurance company. She remained at this job for four years but resigned when the company, to her mind, grew "too big." Soon after that she got married, had children, and took a parental leave of absence for the obligatory time of six months. After that she looked for and got a job as a clerk, but her child suffered from bronchial asthma and could not be with other children, so instead she arranged for a private day mother. However, after a year and a half she quit her job and decided instead to stay home and take care of the child herself. Husband and wife decided to have another child and during her pregnancy she started taking care of other children during the day and continued with that after having her second child. Ingrid says that her husband, a personnel manager in the construction business, is very satisfied with having a housewife. She would like to go back to working life again in a year or two but does not know what her husband's response will be; she hesitates to discuss it with him.

The preliminary results of the interviews in Sollentuna give a slightly different picture from that of Botkyrka. Of the twenty women interviewed, seventeen were gainfully employed, one was retired, two had been housewives ever since they got married. Of the seventeen working women, seven had acquired jobs (after earlier having been housewives), for which they had gone through training in some cases. The remaining ten had returned to their former jobs for which they were already qualified. The social background of the women was more varied in Sollentuna than in Botkyrka. They came from farmers' and workers' homes and in some cases from middle-class families. Let us now look a little closer at a gainfully employed woman in Sollentuna:

Birgitta, 46, with three children, 17, 16, and 6 respectively. Occupation: office-worker. Birgitta went to junior high school for four years and then complemented that with business school instead of high school. "I didn't really know what I wanted to be, but if you start on a commercial career there isn't too much to choose from later." Her first job was in a court services office, and she worked there until she got married. "Then I was a housewife for four years but showed up at my old workplace every now and then when they needed me. . . . In 1964 I resumed my work full time in . . . a job which I managed at home from 1965 up until 1976. Since then I'm employed instead by my husband who is an optician and self-employed." Birgitta manages the store in Stockholm for half of the day and takes care of the bookkeeping at home during the rest of the day.

These two women are very representative of each housing area as far as social background is concerned. Both exemplify the typical effects of their parents' vague expectations or relative indifference to a girl's future. In both cases the women had no notion that they could break through the sex barrier, and chose a traditional woman's profession. After marriage they ascribed a lesser importance to the professional role than to the marriage, which was considered the most important part of their lives.

Ingrid in Botkyrka was able to stay home with her second child and at the same time maintain a personal income, because of the need for day care in the community. In fact, communal day-care centers in Botkyrka are inadequate—there are at present 1,799 places in day-care centers, and 1,646 part-time places, but about 6,000 children are waiting for day-care places. In addition there are 420 communally employed day mothers, but there is still a waiting list for some 3,713 children. In Sollentuna the lack of places in the day-care centers is also great: there are 868 places in day-care centers, 274 in leisure centers, 770 part-time places and 288 full-time places with communal day mothers. The waiting list for these places totals 2,722 children. But even those women with access to day care often prefer to work part time as long as the children are of preschool age. For example, among Botkyrka respondents, ten out of eighteen gainfully employed housewives worked only part time.

The fact that the number of gainfully employed women is so high, despite the lack of day care, has something to do with the fact that it is a single-family housing area. The availability of private day mothers is probably greater, and it is also more accessible than in multifamily housing areas. Also the socially mixed populations of multifamily areas reduces neighborly contact and thereby also informal information on neighbors' wives who are willing to function as day mothers.

If we turn our attention to Sollentuna we find only five women working part time out of eighteen who are gainfully

FIGURE 8.1 One of the daily tasks: buying and carrying groceries from the neighborhood store in the Swedish suburb of Botkyrka. (Ola Heimets)

FIGURE 8.2 A communally employed day-care mother. (Ola Heimets)

employed. In this area the women were older and did not need to worry about small children as much. On the other hand, these older women were housewives when their children were small to a much greater extent than the young women in Botkyrka, since day-care centers are a relatively new development in Sollentuna. Instead, the women had to solve the day-care problem through "self-help." In addition, part-time work was less common, with the consequence that the alternatives were either full-time work or a housewife's existence.

Part-time or half-time work is an alternative that has expanded with the increased participation of women in working life, but part-time employment is also strongly tied to the low-salaried occupations. The social and economic advancement of the family is still dependent on the performance of the men, while the women mainly work to get some stimulation outside the home and to "improve" the family economy (a necessity for many families with new houses of their own). In general they regard work outside the home as a secondary life task. It is inevitable that under these circumstances the main responsibility for children and household work has come to lie with the women. On the other hand, in the cases where both husband and wife work one could expect a relatively equal division of responsibilities and duties between husband and wife. Let us examine more closely two families where the husband and the wife both work full time:

Barbro, 30, in Botkyrka, with one son, 5. Occupation: map draughtswoman, full time. Barbro leaves her son at the day-care center and is driven the 3 kilometers to work by a colleague. Her husband works in Stockholm and drives to work in the family car, which takes 20-25 minutes. Barbro goes grocery shopping during her lunch break. At 5 P.M. she gets a lift back to the housing area, picks up her son at the day-care center, makes dinner, and eats it together with him. The husband, who is an ombudsman, often works late and travels a lot in his job, which means that he is seldom home. Barbro keeps busy in the evening with gardening, washing and ironing, and looking after the child. Once a week she exercises; it is her only evening away from home. On the weekend her husband helps her with the housework. Barbro does not think the division of labor unfair, but she wishes her husband would be home more often—for the child's sake.

Brita, 50, in Sollentuna. Her two sons, 20 and 23 years old, no longer live at home. Occupation: occupational therapist. Brita's day begins at 5:30; she fixes breakfast and wakes her husband at 6:30. He is a clerk in a big trade organization, has flexible working hours, and often does not leave home until 10 o'clock. Shortly after 7:00 Brita walks to the bus and then takes the commuter train to work, which she reaches in 10 minutes. At 4:30 she finishes work and goes straight home (she buys all the food for the following week on Saturdays). She makes dinner, cleans up, makes the beds, and bakes bread several times a week. Brita does not think that the division of labor is unfair. "Of course, I nag a little bit sometimes, but the guys appreciate the things I do."

These two examples show clearly an almost complete identification with the traditional women's role, a role which is highly dependent on upbringing and cultural conditioning. The women's role is reinforced through the confirmation one gets from comparisons with friends and neighbors—especially with neighbors in the single-family housing area with whom there is a relatively intensive social interaction. The social composition of the housing area in Sollentuna is more mixed today than it was fifteen years ago when it was new, but the values are still traditional and markedly middle-class oriented.

Those who differ from the pattern are mercilessly branded as outsiders, and this was exemplified in both areas. The "deviates" in Botkyrka were a couple who had adopted two black children, who did not have a car, and who were vegetarians. This couple was very active in social organizations and had, significantly enough, a complete division of all work tasks at home. This was possible because both husband and wife worked part time, so that one parent was always at home with the children. This couple had close to no contact with the neighbors. They felt the neighbors' standoffishness, but said they did not have time to worry about it because of their many involvements outside the housing area.

On the other hand, the divergent family in Sollentuna initially had very lively contact with the neighbors. In the process of radicalizing their social views, however, they found that the neighbors were locked in a "capitalist" way of thinking. Now they felt uncomfortable in their socially isolated position and did not feel comfortable either with the type of housing: privately owned homes. They wanted to move to an apartment in a multifamily building as soon as the children agreed to this. The husband was a psychologist, the wife a preschool teacher at a day-care center. In contrast to the husband, the wife had long and irregular working hours. For this reason the husband had taken on the main responsibility for children and household. The wife—who had been a housewife herself for a while—reported that she had tried to influence her former women friends among the neighbors by encouraging them to make changes at home and to make demands on the husbands in relation to the division of labor at home. But they seem to have defended themselves by pointing to the husbands' work load outside home and considered it furthermore "too late anyway" to make any changes.

There are many examples that show how difficult it is to assert household individuality without creating negative reactions. Conformity becomes a social necessity in mixing with neighbors, not the least in respect to sexual roles. In view of the extensiveness of neighborly contacts in a single-family housing area, and thereby in the lives of the inhabitants over the years, it is easy to realize that the mutual influences and demands for adjustment are considerable. Young and Willmott mention, for instance, in their well-known study of London that former inner-city residents underwent apparent changes after being moved to a low-density suburban area: they became more object oriented after having been more person oriented (Young and Willmott, 1957). Also in the Swedish areas studied here, people try to some extent to keep up with the Joneses. In the older area in Sollentuna, where many neighborly relations developed into friendships, people appear, however, to be equally person oriented. On the other hand, divorced persons (there were a small number of such women in Sollentuna) are not being invited to neighborhood parties any longer.

The Women's Expectations in Life

The preceding text shows some typical characteristics of the women I met in the two housing areas; it provides an outline of their daily lives and describes how the type of housing and the social environment connected with it appear to affect those lives. In order to further illuminate the question as to whether the women held certain cultural values prior to their choosing a type of housing that seems to give little space for either men's or women's liberation, I would like to let two more women voice their views. What kind of expectations on adult life did they have? To what extent have these expectations been fulfilled?

Marianne, 28, in Botkyrka, with two sons, 5 and 7 respectively. Occupation: housewife and day mother, formerly a clerk seven years ago. "I had pictured my life as a grown-up roughly like this: marriage, two children, a car, and a house. We've built up everything according to the way we wanted it and I'm rather satisfied. Perhaps I hadn't intended to stay home this long, but on the other hand I enjoy being at home and like it here in this area, in Botkyrka and in Sweden. My husband (an engineer) has had an offer to work in Japan for three years, but I could never think of moving that far, especially to a culture in which the woman is so subordinate to the husband. . . . I've never been a career-oriented person, but have been satisfied with being a housewife and a mother. The problem, I suppose, is that I don't look on it as a job but more as routine. . . . My task, I think, is to give the children a safe start in life. I concentrate on their natural abilities and want them to get a good education. Both my husband and I want to concentrate on their sports interest, to see to it that they don't end up in bad company. . . . For the future we plan to get a bigger house, but in the same community. There we want to have a swimming pool, a recreation room, and a hobby room where you can throw darts, and a stereo room where my husband can play full blast."

Berit, 40, in Sollentuna, with two children, 10 and 16 years old. Occupation: housewife for 15 years, employed a year as a stock assistant in a book distribution company. Berit comes from a small village in northern Sweden, where she grew up under poor conditions with a father sick with tuberculosis and six brothers and sisters. After high school she got a job as a maid and then as an office assistant until she met her husband shortly after. "We got married, it was the natural thing to do. The first year after I had the child I felt a certain tiredness, and I felt physically worn out after the second child too, but a year or so after the births I felt that I was myself again. During my 15 years as a housewife I developed a depression without admitting it to myself; I didn't have anybody to talk to. I couldn't discuss it with my husband, I felt ashamed because I really had it good. . . . but the children were tiresome, I wore myself out completely on them, my husband stayed away often for weeks at a time on business trips (as a bookstore representative) and I felt so terribly abandoned. And the children came to suffer because of it. I was very firm with them, did things simply because I'd got it into my head that that was the way it was supposed to be done. I was worried about not sticking to the traditional pattern, but gradually I realized that I couldn't go on like that any longer. . . . The best thing about my present job is my own money. My husband doesn't like when I say that, he thinks his money is mine too. . . . I don't care that my job is unqualified, I don't have it in me to study for something else. Just so that I can be away from home a little while without having to feel guilty about it."

Of the interviewed women, few give an example of the type of housewife's crisis characterizing those highly educated women interviewed by Betty Friedan (Friedan, 1965). It does not appear adequate, either, to relate such problems directly to the type of housing. On the contrary, women who choose or see themselves forced to stay home with the children may feel strengthened in the community of neighbor women. It is demonstrably easier to become part of such a community in an area of single-family housing than it is in the more common Swedish suburbs with multifamily housing and its more mixed population as regards social groups, marital status, age, and ethnic origin. An affinity with "equals" may thus have positive implications, but at the same time the greater homogeneity may be an obstacle to a liberation from the traditional patterns. I have shown with a few examples that it is possible to break the pattern, but that it involves social costs. To deviate from sexual-role patterns, however, presupposes that the family is united in its opinion of the change, e.g., concerning the division of responsibility for children and household.

The Swedish Woman: Today and in the Future

The Swedish woman is probably considerably less progressive than many Americans imagine. Culture and upbringing still favor one-sided choices of occupation, low professional ambitions, and a very strong emphasis on the mother and housewife role. Even in families where the wife has a full-time and qualified job the husband is still considered the breadwinner.

Regardless of whether women are living in suburbs of single-family or multifamily housing it appears as if in Sweden they will largely be tied to the home for a long time to come. Compared to the typical suburb in the United States, most single-family housing areas in Sweden are situated relatively close to larger multifamily housing areas. This means that the women in the single-family houses have almost as easy an access to business and social services as the women in the multifamily buildings. A continued one-sided development of the single-family housing construction will, however, in the long run diminish the preconditions for this closeness between home and services. The situation may thus gradually more and more come to resemble the one in the United States.

A great number of Swedish women are undoubtedly absolute bearers of the traditional view of women and are satisfied with their typical women's professions and with their subordinate position in relation to men and society. The tendency is, however, for an increasing number of women to be gainfully employed, whatever the additional social implications of that may be. Among married women with children under seven years of age the frequency of gainful employment increased during the years 1970–1974 from 47.5 to 55.3 percent. Many women take a job in order to get, on the one hand, a greater variety in life than is provided by homemaking, and on the other, to make possible a higher standard of living for themselves and their families. In a considerable number of households the income of both husband and wife is needed to make homeownership affordable.

There is an increasing minority of women who are growing into professional roles and who are reevaluating the view of themselves they have acquired through their upbringing. An increasing number of women appear to long for a more highly skilled profession than the one they unconsciously chose in their adolescent years and for the chance of being able to leave the one-sided role of mother and housewife through obtaining a place at the day-care center. Despite the fact that the need for day care is much better met in Sweden than in the United States, the rate of expanded construction by far does not keep up with the women's increasing demand for day-care center places.

Of course housing areas with sufficiently developed day care and other services that simplify household work constitute important steps towards the liberation of women. But it is equally important to remove the culturally conditioned ideas that presently decide what the husband and wife are to do and whose work efforts are to be the most important. There is no simple cardinal method for reaching this goal. The work has to be pursued from many different starting points. Shorter working hours and increased possibilities for part-time work for men are some of the many measures that could facilitate the change of attitudes and cultural values.

Notes

1. The social, cultural, and political background of the Swedish variant of suburban development has been thoroughly studied by Anton in the book *Governing Greater Stockholm* (1975).

2. The reason for this is, among other things, the fact that the postwar housing shortage was finally relieved in the beginning of the 1970s as a result of very extensive housing construction over several years. In this situation the construction business concentrated on the building of single-family homes in order to survive. There has been a long-accumulated need in this sector of the housing market. Other important preconditions for the construction of single-family housing have been the rapidly increasing per-capita purchasing power, fast-rising inflation, the high taxes, and deductions of interest rates in computations of income tax (see Daun, 1976).

References

Anton, Thomas J. *Governing Greater Stockholm.* Berkeley: University of California Press, 1975.

Dahlstrom, Edmund. *Trivsel i Soderort,* A community study for social planning. Stockholm: Monografier utgivna av Stockholms kommunal-forvaltning, 1951.

Daun, Åke. *Forortsliv [Suburban life]* . Stockholm: Prisma, 1974.

Daun, Åke. *The Ideological Dilemma of Housing Policy.* PLAN International. HABITAT 76. Periodical for planning of rural and urban areas. Stockholm (1976):21–30.

Friedan, Betty. *The Feminine Mystique.* Middlesex: Penguin Books, 1965.

Gans, Herbert. *The Levittowners.* London: Allen Lane, The Penguin Press, 1967.

Liljestrom, Rita; Gunilla Furst-Mellstrom; and Gillan Liljestrom-Svensson. *Sex Roles in Transition.* Stockholm: The Swedish Institute, 1975.

Michelson, William. *Man and His Urban Environment.* Reading, Mass.: Addison-Wesley, 1970.

Popenoe, David. *The Suburban Environment.* Chicago: The University of Chicago Press, 1977.

Whyte, William H., Jr. *The Organization Man.* Garden City, N.Y.: Anchor Books, Doubleday, 1956.

Young, Michael, and Peter Willmott. *Family and Kinship in East London.* London: Routledge and Kegan Paul, 1957.

9

Toward Supportive Neighborhoods: Women's Role in Changing the Segregated City

Judy Stamp

In its present character, the neighborhood of the American city generally does not meet basic human needs for support and belonging. It was not designed to do so: instead it separates its inhabitants so that problems stemming from isolation are commonplace. As women and their young children are often its only full-time occupants, they are the chief victims of its isolating effects. When we consider the nature of women's relationship to the environment of the city, the important question is whether or not women are going to lend their energies to changing the neighborhood into a vital, supportive setting that meets the needs of "belonging" for those who live there. There are hopeful signs, but there are also serious obstacles in our path. This chapter explores the way in which women are changing neighborhoods to meet the needs of their changing life-styles.

The Power to Change

Women's acceptance of their roles as full-time homemakers reached a peak in the 1950s. Since then, women have made many changes in life-styles. The Women's Movement is a composite of these changes, made by countless women as we seek a fuller expression of our potential. Philosopher and theologian Mary Daly says that the changes—liberation from prescribed roles—begin with women's refusal to be "the other." "[We assert] instead 'I am' without making another 'the other.' . . . The new sisterhood is saying 'Us versus non-being' . . . a new

participation in the power of being." Daly describes "an emergence of woman-consciousness such as has never before taken
place. . . . [Women's] becoming will act as a catalyst for radical
change in our culture. . . . What can effect basic alteration in
the system is a potent influence from without. Women who
reject the patriarchy have this power and indeed are this power
of transformation that is ultimately threatening to things as
they are."[1]

What is the nature of this change as it affects urban neighborhoods? It seems to be coming especially from women and some
men who are trying to combine parenthood and home management with a creative or productive life outside the home sphere.
It is coming from career women who become mothers and from
mothers who become career women.

In the flush of raised consciousness that was the first stage
of the Women's Movement, many young women making personal location choices avoided suburban neighborhoods. If
woman's prescribed role was played out in the sexual ghetto of
the single-family suburb, it was not surprising that women who
were throwing off the prescribed role should also reject the
neighborhood that was structured as the "woman's place" in
the city. Self-development was defined in preparation for a
career and decisions to have children were postponed. A young
woman could avoid the housewives' suburbs, and while she was
studying or working, coupled or single, she could meet her
needs for belonging and for a community among friends at college and university, in special activity groups, and in the workplace. For young women and men the existing residential
suburb offered few attractions and there was no perceived need
for a community that was home based in a different kind of
residential area—a vital, multipurposed "Jane Jacobs" neighborhood.

However, there are hopeful signs that this first orientation is
changing. It is changing because women seeking self-fulfillment
in a career are recognizing that the male-dominated professional
and corporate worlds are just as pernicious to full human development as the housewives' world of the suburb. Competitive corporate and professional routes to success make enormous
demands of time and energy with little time for alternate pur-

suits. Men "on the way up" have traditionally had to put aside other interests, leave care of their families to their wives, and single-mindedly apply themselves to their careers. Though the movement is as yet small, some new career women (along with some men) are rejecting this corporate-defined route to the top. They are unwilling merely to exchange the housewife's specialized role of primary parent and home manager for the career man's specialized role of producer and breadwinner.

It appears that the decision to have children often stimulates reevaluation. Once a woman combines a career with parenthood, she recognizes that she can no longer accept detachment from a community that is involved with children. She cannot simply choose a high-rise apartment that is close to work and offers adult recreational amenities, nor a retreat in the country, accepting a long commute to work. She needs to make a commitment to her home and to a community where her children's lives are centered, and she needs to minimize time spent commuting. In sum she needs to consider how to reconcile the demands of parenting with the established demands of her job. Similar problems are faced by women who have stayed home to raise children and then decide to change life-style and prepare for or pursue a career. It becomes evident that the large split-level house in an outlying suburb is not the perfect place to raise children. She must now consider the time and cost of commuting to centers of work or learning, and the difficulties of arranging child care. She no longer has unlimited time to chauffeur children or to manage a large home. Any changes she makes that take her away from home or that demand periods of undivided time within it must be added to her role as primary parent and home manager.

Women moving from either home or career to more encompassing life-styles need help. They can no longer operate in isolation. A married woman may turn first to her husband for his participation in parenting and home management. Some husbands are making the transition to full partnership in the home. Others find it difficult to do so, whether for psychological or job-related reasons. Single parents do not have the option of shared parenting. Regardless of her situation, a woman soon realizes that she must have support in parenting beyond the confines of the nuclear family and this becomes the incentive to relate to a child-centered community.

There are strong indications over the past decade and across the city that women are coming out of isolation: forming significant friendships with other women, entering paid employment in greater numbers, and coming together in groups that provide the important impetus of support for members who are seeking growth and self-development. The establishment of drop-in centers and school-based groups means that many of these networks are neighborhood based and have present and potential benefits for neighborhood residents beyond the group itself: children, the elderly, and singles outside nuclear families.

These are the hopeful signs that indeed women are moving to reestablish the neighborhood as a vital, supportive setting for human growth. We are seeking new models that will allow us to nurture and create as well as to produce and consume; to feel as well as to think; to be independent as well as dependent; and to give time to children and other relationships as well as to a career. So while we must still occupy the built environment of the city in its present form, we are beginning to break down its isolating barriers within our groups, and within neighborhoods, and assert that its function will no longer remain as it was. The old form will no longer have the power to cripple us by stifling our growth, and this may be the most powerful step toward reshaping the form itself and breaking down the barriers of segregation between "us" and "the other." We must keep searching for the mechanisms to do so, for there is still a long way to go.

Changing Neighborhoods: A Personal History

My interest in the way women change neighborhoods stems from my own choices and experience of neighborhoods as a mother and employee, as well as from the viewpoint of an urban geographer. It is therefore relevant, I believe, to share that experience as a personal "case study."

It is evident that those of us who have young children are not expecting to change the urban structure by overthrowing the bastions of power at their center. Nor are we preparing well-researched, documented plans for social change such as are produced in the planning departments of universities, government, and industry. Our lives do not leave time for that kind of effort. What we are doing is evaluating existing neighborhoods within the present urban structure and choosing among those that can best meet our needs. And within the neighborhoods we have chosen, we are making changes that are pragmatic adjustments to our pressing needs of the moment—they are at the personal scale, neighborly, and immediate. Thus we change neighborhoods, first, when we move to a new location more suitable to the needs of a changing life-style (perhaps to minimize commuting time, or to get rid of an expensive suburban mortgage), and second, without moving, when we change our present neighborhood by participating in supportive networks and establishing our own centers in the network. In geographers' language this changes the neighborhood from a homogeneous (or "formal") region of isolated homes to a "functional" region of interaction and mutual support. These changes must be evaluated against the background patterns of deprivation, isolation, and segregation evident in any description of "women's life-style regions."

The first neighborhood I chose independently as a teacher-student and a single parent was Highland Park, Michigan, an enclave suburb of Detroit. I moved to Highland Park when my children were five and two, and I had already been teaching geography at Wayne State University in downtown Detroit for four years. I had acquired sufficient knowledge of the social geography of Detroit to base my choice of a new neighborhood on three important criteria: proximity to my job, the heterogeneity of the neighborhood population, and the small size of the municipality.

A most important location criterion was to be close to my job at the university. My previous experience of commuting for three hours (nearly one hundred miles) daily to and from Ann Arbor—with outlying child care thrown in—convinced me of the importance of proximity to workplace. Highland Park was three miles from the university, a ten-minute drive on wide, nearly empty, streets.

Equally important to me however, was that I live in an ethnically mixed neighborhood that reflected in part the diversity of people in Detroit. I had grown up in a white, "middle-class" suburb in Johannesburg, South Africa and wanted no part of the limiting outlook such an environment fostered, either for myself or for my children. My neighbors in Highland Park were Black, Arabic, Jewish, Southern White, Scottish. . . .

A third criteria was the small size of the municipality, since I was planning to work on community geographical studies with Wayne State students and Highland Park residents. The city, with its population of 37,000 in three square miles, seemed small enough that problems could be identified and small-scale solutions could be presented to the government for implementation.

In moving to Highland Park I was aware that the public school system was a failing institution, unable to compensate for the effects of the poverty-stricken surrounding neighborhoods. As a result it had been abandoned by middle-class parents (white and black) who could afford to send their children elsewhere. This left a trouble-ridden, low-income school population. My own choices were enlarged by my relatively high income as a university professor, and I chose to send the children to an "alternate" school and to a cooperative nursery school. The choices added considerable chauffeuring time to my schedule and robbed the children of a natural mobility and close friendships within their own neighborhood. Car pools were formed with other nearby parents who were able to afford similar private education for their children, which led to close friendships between "high-income" families. Friendships with "low-income" families and with children at the public school were not as close. Different patterns of childrearing and child behavior also resulted in limited interaction between these groups.

The small size of Highland Park did indeed have benefits, when during the course in "community geography," students and residents gathered data on neighborhood resources and presented the results to block clubs as suggested problem solutions. One outcome of our work with local teenagers was the preparation of a recreation plan for submission to the city council. Another important example of the benefits of the small municipality was the effectiveness of the Michigan municipal-employees residency rule. This required that all municipal employees live within the boundaries of the city where they worked. Councilmen, city administrators, policemen, and teachers lived in close proximity to factory workers, retirees, the unemployed, and women on welfare. Although the class system was not changed by the lack of income segregation at a neighborhood scale, often interpersonal problems were handled in a personal, neighborly way. A family with problem teenagers on our block, for example, was visited regularly by a policeman-neighbor who acted as "big brother" to the boys. Other neighbors were also supportive of the family, yet strongly discouraged the boys' early antisocial behavior. After two years the boys had settled in as helpful, friendly members of the neighborhood.

Poverty was the central fact of life for most, however, and its problems could not be overcome merely with neighborly goodwill. When I lost my job at Wayne State University after two years in Highland Park, the loss of my own high-income status became a major factor in my decision to move. I would no longer be able to afford the alternate school that had become an important "community" for my daughter. More important, my children were moving into a new stage of childhood where their range of movement would normally extend beyond the front yard of our own home. And while I, as an adult woman, had learned techniques for getting around Detroit with minimal fear for my safety, I did not have the same feeling of confidence that my small children could move freely on foot in the neighborhood and, later, on public transportation. My daughter's best friend now goes to the neighborhood grocery store only when accompanied by her large Airedale dog for protection. Another friend left the neighborhood for the suburbs because her teenage daughter could not walk one block to the bus stop without being harassed by cruising male motorists who frequented the "neighborhood" pornographic theaters along Woodward Avenue. As they grew older the children could not as easily be shielded from the violence of the city.

I moved to Toronto, Ontario. The major reasons for my move to Toronto were in part personal and in part to facilitate a life-style I wanted for myself and my children. I wanted a neighborhood where both I and my children could enjoy the freedom of comparative safety and the freedom of mobility in the heart of a dynamic city, and I could pursue the unfolding directions of my career. These freedoms are denied to women and children in most American cities. My street, Brunswick Avenue, is a microcosm of the city, with more than fifteen ethnic groups represented; the children's school has fifty-two! We are three blocks from subway and bus stops, and my nine-year-old daughter can make short, unaccompanied trips via subway. Bicycles provide local mobility for big and little people. The neighborhood network takes many forms and is never more active than in the summer when we move out onto our front porch "living room" and share conversations and meals with neighbors and friends who drop by.

My work position has changed—from an academic who studied community geography and attempted to facilitate local change— to a community worker also studying the geographic implications of neighborhood change and changes in women's life-styles. Our collective of five women "parent liaison workers" has established Programs for People with Children (PPC) in several neighborhoods of inner-city Toronto. One program is a Parent-Child Drop-in Center that provides an informal, friendly gathering place for children and adults from nearby high-rise buildings. We have also established several support groups for women with preschool children and sponsored a network of communication between many existing groups of women in the inner city.[2]

The work has put me in touch with the ways in which women with different life-styles are seeking support in different neighborhoods. We have a support group of women on welfare who are living in high-rise public housing. The stumbling blocks to the formation of a community are the fear and mistrust of the neighbors and a chronic depression and apathy. This seems to result from life-styles from which all semblance of self-direction and control is gone. Activities that arouse interest in the group are those that offer a break from constant child care and from the confines of cramped high-rise apartments. We made attempts at forming a support group in a neighborhood where both men and women work or where the woman often takes on work for periods when the man is unemployed. It was soon evident that women who carry two jobs have no time for the relaxation and comfort of a support group, however much they may want it. In this neighborhood, we have resorted to home visits and keeping in touch by telephone to provide liaison and referrals of many kinds.

Groups of husband-supported women are located mostly in the suburbs. While children are still small the parenting career becomes all absorbing, and group meetings frequently focus on parent-effectiveness training. But women in these groups are making other changes in their lives such as preparing for post-parenting careers, and these changes are shared with group members.

Women's groups all over the city, including those we initiated, are being facilitated with skills given by trained personnel from several organizations. For example the YWCA in Toronto does an excellent job of training leaders and facilitating different kinds of groups. There are "Take-a-Break" groups for mothers of young children (on which our PPC support groups are patterned), "Focus on Change" and "Life Skills" groups for women planning postparenting careers, and special groups to meet the needs of immigrant women. Another group-facilitating organization is the "Self-Help Collective" of the Women's Counselling and Referral Service, which helps new support groups of women at the rate of about one a month.[3]

My own evolution from isolation in a nuclear family (with personal ambitions centered on my own career) to enthusiastic participation in cooperative action is not an isolated case. I have been part of a fluctuating, growing movement of cooperative, supportive action among women and men first in Detroit and now in Toronto. It is a movement without clearly defined goals, structure, or membership, but it is nonetheless a potent force for changing the structure of the city as it continues to encourage changes in my life and in the lives of other citizens who are my friends and neighbors.

Notes

1. Mary Daly, "God is a Verb," in Uta West (ed.), *Woman in a Changing World* (New York: McGraw Hill, 1975), p. 157.

2. "Programs for People with Children" was funded by a year's grant

from the Canada Works Division of the Canadian Government and was sponsored by the Toronto Board of Education. Within this framework the five staff members had considerable autonomy to plan and develop their own programs.

3. All these groups are listed in "The Parent Resource People's Guide to Toronto Area Support Groups," available from the Toronto Board of Education, Programs for People with Children.

Women in Environmental Decisionmaking: Institutional Constraints

Introduction

David Morley

Part 3 contains chapters dealing with the constraints placed on women by the institutions and decisionmaking processes associated with the design and delivery of human environments. Each chapter is concerned both with the roles that women play in existing environment-producing organizations and with the implications of those roles for the form of future environments in relation to women's needs. The emphasis therefore is on women and decisionmaking in institutional settings.

The first three chapters (by Ellen Perry Berkeley, Jacqueline Leavitt, and Anonymous) deal with education and practice in the environmental professions—architecture and urban planning. The fourth chapter (by Ronald Lawson, Stephen Barton, and Jenna W. Joselit) deals with the organization of grass-roots reform by the tenants of particular housing environments, while the final chapter (by Richard W. Butler and Susan Phillips) considers women in municipal government. Women are viewed in a variety of organizational frameworks: as students, educators, professionals, community leaders, politicians, public servants, and users—all making direct input into the complex of public and private institutions that control the development and form of human environments. Berkeley's review of women in architecture reveals a familiar pattern. Women have been placed in a peripheral position in the profession. That this should have been the case in the nineteenth century is perhaps less shocking than the extremely slow progress of women in the architectural profession during this century. Exceptions to this resistance to women, like the Cambridge School at

Harvard, serve only to highlight the norm.

Breaking out of the peripheral status has been very difficult—
the proportion of women in the profession actually declined
between 1950 and 1970, and although that figure is now increasing it is still below 5 percent. If these facts are bleak, the
emerging style of women in the architectural profession gives
reason for hope. Berkeley cites instances of women architects
grouping to work and learn together with results that suggest
the evolution of a new style of environmental professionalism,
involving greater sensitivity towards users, closer association
between architect and client, emphasis on the design implications of changing women's roles, and the demystification of the
architectural and design process.

If architects have traditionally displayed a sense of confidence
in their roles, urban planners apparently do not. Leavitt's chapter deals with the same issues as Berkeley's, but with regard to
women in planning. Her conclusions are essentially gloomy:
that planning itself is marginal to the process of shaping the
environment and that women's role in the planning process is
doubly marginal. While women are estimated to occupy over a
quarter of the total number of planning positions, only 10 percent of professional positions are held by women, and perhaps
as few as 2 percent of executive appointments. Women in planning earn less than men with the same experience and qualifications, and are generally discouraged from staying in the profession. It is estimated that 50 percent of them disrupt or terminate
their careers. With regard to the opportunities for women planners to play an advocate role on behalf of women users of the
urban environment, Leavitt concludes that women planners
tend to conform to the dominant male ethic of the profession
and become separated from their identification with women.

This picture of alienation and rejection is reinforced in the
anonymously authored chapter on discrimination against
women in environmental design education. In fact, what this
study does is to show the origins of the unequal career development experienced by so many women. Whether as student,
staff, or faculty member, women in the university school of
architecture under study are aware of the blocking of their
aspirations and the limiting of their achievement by discriminat-

ing practices (explicit or implicit) on the part of the male members of the institution.

If the environmental professions present an uncertain prospect for women concerned with changing the basis for environmental design, the study by Ronald Lawson, Stephen Barton, and Jenna Joselit of women's roles in the New York tenants' movement presents at least a potential for change. Here we are looking at the formation of grass-roots reform organizations operating in the domestic setting with some freedom from the constraints of the established social hierarchies that are reflected in the development of formal professional organizations. It might be assumed that in this setting, because they are the primary occupiers of such spaces, women's roles will be more established and significant.

The authors identify a common profile of reform movement activity. Women form the dominant, active membership of tenant organizations at the local or building level. They have the local contacts and personal relationships necessary to mobilize an active response to inequities. However, the district and city-wide tenant organizations tend to be dominated by men, especially at times of intensive political activity and high leadership visibility. Women do seem to have a greater chance of becoming overall leaders when the level of activity drops and becomes routine, and when there are fewer political returns from active participation. Some hope emerges from the fact that this pattern seems to be changing; certainly in the New York tenant movement, and probably more widely in resident and other community-based groups, leadership is frequently in the hands of women. The increase in women's self-awareness and confidence during an era of increasing impact of the Women's Movement is having its effects.

Women's newly found confidence in playing public affairs roles cannot lead to significant change without their election or appointment to positions on decisionmaking bodies. Butler and Phillips' paper in this section considers women's involvement in municipal government in one Ontario city. While these findings are limited in application, some important implications can be drawn. Neither through group pressure on decisionmaking bodies nor through election or appointment to these bodies, did the

women of London, Ontario, play an active role in transferring
their concerns to the public arena. Only in the conventional wom-
en's interest areas was their presence felt (i.e., education, social
services, housing, arts and culture, and day care), but even here
women were never a majority or even a parity of a committee.
The overwhelming attitude of the male members of committees
was that there was no need for special women's representation
since their views did not differ substantially from the men's!

Women clearly have enormous difficulty in translating their
strongly felt interests into the political and bureaucratic arenas.
Despite the awareness and sensitivity of individual women
towards their environments, it seems likely that significant
change will come only after legislatures at all levels of government enact it, and that may only happen as a result of political
pressure exerted by women.

It is difficult to respond to the chapters in Part 3 without a
feeling of gloom and despondency. Environment-creating institutions are seen to be the tools of the existing male-dominated
society. They create environments that are symbols of that
societal authority. While the basic form of the environment is
shaped outside the control of the environmental design professions, even here women play marginal roles and do not get appointed to the more influential senior positions. Those women
who do become active architects or planners are under great
pressure to conform; in fact, conformity is a key requirement
for any successful professional career. Such compliance with
established conventions is usually ingrained in women during
their professional training.

Women play an insignificant role in the bodies that oversee,
control, or otherwise influence political decisions leading to
environmental design (planning commissions, municipal boards,
chambers of commerce, etc.). Women's organizations outside
of these established settings do not effectively confront the
environmental discrimination and inequity suffered by women.
All this information may be profoundly disturbing for both
feminists and liberated males, but despite signs of inroads recorded in the media (but not reflected in the studies included
in this book), these findings must be faced before more forceful
action for women's environments can get underway.

10

Architecture:
Toward a Feminist Critique

Ellen Perry Berkeley

The acerbic Samuel Johnson once commented: "A woman writing a novel is like a dog on its hind legs; one is surprised not that it's done well but that it's done at all." A woman practicing architecture, until recently was as remarkable as a dog walking on its hind legs. It hardly mattered whether the job was done well because women were peripheral to the profession, denied even the most meager legitimation. Women architects of the nineteenth century (and later) have claimed special aptitude for domestic architecture,[1] but while this has given women a certain status, the men guaranteed that the status was low. A ruling handed down in an 1876 editorial is typical: "the planning of houses is not architecture."[2]

Women have come some distance since then, even though architecture is still very much a "man's profession." This chapter will trace the history of the past 100 years in the education of women for the practice of architecture and will suggest some of the possibilities for the future.

The Earliest Women Students

The nation's first school of architecture, at M.I.T., opened to men in 1861 and to women in 1885.[3] Cornell, the nation's second architecture school, had already graduated three women

This chapter is based on an edited version of a paper included in a forthcoming book, Judy Loeb (ed.), *Feminist Collage: Educating Women in the Visual Arts* (New York: Teachers College Press, Columbia University, n.d.).

by 1880.[4] The land-grant schools, unable to exclude women, were often grossly inhospitable to those who couldn't be "counseled" away; only a stubborn and single-minded woman finished the course at the state universities in the early decades of the twentieth century. Like the men, a few women studied abroad; the outstanding Julia Morgan, architect of Hearst's San Simeon and protégée of Bernard Maybeck, was the first woman accepted at L'Ecole des Beaux Arts, in 1898.

Academic training was not the only route into the profession for women or men. Apprenticeship was widely accepted; the difficulty was in finding a sponsor who would accept a woman.[5] Private tutoring was another route, both for the affluent gentlewoman eager to acquire gentlewomanly skills and for the woman eager to use her mind in the days of the new feminism sixty years ago.

But the major place for an architectural education, for both women and men, was increasingly at the "collegiate schools of architecture"—the schools within the established centers of learning. In fact, some of the most prestigious schools have accepted women only during our lifetime. Just before World War I, when total enrollment in the nation's twenty collegiate schools of architecture was 1,450, the largest school (University of Pennsylvania, with 216 students) was closed to women and remained so until after World War II.

The Extraordinary Cambridge School

This experiment began with a gesture by Harvard in 1915, and it ended with another gesture in 1942. Between those years, almost 500 women passed through an extraordinary professional school open only to women.[6] The school began when Harvard, which could not see itself instructing women directly, asked one of its faculty members, Henry Atherton Frost, to instruct a young woman in architectural drafting. He tutored her in his own office; she was soon eargerly joined by five others, and "The Cambridge School of Architecture and Landscape Architecture" burst into existence—soon expanded in size and scope, and staffed with Harvard's best teachers. ("They supplemented their salaries," recalls G. Holmes Perkins, one of these young teachers, "otherwise the school couldn't have made it.")

Frost encouraged what he saw as the special interest of the Cambridge student: "in housing rather than houses; in community centers for the masses rather than in neighborhood clubs for the elect; in regional planning more than in estate planning; in social aspects of her profession more than in private commissions." To Frost, "her interest in her profession embraces its social and human implications." A year before the school closed, he proposed an expanded M.Arch. of "research and design in the direction of (for want of a better term) socialized architecture." How extraordinary that might have been. The Cambridge School was already pioneering in its integration of the study of architecture and landscape architecture—an important direction that would later be "pioneered" by Harvard in the 1940s.

Why did the school die? It had produced incredibly determined and able practitioners—83 percent of all graduates (and 60 percent of all married graduates) were professionally active in 1930.[7] It died, I believe, because some people didn't realize its excellence, and because others did. Let us review its final days. Since the Cambridge School was unable to offer degrees (only certificates were available) unless it became affiliated with an accredited college, Frost began seeking such an affiliation in 1928. The trustees of Smith College voted on affiliation in 1932, and Smith became full owner of the Cambridge School in 1938; the new name became "Smith College Graduate School of Architecture and Landscape Architecture, Formerly the Cambridge School." But this affiliation, which had been supported by the great president of Smith, William A. Neilson, was not appreciated by his successor who could only see the Cambridge School as a financial nightmare. In 1940, the new president of Smith warned Frost: "I am much afraid that unless we can substantially reduce the present deficit the Trustees will decide to give up the school at the earliest possible moment"; three months later, this happened.

Harvard also saw the Cambridge School in economic terms—these were spirited and hard-working women, but this was not their primary value. One student would recall thirty years later: "no one was fooled for a minute . . . they needed us to replace the men being drafted." For the duration of the war, according to the agreement reached in 1942, the Cambridge School would "cease" and Harvard would accept women students in its architecture program. A considerable battle ensued at the time about whether Harvard would accept women as candidates for *degrees* (it did), and whether Harvard would continue the policy after the war (it did). The Cambridge School never reopened, even though Harvard's hospitality to women cooled in the postwar period. In 1951, the dean of Harvard's Graduate School of Design claimed (without substantiation) that 95 percent of the women with degrees in architecture had retired from the profession and become housewives.[8]

Up and Down, but Mostly Down

Women have never been numerous in the profession. An article in one of the architectural journals, in 1948, was titled "A Thousand Women in Architecture."[9] But this figure included many who had merely studied architecture. Only 231 women answered the magazine's questionnaire, and of these only 108 were practicing.

The history of Alpha Alpha Gamma gives further—and sadder—evidence of the profession's resistance to women. Women students in architecture were numerous enough to form organizations at Washington University and the University of Minnesota as early as 1915. By 1922, these groups became a national organization—Alpha Alpha Gamma—which, at its height, had eleven student chapters and nine alumnae chapters. By 1948, however, women's zeal for the study of architecture had waned or been stifled; alumnae were more numerous than students, and the national group reorganized itself as the Association of Women in Architecture (with Alpha Alpha Gamma as its undergraduate affiliate). Whether this marked the "coming of age" of Alpha Alpha Gamma is debatable. The national group was disbanded about 1969; one chapter still survives in Los Angeles.

One further item: the 1950s saw the dissolution of the Women's Architectural Club of Chicago, founded in 1921 "to further the interests of women in Architecture."[10] Bertha Whitman, first woman graduate in architecture from Michigan (1920) recalls: "After about 1950 there were not so many women architects in Chicago, and it was hard to maintain a club. The AIA asked them to become a branch and it deteriorated into nothing, [equivalent to] wives of members.

After World War II, women lost ground in many jobs and professions. In architecture, during the twenty years from 1950 to 1970, the proportion of women declined from 3.8 to 3.6 percent, although the profession itself was expanding during this time. Women went back to their homes, men back to business as usual.

The New Numbers Game

In 1973, the American Institute of Architects was urged to appoint a task force to study the status of women in the profession. The report of that task force, published in 1975, stated that women were only 1.2 percent of all *registered* architects and 3.7 percent of the *total* architectural population in the United States. These figures were out of date at the time they were published, however; the total number of registered architects was by then 60,000 and no one knows, or is telling, how many of these 60,000 were women. The last few years have seen an increasing number of women graduated from the schools and later licensed, but the percentage of women among registered architects is still very low—probably less than 5 percent.

The percentage of women in the schools is increasing steadily, says the Association of Collegiate Schools of Architecture. In 1973, for instance, women were 8.4 percent of all architecture students, up from 6 percent in 1969. But the number of women in several architecture schools is quite high—25 percent or higher—so that if the average in all the schools is still below 10 percent,[11] some schools have very few women indeed! Whether a significantly higher percentage of women will be attracted to (and accepted for) the study of architecture depends on many factors. In a profession that has been dragged reluctantly into almost every social protest, a cautious optimism seems in order.

The Feminist Critique

It is important to focus on the possibilities suggested by the presence of more women in the architectural profession. Simply having more women architects would be a hollow victory; I believe that the real problem for a thoughtful woman is not whether she is *accepted* into the profession, but whether she *wants* to be accepted into the profession as it is now.

Many women (and men too) believe that the profession is not doing its best for the "users" of buildings (the hospital patients, office workers, residents, and so on), and some of these women are bringing a feminist perspective to this critique. Among the earliest have been these. One architecture student proposed in her graduate thesis an entirely new "environment for birth," in which childbirth is considered a natural event and not an illness.[12] Another student investigated the physical barriers to women who are accompanied by young children—the stairs and doors that do not permit a baby carriage to pass, and so on.[13] Another student evaluated several well-known housing projects that were built for married students, but evaluated them from the viewpoint of the young mothers in the projects. She concluded that the daily life of these women was not carefully considered in the design of these projects, and as a result the daily life of these women was filled with inconvenience and loneliness.[14] The feminist critique is not a critique without action; one architectural office composed entirely of women designed a low-budget project for a restaurant being run by women. To save money on the construction, the architects designed interiors that could easily be built by the client. Then, knowing that women often lack basic carpentry skills, the architects instructed the client in the skills needed.[15]

Some women faculty members in the architecture schools have developed entire courses on issues important to women. One course at Columbia University has studied the impact of urban planning on women in America. The course concluded that the assumptions made by planners about women have often been out-of-date and rigid, confining women to roles (in the home and in society) that women do not want and in fact do not any longer fill.[16]

Such courses and projects in the architecture schools are still rare, perhaps because they require the approval of professors and administrators who are mostly men. It is for this reason that the so-called "alternative institutions" for women have been created by women, in many fields.

The Women's School of Planning and Architecture

I was one of the seven women who started the Women's School of Planning and Architecture—the first such school to be completely founded, financed, and run by women.[17] (We call it WSPA, pronounced "wis-pa.") We held the first session of WSPA during August 1975, the second during August 1976, and a third and fourth during 1978 and 1979. Each time we rented facilities at an existing university—in Maine, California, Rhode Island, and Colorado—and had more than fifty women living and learning together for the intensive two-week session.

The reasons for the creation of WSPA are summed up in the poster announcing the 1976 session: "Our purpose remains twofold—to create a personally supportive environment for the free exchange of ideas and knowledge, and to encourage both personal and professional growth through a fuller integration of our values and identities as women with our values and identities as designers." An informal account of what we did will further explain our purposes in starting WSPA:

- We wanted to avoid the hierarchical system prevalent in most traditional schools. We hoped that every "participant" could be a teacher in her own way, and to a rewarding extent she was. In addition, some participants from the first session became "coordinators" (our term for organizers and teachers) for the second session.
- We wanted to bring together women from all fields involved in the design of the built environment. We had architects, landscape architects, planners, weavers, carpenters, interior designers, environmental psychologists, and others. We learned a great deal about our work, our world, ourselves, and we left with new strength in our combined ideas and abilities.

- We wanted to give every woman a sense of her own validity; we wanted to honor the special interests and skills of every woman. In a profession composed primarily of men, women are often made to feel different and unworthy; we wanted our women to feel different if they chose to, but no less worthy.
- We wanted to have women of all ages and all levels of experience. The age range, in fact, has been eighteen to fifty-eight. The mix was extremely stimulating, and important to everyone: to the student looking for "role models"; to the teacher reevaluating traditional ways of relating to students; and to the practitioner seeking contact with new people and new ideas.
- We wanted to provide (and experience) a new kind of living-and-learning situation. And we did—talking, laughing, crying, learning, working, and playing together almost twenty-four hours a day for two jam-packed weeks.
- We wanted—not least—to offer courses and approaches not found in the traditional schools. Thus, we evaluated the built environment from a feminist view, probed our ideas and values in new ways, discussed new professional offices in which cooperation has replaced hierarchy, studied planning by interviewing local women (mostly nonprofessionals) who were actually changing their own communities, learned carpentry, and so on. Our second session expanded on some of these subjects and added others: politics and ideology in planning, architectural tapestry, energy-conscious design.

Our third session centered on a single theme, "Workplaces and Dwellings: Implications for Women," and drew on the experiences of women working in the public and private sectors of development. The theme for the fourth session, "Designing the Future as if Women Mattered," was chosen with the "expectation that the next few decades will witness a critical juncture in history—the transition from a rapidly growing and resource-consumptive industrial society to a post-industrial society." The implications of a conserver society, for women *and* for environmental design, had nowhere previously been discussed.

During each session, the schedule left room for spontaneous discussion on diverse subjects and on projects brought to WSPA by participants.

WSPA has meant different things to different people. For some it has been an impetus for major change in professional direction. For others, it has been an eye-opener in the possibilities of a supportive community. For those of us involved as coordinators, it has been an occasionally agonizing attempt to create a new model of education, of community, of organization, and of professional responsibility. WSPA has been an attempt by women to pursue goals we consider important and to pursue them in ways we consider honorable.[18]

Toward a New Professionalism

The real questioning by some women architects, it seems to me, is toward a new definition of professionalism—what one does, why, how, and for whom. And the new feminism could well be stronger than the old professionalism.

Some design professionals, for instance, have been urging women who lack a design background to honor their hopes and dreams about the environment.[19] Others have been working with clients and each other in a new way, which is equally important.[20] Still others are trying to make the larger public aware of women's needs so that the built environment will not be as frustrating and demeaning to women in the future.[21] The special concerns of women have previously received scant attention from a predominantly male profession.

Meanwhile we are looking toward a time when men and women will share in the responsibilities of home and family[22] while sharing in the challenges of productive and creative work. Until more feminists become architects—or until more architects become feminists—society will be stuck with such absurdities as:

- In a major new office building, only the men's rest rooms are provided with lights to encourage reading. (Is it assumed that women would be "wasting company time"?)
- A man can't take his little daughter to the public men's

room or to the ladies' room. (Is it assumed that baby-tending is not a daddy's job?)

- Tiny closed-off kitchens are unpleasant to work in and disruptive of social relationships. (Is it assumed that opening a kitchen to public view is unaesthetic, but that making the lady of the house into a scullery maid is "refined"?)

I have emphasized function over form in this chapter to emphasize the fact that architecture is more than a visual art; indeed, some of the worst of the "form making" in twentieth-century architecture had denied all human needs—both female and male—and architects of both sexes are rebelling against the arbitrariness of such visual and sculptural acrobatics. Whether women architects will find their own imagery, special and exclusive to women, is another question. Not many women architects seem willing or able to think about this question, although the phallic skyscraper comes in for some light-hearted ridicule (and heavy-handed abuse) from time to time. My own view is that a skyscraper can be humane or inhumane, according to many qualities of form and function. My plea is for an architecture that meets people's needs—and this plea is for an architecture that meets people's needs—and this includes aesthetic needs too. Perhaps I am wary of any special imagery being foisted on people just because an architect (of whatever sex) thinks it will be good for them.

Women and Change

I am not a prophet and have written too often about events or ideas that petered out soon after I pegged them as the wave of the future. But I can't resist thinking that for the architectural profession to survive in any real sense—that is, through doing well at important tasks—it must respond in precisely the directions that have been suggested by a number of women.[23]

What are these directions? For one thing, a new link with the great mass of nonprofessionals, accepting them as people with their own values, not as tasteless slobs to be manipulated for a fee (if they *have* the fee). From this follows all else: a new working relationship with clients; a new sensitivity to "users";

and a new demystification of architectural ideas, skills, and jargon.

Some men surely want this and don't just say so because it is still fashionable to want to be "relevant." Conversely, some women surely want to be in the profession as it is, want membership in an elite body, and do not want that profession to change. Yet it will change, and partly because of women. It will lose some of its elite status as the percentage of women rises, and the profession will thus open even further to women. Men know well what they have been doing: keeping women out of their clubs and professions, out of their world.

What women make of their presence in the architectural profession is a great unknown. I defend any woman's right to do any kind of architectural work she wants (including the work that the stereotype finds her "best suited" for: namely, domestic architecture), especially if she does so in a way that responds to women's changing needs and life-styles as well as to men's. Housing is the basic shelter of a society, no less important than all its monuments and public buildings. New kinds of housing can encourage new social relationships or can accommodate existing relationships that are still struggling within constricting forms of housing.

I also defend (reluctantly) any woman's right to do the same oppressive, mindless, arrogant work that men often do; women shouldn't have to be superhuman. But if women allow themselves to be *at least* human, and if the schools do not press them into a mold that badly needs reshaping, women architects in the next decades could really be "something else!"

Notes

1. Lulu Stoughton Beem, writing in *Inland Architect*, October 1884: "Women are naturally better judges of color, better in the blending of fabrics, besides knowing intuitively what is wanted about a house—wants too small for men to perceive."

2. *The American Architect and Building News* 1:1 (September 30, 1876). Note that this editorial, which went on to establish the "proper place" of women in the profession, appeared in the first issue of this journal.

3. Caroline Shillaber, *MIT School of Architecture and Planning, 1861–1961: A Hundred Year Chronicle* (Cambridge, 1961). The entire institute only opened to women in 1883.

4. Arthur C. Weatherhead, *The History of Collegiate Education in Architecture in the United States* (Los Angeles, 1941), p. 33 (the only mention of women in Weatherhead's 252-page dissertation).

5. The prevailing view at the turn of the century: it was tolerable to have a woman as a student, and you wouldn't mind marrying one, but you certainly wouldn't want one as a colleague. See "The Admission of a Woman to Associateship in the RIBA," *The American Architect and Building News* 63 (January 21, 1899):20–21. The Royal Institute of British Architects admitted its first woman only in 1899—and only after a royal battle. She had passed all exams but, it was explained, while Oxford and Cambridge ladies were allowed to sit for examinations, they were not given degrees. By admitting women, the RIBA would be "conferring degrees, . . . going against the general principle of all institutions and associations of this kind." (A similar debate took place at Harvard in the 1940s.)

6. The 1942 alumnae register had 755 names, but some were cross-referenced for married names. The "best guess" of 450 to 500 is from Dorothy May Anderson of Washington, D.C., who went to the Cambridge School, taught there, and did a recent report on its landscape architects for the American Society of Landscape Architects (its Committee for Women in Landscape Architecture). For further information on this committee, write to the ASLA, 1750 Old Meadow Rd., McLean, VA 22101.

7. Much of this material on the Cambridge School comes from Doris Cole's book, *From Tipi to Skyscraper: A History of Women in Architecture* (Boston: i press inc., 1973). Her chapter on the Cambridge School was also published in *Architecture Plus* 1 (December 1973):11, 30–35 and 78–79.

8. "The Architectress," by Joseph Hudnut, *American Institute of Architects Journal* 15 (March 1951):111–116; and (April 1951):181–184 and 187–188. This is a loathsome and patronizing article, but an important indication of the attitudes of the time.

9. *Architectural Record,* 103 (March 1948):105–113; and (June 1948): 108–115. Of the eighteen women whose work was illustrated, four had studied at the Cambridge school.

10. A poignant reminder of the isolation of women architects is this statement in a 1942 issue of *The Architrave* (the "occasional publication" of the Chicago club): the Women's Architectural Club "was, at the time of its beginning, and is now, so far as it is possible to ascertain, the only professional organization of women architects in the United States." This wasn't accurate, of course; alumnae chapters of Alpha Alpha Gamma

had been in existence since 1926.

11. "The Affirmative Action Plan for the Integration of Women in the Architectural Profession," published by the AIA Task Force on Women in Architecture, 1975, suggests that the percentage of women in all undergraduate and graduate architectural programs be *increased* by 1976–1977 to 10 percent of total enrollment (and by 1979–1980 to 23 percent). For further information on the AIA's Affirmative Action efforts, write to the AIA, 1735 New York Ave. NW, Washington, D.C. 20006. The Association of Collegiate Schools of Architecture, which has data on ninety or so member schools, is at the same address.

12. Wendy Bertrand, at the University of California at Berkeley.

13. Martha Rush, at Pratt Institute; this project was only a short video-tape, but it opened up an entirely new definition of "the handicapped" (in relation to buildings) as including more than just those using wheel-chairs and crutches.

14. Reena Racki, at M.I.T.

15. The Open Design Office, of Cambridge, Massachusetts.

16. Jackie Leavitt, the driving force behind this course, has expanded the initial inquiry to include open lectures, a studio project, and continuing research. Among other faculty members who have brought a new consciousness to architectural education are Dolores Hayden, at M.I.T., on many aspects of "sexual politics"; and Mimi Lobell, at Pratt, on the "feminine principle."

17. The founding coordinators of WSPA are Katrin Adam, Ellen Perry Berkeley, Noel Phyllis Birkby, Bobbie Sue Hood, Marie Kennedy, Joan Forrester Sprague, and Leslie Kanes Weisman.

18. Our intention has always been to reevaluate our program continually as we proceed, and WSPA is evolving as I write. We can expect future activities to be different in format and content, perhaps quite drastically different. For information on past or future activities, write to WSPA at Box 311, Shaftsbury, VT 05262.

19. "A Woman-Built Environment: Constructive Fantasies," by Noel Phyllis Birkby and Leslie Kanes Weisman in *Quest: A Feminist Quarterly* 2, no. 1 (summer 1975).

20. "We really *care* what the client wants," Joan Sprague once said to me, and I recall her astonishment, not that the Open Design Office was doing this, but that most offices were not. In some cases it means providing only minimal technical assistance—helping people to help themselves. It may not pay well or photograph well, but it serves a real need.

21. Clare Cooper, in her excellent book *Easter Hill Village: Some Social Implications of Design* (New York: Free Press, 1975) points to the "dichotomy of male-dominated provision vs. female-dominated consumption of a

home environment." This housing project was most deficient in the *spaces between buildings,* in the lack of play areas and the lack of privacy in the yards—in short, in items men find unimportant but women at home with children find critically important.

22. See my own article on the "servicehus" of Sweden, in *Architecture Plus* 1, no. 4 (May 1973):56–59. The "service house" can be defined as multifamily housing with certain services readily available for purchase (or already included in the rent): food from a central kitchen, day care, and assistance on all kinds of daily chores and emergency needs. See also Dolores Hayden's important historical data on cooperative housekeeping: "Collectivizing the Domestic Workplace," *Lotus* (Milan, Italy) 12 (1976), reprinted as "Redesigning the Domestic Workplace," *Chrysalis* 1 (1977).

23. For the most comprehensive look at women in architecture yet published, see *Women in American Architecture: A Historic and Contemporary Perspective,* edited by Susana Torre (New York: Whitney Library of Design, 1977). This volume accompanied the exhibition at the Brooklyn Museum organized by The Architectural League of New York through its Archive of Women in Architecture. For information on the use of the archive and the loan of the exhibition, write to the archive at 41 East 65 St., New York, NY 10021.

11

Women in Planning:
There's More to Affirmative Action
than Gaining Access

Jacqueline Leavitt

Planning is a problematic profession. It is not as old as the established professions of law, medicine, and religion, and it has some of the characteristics of a semiprofession, such as social work. Planners often have difficulty in defining their professional identity. An occupation with marginal professional status, planning is doubly marginal for women who are caught between professional and female role demands. Traditionally, planning neglects the needs of women in and out of the profession. Because the planning profession is growing, and with it the proportion of women receiving planning degrees, there is increased interest in what occurs when women gain access to the profession and whether their increasing numbers are having an impact on its content and practice. One approach that can help us understand the impact is to look at how career patterns in planning differ between men and women and among women, as well as the reasons for those differences. Are women entering planning in greater numbers only to withdraw after a period of time? Further, do female planners interpret and represent women's concerns within the planning profession, and in what way does this relate to their career patterns?

There is reason to hypothesize that the career patterns of female planners resemble those of other women in the non-professional ranks of the labor force. Thus, although the drop-out pattern during childrearing years for the twenty-five to thirty-four age group has become less common in general, it will not be surprising to find discontinuous or part-time careers for female planners.[1] One study has shown that the percentage of those women who return to their employment following maternity leave from low-skilled work ranges from 30 to 40 percent; 75 to 80 percent in most professional and managerial positions; and 95 percent in medicine and teaching.[2] Based on a 1971 study of 200 women planners, one researcher hypothesizes that about half the women receiving master's degrees in planning would have careers characterized by discontinuity, disruption, and part-time work for reasons related to child-rearing.[3] However, there is reason to suspect that planning shares characteristics with the professions that permit irregular career patterns. Based on a small sample conducted by this author, women who leave planning for whatever reasons appear to move in and out of the profession without necessarily losing titles, responsibilities, or taking salary cuts.

This chapter grew out of observations of the work histories of colleagues who dropped in and out of planning. While some of these women are active in issues central to the Women's Movement, it did not appear that the reasons for their discontinuous career patterns could be attributed either to child-rearing or to feminism. With the intent of finding out why career patterns were irregular and if there was any relation to feminism and female advocacy, ten interviews were conducted with both sexes, preliminary to documenting the work histories of 200 male and female planners. The results of these preliminary interviews are incorporated into this chapter.

Growth of the Planning Profession:
Women in Planning

First it is necessary to establish the element of subjectivity involved in the identification of planners. There are planners in both private and public agencies; not all practitioners have planning degrees—some are trained as planners and others educated in planning-related fields; not all planners belong to the American Institute of Planners (AIP), and not all AIP members are in the planning category or are degree-carrying planners.

In 1917, twenty-four men started what is now known as the

American Institute of Planners. If one indicator of growth in the planning profession is membership in the AIP, then the rolls reveal a steady increase from the hundreds in 1940 to the thousands in the fifties and sixties. Membership in 1974 was estimated to be 10,000.[4]

Another indicator of growth in the profession is the increase in the numbers of institutions offering a planning or planning-related degree—from 1909, when a single lecture was given at Harvard University for students in the department of landscape architecture, to 1929 when the first three-year postgraduate course was given there, to 1976, when eighty-five institutions offered related degrees (fifty-five specifically in planning). Total enrollment in master's degree programs for 1976 was almost 5,000, a figure that increases to about 6,400 when bachelor and doctoral programs are added.[5]

Part of the recent growth in planning is due to the increasing numbers of women in the field, although as in other more established professions, women are not equally represented. The percentage of women in established professions in the seventies is lower than at the turn of the century: women made up 12 percent of all professional workers in 1900, and 10 percent in 1970.[6] Although the growth of female professional and technical workers between 1972 and 1985 is expected to be slower than between 1960 and 1972, one source projects an increasing need for planners because of the issues surrounding environmental protection, urban renewal, and mass transportation resulting from population growth and concentration in metropolitan areas.[7]

Precise figures of the number of women planners who are practicing currently are difficult to cite. There is no one directory of licensed planners because there is no uniform licensing requirement as in medicine or law. Surveys were made in 1971, 1972, and 1974 by the American Society of Planning Officials (ASPO) of authorized filled positions.[8] Women in planning agencies in 1974 occupied 25.6 percent of all authorized positions, filling 16.9 percent of the specialized professional, 16.5 percent of the drafting, and 10.1 percent of the professional slots (compared to 23.7 percent of technical positions). In contrast, women in clerical and secretarial positions were overrepresented at 67.4 percent.[9] In 1971, the AIP adopted a policy on Equal Treatment of Women Planners.[10] Later, targets were set requiring that by January 1975 women were to comprise 20 percent of positions in each of three categories: planning staff, management and supervisory personnel, and students in planning schools. In fact, only the percentage of women students in planning schools meets these guidelines.

What are the factors that contributed to male domination in planning? The most obvious reason in the period between 1920 and 1940 is that women were likely to be educated in the existing women's colleges. The first planning curricula were not offered until the late twenties at schools not likely to attract women. Women interested in what would be social aspects of planning were directed to the social-work schools, and those interested in housing could find an outlet in schools with curricula in domestic science. Two notable exceptions are Edith Elmer Wood and Catherine Bauer Wurster. The former took degrees in social work and political economy, the latter some courses in architecture. Both gained entry to careers as "housers" through volunteer work and apprenticeships.[11]

A study of planning commissioners made in 1950 is informative about the early role of women in the profession. Sixty city and county planning agencies were surveyed; only fourteen of the larger cities gave women "an official voice in the planning process." Of the sixteen reported commissioners who were women, twelve were housewives who occupied positions in women's club work; 2.2 percent of commission members were housewives; and four of the sixteen women identified with careers in the professions of planning, banking, law, and architecture. Males who were in planning and related professions (architecture and engineering outnumbered planning) accounted for sixty-eight (or 12.1 percent) of the 558 total occupations reported. The greatest representation by occupations, 30 percent, was drawn from industry, trade, banking, real estate, and building.[12]

Not until the late sixties and early seventies did women begin to take advantage of more formal educational opportunities to study planning. The growing demand for planners to work on social-service programs and the fact that more women were going to school may explain in part the changing sex composition of planning schools. It is also possible that it was not until the end of the sixties that women began to find planning compatible as well as accessible—a profession that consciously or unconsciously, lent itself to easy or flexible management of career and home lives.

A preliminary analysis of membership in the American Institute of Planners and of graduates of Columbia University's Planning School indicates that there were probably one or two, possibly three, women in any given planning education institution for each year prior to 1968. For the first time in 1968, the American Society of Planning Officials collected nationwide data that showed breakdowns by sex and minority groups.

Table 11.1 summarizes the absolute growth from 1968 to 1978 of men and women planning graduates.[13] Even though these figures might seem to show that women have made real progress in gaining access to the planning profession, it is important to note that over a fifty-year period, women receiving degrees represent only about five percent of all degree-granted planners.

We may speculate on the reason for this rise in numbers of female planners. The influence of the Women's Movement and

TABLE 11.1 Planning Degrees Granted to Females and Males, 1968-1978*

Year	Total	Female Number	%	Male Number	%
1968	610	46	7.5	564	92.5
1970	911	155	17.0	756	83.0
1972	1128	173	15.3	955	84.4
1973	1302	246	18.9	1056	81.1
1974	1564	350	22.3	1214	77.7
1975	1831	483	26.3	1348	73.6
1976	1905	534	28.0	1355	71.1
1977-78	2500	775	31.0	1725	69.0

* Surveys not taken in 1969, 1971
  Source: American Society of Planning Officials.

passage of affirmative action legislation undoubtedly played a role—as we have seen the profession itself responded somewhat to membership pressure and established guidelines for increasing the numbers. It is doubtful that females were displacing male applicants, but rather that more females were attracted into planning and/or away from other fields at the same time that males were more attracted to other fields.

Another factor is critical in considering women's entry into the planning profession. Men are paid more and promoted to higher positions than women. ASPO surveys of public agencies from 1968 to 1971 show that: "At no point do female planners' median salaries equal those of their male counterparts, despite an equal educational background and the same amount of planning experience. The greatest difference in salary is found at the highest levels of planning experience."[14] For example, with more than ten years of experience and holding a Master of City Planning, males earned $18,000 compared to $13,344 for females. With six to eight years of experience, men earned $15,534 and women $12,500; and with two years or less of experience, men earned $10,471 and women $9,992.[15] In 1977, the overall median salary for women in public and private agencies responding to ASPO's survey is still about $4,000 less ($16,000 compared to $20,000 for men); the survey no longer shows that the differential increases with experience.

Women employed in planning agencies are heavily concentrated in the lower ranks. In 1974, of 670 agencies reporting to the American Society of Planning Officials there were only eight women planning directors. Within the professional organization itself, a woman was president for the first time in 1977; between 1974 and 1976, two women were vice-presidents; and in 1970, one woman was, in what is often regarded as a sex-linked position, secretary-treasurer.

Based on purely objective criteria, women have good reasons to view themselves as marginal within the profession. Women have gained access to the profession; however, one of the difficulties in measuring the impact of the increased numbers is the lack of concentration of female planners. What exactly constitutes the critical mass necessary to have an effect on professional practice and content? While far from conclusive, we might argue that there have been some changes if not gains. The continued existence and renaissance of women's caucuses at professional conferences is one indicator. For example, a small group of women were able to get the AIP to reluctantly endorse the Equal Rights Amendment in 1977—this was undoubtedly helped by the presence of women on the board. Secondly, there is evidence of planners seeking information on issues that affect women, wanting to know what methods and information they can use in order to be responsive to women's needs and to respond as women. There are women's planning groups in some areas of the country, and there is to be a task force addressing issues concerning women sponsored by the American Planning Association (the merged organization of ASPO and AIP). Impact has been made through at least one lawsuit brought by women employees, including planners, against the Boston Redevelopment Authority over inequities in pay structure, advancement, and job structure.[16] As negligible as these gains may seem, the impact of the increase on women practitioners in terms of daily planning activity is even less evident. Indeed the integration of what are explicitly women's needs into the content of planning may be less likely to occur in part because of withdrawal patterns.

Marginality and Powerlessness: Patterns of Withdrawal

Planning as a profession may be characterized as marginal if we consider its relative lack of power in the decisionmaking process. Planners may have command over a specialized body of knowledge, but this cannot be equated with power.[17] Even when planners have direct access to political leaders, they have only one input into the political decision process.[18] Contrary to the popular image that planners have a strong influence on public decisions, in reality planners often find that planning decisions are largely made after the trends and investments of private real estate, development, and finance markets are apparent. Planners often find themselves powerless in affecting social change, even though an interest in social reform initially attracted many of them to the profession.[19]

If planning is marginal in society because it lacks power, the relative powerlessness of planners has intensified due to internal changes within the profession. "Twenty to thirty years ago (1930 to 1940), the tempo of the planning office was leisurely";[20] the planner was typified as a single person servicing a small town or neighborhood. In 1940, when planning was gaining currency, twenty-seven cities out of a total of thirty-seven had an average staff size of five persons, excluding the atypical staffs of Los Angeles and New York.[21] In 1976, the one-person office is operating only in cities with populations under 10,000. Authorized staff positions in cities with populations less than 50,000 range from one to eleven.[22] In cities 50,000 and over, the median number of authorized professional planning positions ranges from five to forty-seven. Therefore there is greater likelihood that planners will work in an office that is characterized by the specialization of tasks. Consequently, there may be a tendency to have less interaction with other planners in the same agency and for each individual to have a narrower range of responsibility, particularly in the larger bureaucracies.

Compared to other professions, such as social work or teaching, where professionals are required to keep fixed hours to meet clients, planners can achieve somewhat more flexibility. However, projects are rarely self-generated, and content, even emphasis, of work activities, is set outside the planning agency. Also, over the past decade there has been a shift towards involvement by planners in implementation, a response to the legal and business administration professions' increasingly larger role in planning, and to protests by community groups. Several studies show that planners feel more satisfied with a project they have worked on when it entails creative thinking. But the number of planners who can be involved in this way is limited by the nature of most projects and the style of the profession.[23]

We know very little about withdrawal patterns of planners or other professionals. Average job tenure for planners in 1977 was 3.3 years—an increase from the 2.1 years of 1971, which reflects a tightening job market. It has usually been assumed that job movement is related to job mobility. However, we may expect that women's career patterns differ from men's and that tenure and withdrawal patterns will involve child-related and other factors.

A recent study by Terry Ann Vigil of 200 female planners suggests that women's career patterns are significantly different from men's.[24] Most striking was the finding that large numbers of women planners have either worked part time or interrupted their careers for some period of time. Her sample of 200 showed that "50 percent of women planners receiving their master's degree in 1971 are seriously affected by continuity-discontinuity. What is significant is that most women planners are highly professionally committed and either never leave their career or attempt to continue it through part-time work or re-entry into planning. Only the need to raise children appears to interrupt their careers to any extent."[25]

Preliminary data from interviews conducted by this author with seven women planners reveal that reasons for leaving planning are complex; there is rarely a single reason or a clean break with planning. Three women left voluntarily, and only one of them left planning permanently (though she did go into an extension of planning). A combination of reasons led to her withdrawal, including feeling ineffective about her work, having difficulty with a male supervisor, and having a child. In two other cases, the decisions to leave may be traced to a feeling of powerlessness; one from losing battles around urban renewal plans, the other from not being able to deliver funding for a housing project. The two women who withdrew temporarily engaged in free-lance advocacy planning—a situation where even greater job frustrations were encountered.

The job situation of the two women with continuous careers in planning differs markedly from that of those who withdrew. One woman had a job in the same agency for twenty-seven years. While rearing children she worked on a part-time schedule for eleven years before returning to full-time duties. The agency more or less accommodated itself to her needs during her child-rearing years, but she points out that the concessions made to her were not institutionalized gains, despite pressure from herself and other workers for a workplace child-care facility. This woman recently refused the offer of a higher position that would have required her to put in longer hours, but she is active in community affairs, which, broadly speaking, are planning related, sitting both on a community board and on the board of a housing co-op. The extracurricular role may reduce conflict between home and work roles or it may afford her a different kind of gratification from her salaried job, thus removing the need for withdrawal.

Another woman, who had worked in a community planning office continuously for six years, only contemplates withdrawal as a temporary situation for travel or study reasons. She sees her career moving away from planning and towards community organizing, a function she now combines with her planning duties.

What appears to distinguish these two women from those who withdrew for other than child-related reasons is that they are working in more or less sheltered environments. It is probable that each has found a work environment compatible with her expectations of personal and professional life, and that they can manage their careers in such a way as to continue working in the same environment. In particular, the woman working in the community planning office is able to wage battles similar to those of the women who withdrew temporarily, but from the vantage point of an established advocacy office.

Female Advocacy in Planning

One female planner, beginning her career as an intern at a regional planning agency, stated, "women planners need to be advocates for other women."[26] Can this occur while women planners are a minority? It has been recognized that hiring more women or minorities does not necessarily ensure that the needs of their group will be met by a particular government agency. But the hope for greater equity through affirmative action is expressed by Kranz who writes: "We do expect that minority and female 'representatives' *as a group* will mirror more closely the needs and wishes of their group, whether overtly or subconsciously, than nonminorities do; that they will be seen by others as symbolically representing 'their' group, and that on *most* decisions within the bureaucracy and services to the public, a bureaucracy containing the ideal-type representation of minorities and women will govern 'better' than one that is not unrepresentative."[27]

If there were a feminist awareness on the part of planners, and if the profession altered its perspective, several types of issues might be raised. At the National Woman's Convention in Houston, Texas, in 1977, delegates adopted twenty-five of twenty-six resolutions.[28] The resolutions included topics such as child care, battered women, health, and housing as a component of minority, older-citizens, and sexual-preference resolutions. The resolution on statistics called for a breakdown of federal data that has previously not identified women and minorities sufficiently to demonstrate the exact details of being disadvantaged. These topics have a direct relevance to planning.

There are several reasons why these concerns may not be part of current planning practices: community facilities like child care and halfway houses are often defined as either child centered or as welfare related. From the traditional planning perspective, women's needs or changing roles are secondary, even though women are often the majority of clients.

Planning for these facilities is funded by agencies acting in a relatively autonomous fashion; it also is carried out outside the housing, transportation, environmental agencies where the funds originate and where planners concentrate their attention. While these reasons may appear rational, there is a more fundamental reason that reflects the present structure and largely conservative nature of the planning profession. Planning largely ignores the needs of special groups, specifically women, and takes for granted the nuclear family and the average person or group.[29] We can see this most clearly in housing. Housing for the elderly is fundable and fashionable, and thus women are an indirect beneficiary of the attention paid to this special group. But housing for the single-parent family and for those whose sexual preference is other than the nuclear family is an issue to which planning pays little heed.

People who were interviewed offered four reasons that might underlie the lack of interest the profession has towards issues concerning women: (1) there is no guidance from the profession; (2) men are the policymakers; (3) there is no grass-roots pressure; and (4) there is no pressure from women within the profession. In some ways the first and second reasons are the same in that professional orientation is unlikely to change when it is predominantly male oriented.[30] The difficulty with expecting change to come from grass-roots groups is that usually the term is used to mean minority and poor communities where the official Women's Movement has had little if any impact. Women in the profession who are most likely to resemble the women typified by the Women's Liberation Movement are often caught between professional and female demands.[31]

Although women have entered the field of planning in increasing numbers, there is little evidence that planning agencies are prepared to accommodate the organization of work to female needs, even if sex-role stereotyping is accepted. This is particularly apparent in issues surrounding childrearing.[32] Consider the following:

> Planning agencies have mentioned in General Plans the assumption of a shorter work week and more women in the labor force, plus the goal of day care centers for working mothers. However, planning agencies have not provided any leadership in this field. One woman in our office currently works 30 hours a week in order to be able to take her young children to school and pick them up at a reasonable hour. She is considered part-time and therefore receives no benefits such as paid vacations or holidays, sick leaves, or automatic periodic pay raises.[33]

Thus, women planners may often find that a profession that pays at least lip service to "user needs" does not even acknowledge needs of its own workers.

If the planning profession does not accommodate the needs of its own practitioners, is it likely that those who are being discriminated against will advocate other women's needs? Interviews with women planners reveal that different patterns of response to women's issues may occur among female planners and that the response varies by career pattern among women. It is difficult to draw conclusions from such a small sample, but the results do suggest the possibility that planning may be compatible for women who wish to manage their career and a personal life. The emphasis between the personal and political concerns may be influenced by external events. The women who withdrew for two years practiced planning during a time when the civil rights, antiwar, anticareerism, and the women's movements were flourishing. We may also speculate that the presence of women who have discontinuous careers helps create an environment for change within the bureaucracy. Women involved in the Boston Redevelopment suit mention that workers were stimulated by the Women's Movement then active in Boston. Certainly in a field like planning the legacy of the civil rights movement suggests that the professions respond to external pressure; we might expect feminist planners outside the bureaucracy to be able to exert a similar pressure.

Of course it can be argued that this pressure is futile if the profession is, to begin with, marginal and has little effect on women's daily lives. Yet, even at the workplace, conditions are such that women's continuous career patterns are problematic. The type of structural change needed to ensure continuous career patterns, if only childrearing is considered, could lead to the profession practicing what it preaches. Female planners might then find it more legitimate to be advocates for the woman's perspective, and withdrawal patterns may then be a reflection of the legitimacy of different types of career patterns for both men and women.

Notes

1. Myra H. Strober, "Women and Men in the World of Work: Present and Future," in Libby A. Cater, Anne Firor Scott, and Wendy Martyna (eds.), *Women & Men: Changing Roles* (New York: Aspen Institute for Humanistic Studies, 1975), p. 122.

2. Terry Ann Vigil, *A Manpower Study of the Professional Woman in Planning* (unpublished thesis submitted in partial fulfillment of requirements for the degree of Master of Regional Planning, Graduate School of Syracuse University, 1972).

3. Michael P. Fogarty, Rhona Rapoport, and Robert N. Rapoport, *Sex, Career and Family* (Beverly Hills, Calif.: Sage Publications, 1971), p. 26.

4. American Institute of Planners, "Founding and History, 1917–1951," in *Handbook and Roster* (Cambridge: Institute Headquarters, 1951).

5. Linda L. Corby and Frank S. So, "Annual ASPO School Survey," *Planning* 41, no. 3 (Chicago: American Society of Planning Officials, 1975):50–51; and figures provided from reports on planning degrees

granted, enrollment, and planning-related degrees granted, enrollment by sex and minority, 1968–1976, American Society of Planning Officials.

6. Athena Theodore (ed.), *The Professional Woman* (Cambridge, Mass.: Schenkman, 1971), p. 3.

7. U.S. Department of Labor, *1975 Handbook for Women Workers* (Washington, D.C.: U.S. Government Printing Office, 1975), p. 254.

8. The surveys made in 1971, 1972, and 1974 are not completely comparable because of different samples. See Karen C. Hapgood, *Women in Planning: A Report on Their Status in Public Planning Agencies* (Chicago: American Society of Planning Officials, 1971), PAS no. 273; Lisa B. Yondorf, *Women and Blacks in Planning* (Chicago: American Society of Planning Officials, 1972), PAS Memo no. m-10; ASPO, *Expenditures, Staff, and Salaries of Planning Agencies, 1974* (Chicago: American Society of Planning Officials, 1974), PAS no. 299.

9. ASPO, *Expenditures, Staff, and Salaries of Planning Agencies, 1974,* p. 7.

10. American Institute of Planners, "Equal Treatment of Women Planners," (Washington, D.C.: American Institute of Planners).

11. See Eugenie L. Birch, "Women-Made America: The Case of Early Public Housing Policy," *Journal of the American Institute of Planners* 44, no. 2 (April 1978) for a discussion of the careers of Edith Elmer Wood and Catherine Bauer Wurster.

12. ASPO, *The Planning Commission—Its Composition and Function* (Chicago: American Society of Planning Officials, 1950), Information Report no. 19, p. 11.

13. According to figures provided by ASPO, I have calculated that from 1958 to 1976, 10,200 master's degrees in planning were awarded by sixty-four planning schools in the United States and Canada. Figures for women planners are available from 1968 through 1976 from ASPO; this figure is almost 2,000. I have estimated figures for women planners for the period prior to 1968, based on a review of women graduates from Columbia University and on female members of AIP, selecting a medium-range estimate. Similarly, I have estimated the numbers prior to 1958. The figures are then as follows: approximately 11,500 planners educated in institutions between 1929 and 1976, of which an estimated 2,270 are female and 9,230 are male.

Jerome L. Kaufman in "Contemporary Planning Practice: State of the Art," in David R. Godschalk (ed.), *Planning in America: Learning from Turbulence* (Washington, D.C.: American Institute of Planners, 1974), estimates that in 1973 there were 16,000 planners of whom 13,000 belonged to both AIP and ASPO, and another 3,500 who belonged to neither of the two national planning agencies.

Robert A. Beauregard in "The Occupation of Planning: A View from the Census," *Journal of the American Institute of Planners* 42, no. 2 (April 1976), reports that the 1973 Census of Occupational Characteristics indicates there were 9,214 planners of whom 89.5 percent were male and 10.5 percent were female. Beauregard also estimates, drawing on statistics other than those from the Census, that there are more than 14,700 planners, plus those who do not belong to AIP or ASPO.

14. Hapgood, *Women in Planning,* p. 8.

15. Michael J. Meshenberg and George C. Turnbull, Jr., *Salaries and Tenure of Professional Planners: 1977* (Chicago: American Society of Planning Officials, 1977).

16. Catherine Samuels, *The Forgotten Five Million: Women in Public Employment* (New York: Faculty Press, Inc., 1975), p. 76.

17. See Paul D. Montagna, *Occupations and Society: Toward a Sociology of the Labor Market* (New York: John Wiley & Sons, 1977), particularly chapter 9, "The Professions: Approaches to their Study," for an overview of three major approaches to a study of the profession. In this chapter, a brief description is presented of the powerlessness of planners in relation to decisionmaking, the substance of work, and the lack of control over one's work in regard to substance. These aspects of work reflect the planning field regardless of whether one school of sociology sees the field as a profession or not.

18. For a paradigm of models that may help explain how planners relate to decisionmakers, see Jurgen Habermas, "The Scientization of Politics and Public Opinion," in Habermas, *Toward A Rational Society* (Boston: Beacon Press, 1968), pp. 62–80.

19. See Vigil, *A Manpower Study,* p. 66, shows that 47 of 200 respondents or 23.5 percent said they "wished to accomplish change." See also John W. Dyckman, "What Makes Planners Plan?" in Andreas Faludi (ed.), *A Reader in Planning Theory* (Oxford: Pergamon Press, 1973), p. 245; and also in Faludi, *A Reader in Planning Theory,* Francine F. Rabinovitz, "Politics, Personality and Planning," pp. 265–376.

20. ASPO, *Principles of Organization for Planning Agencies* (Chicago: American Society of Planning Officials, 1961), Information Report no. 146, p. 1.

21. Robert A. Walker, *The Planning Function in Urban Government* (Chicago: University of Chicago Press, 1950), pp. 185 and 187.

22. ASPO, *Expenditures, Staff, and Salaries of Planning Agencies* (Chicago: American Society of Planning Officials, 1976), PAS no. 317.

23. Howell S. Baum, "Organization in the Work of Planners, An Empirical Study of Problems Planners Experience," draft paper presented to the Southeast Region of the Association of Collegiate Schools of Planning,

March 30–31, 1978, Charlottesville, Virginia. Anthony J. Cantanese, *Personality, Politics and Planning* (New York: Sage Publications, 1978), describes the styles of planning directors and the development of planning projects.

24. Vigil, *A Manpower Study.*

25. Ibid.

26. Discussion with Theresa Eason, planning student and intern at Columbia University's Division of Urban Planning, December 1977.

27. Harry Kranz, *The Participatory Bureaucracy* (Lexington, Mass.: D. C. Heath & Co., 1976), p. 103.

28. See proposed *National Plan of Action,* adopted by the President's National Commission on the Observance of International Women's Year, October 20, 1977.

29. See Jerome L. Kaufman, "An Approach to Planning for Women," in Karen C. Hapgood and Judith Getzels (eds.), *Planning, Women and Change* (Washington, D.C.: U.S. Department of Housing and Urban Development, and Chicago: Planning Advisory Service, Report no. 301, 1974), pp. 73–76.

30. Pat McCormick, "Notes from a Woman Planner," paper distributed at the American Institute of Planners Conference, San Francisco, October, 1971, p. 1.

31. Arlie Hochschild, "Making It: Marginality and Obstacles to Minority Consciousness," pp. 194–199 in Ruth B. Kundsin (ed.), *Women and Success* (New York: William Morrow & Co., 1974).

32. See Hapgood, *Women In Planning,* pp. 12–14. There is a lack of standardization with respect to maternity leave as Hapgood points out.

33. AIP Women's Right Policy Planning Committee, "A Policy Paper Concerning Women in Planning." Transmitted to the author by Jerome L. Kaufman, October 1977, unnumbered.

12

No Academic Matter:
Unconscious Discrimination
in Environmental Design Education

Anonymous

Introduction

By law, universities in the United States are required to prepare affirmative action plans specifying policies for female and minority recruitment and career development in each department. Although such a plan may identify a department's numerical strengths and weaknesses, it usually says very little about the day-to-day experience of its women and minority members. Since unequal education and career development are often the results of attitudes rather than policies, this chapter describes discrimination in qualitative rather than quantitative terms by discussing everyday behavior. It deals first with unequal education and career preparation as experienced by students and, second, with unequal career development as experienced by staff and faculty.

In the spring of 1976 a questionnaire was circulated to several hundred members of a school of architecture, asking for information about incidents that respondents felt indicated discrimination on the basis of race or sex. Taking the first fifty responses to their survey, the committee selected comments and anecdotes that they believed illuminated the day-to-day problems

The authors are a group of students, staff, and faculty at a school of architecture in a U.S. university. Because we wish to publish this study as a description of typical problems that women and minorities face in the environmental design fields rather than as a discussion of a particular department or of particular individuals, some details have been altered to assure the anonymity of the school, the respondents, and the authors.

experienced by many women and members of minority groups in the institution. They chose what they thought were typical incidents, characteristic of many schools in the field of environmental design and in other professional fields dominated by white males, such as law, medicine, and business.

Using the incidents furnished by the respondents, the authors tried to explain the paradoxical nature of discrimination—especially the alternation between too much attention, through race or sex being made an issue in inappropriate ways, and too little attention, or apparent "invisibility," as a result of white male exclusiveness. The conclusions were received with both extremely positive and extremely negative reactions. Some members of the department were relieved to be able to approach the issues publicly, some were embarrassed, and others felt the authors were far too critical of white males.

Unequal Education and Career Preparation: The Students' Experience at School

Often sexist and racist attitudes are expressed in such a way as to make the victims feel totally isolated in their anger. Those who provoked the anger may defend themselves by saying "I didn't mean it," or "You're oversensitive," or "It's trivial," but repetitions of such incidents over several years can add up to unequal education for minority students, women students, and especially minority women students. Their experiences can be categorized as reflecting invisibility, hostility, and spotlighting.

Perhaps the sense of *invisibility* was most often mentioned by students:

> I have answered a question in a class and had the teacher basically hear it but not acknowledge it, and then when a male in the class gave the same answer it was accepted as correct and the discussion went on from there. I was, in that case, invisible.

> Several members of the architecture faculty appear not to listen or to take what I say seriously because I am a woman. They attend to the same things said by a man.

> My design professors . . . either avoid contact with or are uncomfortable with women students . . . or is it me?

Invisible female presence is underscored by sexist language, which assumes all humans, or all architects, or all students are male. Thus phrases like "man and his environment," the "man-made environment," drafts*man*, "the architect and *his* skills," grate on women who are specifically excluded. Various fellowship announcements and course materials also go on in this vein. Even more serious examples of ignoring the female and minority presence are textbooks that mention only the work of white male architects, excluding the work of women and minority architects.[1] At the same time, courses and texts often rely upon crude stereotypes concerning women and minority users of buildings:[2] design instructors will encourage students working on housing to design the windows so that *mothers* can supervise their children while performing other domestic chores; or faculty will use a downtown athletic club as a design problem, mindless of the frequent exclusion of women and minority members from such facilities.

Students also complained bitterly of condescending attitudes expressed by faculty:

> In building technology courses, I have known professors to assume that the women would not do well. Here it is often a question of background, not sex. Women here are clearly as capable as the men, but in the architecture department the women are likely to come from more humanistic backgrounds than male students. That does not mean they won't grasp a scientific concept if it is clearly explained to them.

In conclusion we note an educational study by Rosenthal and Jacobsen in which a teacher had communicated to a randomly selected group of students high expectations and confidence in them. Sensing this support, the students' morale was boosted so that they actually did perform better than those to whom this support was not given.[3] In many architecture programs the opposite may happen; women and minority students sense that faculty have little confidence in them or low expectations of them.

In addition to blatant, outspoken condescension and hostility there are a number of ways of subtly implying a lack of belief in a student's ability. This can be a heavier deadweight than direct criticism because it's much harder to discuss or to fight back against. Some teachers pay too much attention to women and minority students, "spotlighting" them, as one feminist critic calls it.[4]

> A professor for a course I'm in now treats the women in the class as "cute, dumb, little-girl" architects who need special help. . . . We do . . . but not in the overbearingly patronizing way that it's given!

> I feel that my work isn't judged as an individual in the class, but as "that woman" in the class! I feel compelled to perform on behalf of all the women in the school, and that I am judged in that way.

For women students, hostility or spotlighting may be particularly uncomfortable if it comes in the form of sexual innuendo.

> I have been acutely aware of design professors avoiding close contact with the women students. Either a distance is kept with sexist joking and "flirting," keeping the woman in her place by making sex more important than her study of design . . . or else the professor has some internal fear of a potential involvement with the woman student and so maintains a cold, studied distance.

> I have seen one of my design teachers exhibit one behavior to the woman students (playful flirtatiousness), and another (competitive comradery) to the men in the class. . . . I don't particularly enjoy such game-playing, it got in the way of learning from this teacher who clearly is very knowledgeable. The women students who did respond in like manner (by flirting) would receive more attention, but at reviews got even more strident criticism.

Field trips for a studio were reported by another student: "the men were irritated because the women were getting so much attention." Another student described a design teacher who constantly flirted with women students. Many complaints, according to one respondent, resulted in a plea for some teachers to "clean up their act!" That was perhaps a more fortunate outcome than the woman student taking the blame on *herself*: "One design professor loved to chat rather than talk about my work, but I loved to chat, too. I felt frustrated at the end of the term, but nonetheless wholly responsible." For both women and minority students, the immediate solution may seem to be avoidance of certain faculty:

> There is a grapevine among the women students about which faculty members have trouble relating to the women students. The mere fact of the existence of this type of underground information bespeaks that the women students consider it a serious problem. Sexism clearly affects their ability to learn from a professor, and thus relates to the overall value of their education.

The Students' Field Experience

Employment in the architectural profession often occurs while students are still in school. This outside employment may have a profound effect on an individual's sense of self as a professional. Since the architectural profession's affirmative action record is so bad, any school's push for minority and female career preparation is severely handicapped.[5] No school has much power to change professional discrimination, but serious attention to job placement for women and minority students can help. One woman student wrote about "very obvious discrimination":

> Walking into a lumber yard in carpenter's work clothes has elicited any number of remarks, which have had the net effect of making me wonder if I was not deformed in some way. Working-class men when threatened are directly offensive, whereas professional colleagues tend to make less obvious cracks, like alluding to your personal appearance.

Two women students mentioned their frustrated desire to specialize in some aspect of construction or contracting, and their conclusion was that male chauvinism in this area makes it wiser to work in an office. Office work is far from easy however. One woman student complained:

> I came to graduate school because I was unsatisfied with what I was learning in my job and I think it was because of discrimination. I would rather work for myself than in an office. I feel depressed

and pessimistic about earning a living. . . . I am tempted to withdraw [so] I don't have to hear the kind of crap . . . [such as] constant surprise when I tell people what I do: "Oh, really?" "Very good!" or "You don't look old enough."

Another discusses career frustration:

> After working as the only woman in the design sections of two different offices, dealing with clients' unbelief ("You're too young and pretty to be an architect") and lecherous advances disguised as desk discussions of my work, I got fed up. I decided to try to specialize in an area of research where I could work alone, and have greater control over my professional contacts.

Coping with Unequal Status

Alienation and anger come through very clearly when students describe the ways they try to cope with discrimination:

> My personal experience has been one of constant struggle against being overwhelmed by a strange and very cold environment . . . which espouses a value system and a life-style which I find to be narrow, parochial and one-dimensional. I say this with the knowledge that there are other places I could go and find environments which are much more pluralistic and accepting of a variety of life-styles and cultures. I have found living with the acute awareness that one is essentially a stranger in a strange land, emotionally and psychologically exhausting and draining. Nevertheless, I value the experience because it has forced me to confront and begin to cope with the realities with which I will have to live in my professional life. [Minority woman]

In addition to the psychological drain, many minority and women students see the "educational opportunity" for which every tuition dollar goes shrinking before their very eyes. Discrimination at the blatant "we-don't-allow-women-and-minorities-to-study-here" level has been curtailed, but subtler forms still flourish:

> I feel it is important to demonstrate that it was not long ago when very blatant discrimination was acceptable, and that many of the

same people are still prominent members of the department. [Woman]

Nearly every woman and minority student anticipated frustration and difficulty in trying to fulfill their career plans once they left school. Nearly all felt that the anticipated difficulty has and will force them to modify their plans. Many assumed they will have to work twice as hard as white males to meet their goals:

> I definitely anticipate difficulties. My only plan to deal with this is to try harder than most men. [Woman]

> I have long known of discrimination! Well, I must make sure my skills and qualifications are impeccable. [Minority student]

In general, black students (male and female) had a focus for directed anger:

> I know the law and I'll take court action if necessary.

> I must know the laws and be ready to stand up for my rights in court. I will not be defeated in my will and spirit although I may lose a battle.

Many of the women, on the other hand, didn't seem to know where or how to express their rage. Middle-class upbringing, which labels aggressive behavior as unfeminine, led to real conflict in regard to their responses: "I've never confronted a teacher about his attitude but I'm getting close to it." Women also expressed a desire to avoid confrontation that might limit their career options, just as women and blacks had decided to avoid certain design teachers: "I feel I will have to avoid working with certain kinds of men because of the psychic and emotional strains and hence I feel more limited in some ways."

Almost all of those responding strongly expressed their need for role models to look toward as a successful example, and as someone who could give advice, understanding, and encouragement. Over and over again, women students mentioned the importance of women architects on the faculty.

The women on the faculty are my role models. Seeing them tells me I can do it.

Professor X (a woman) is really important. She takes herself and her work very seriously—it is good for male faculty, to help them understand how seriously women *students* take themselves and their work.

One black student was made to feel uneasy about his professional needs: "As childish as this sounds, I would like to have had a faculty role model during my stay here to talk to." In addition to the need for role models many black students felt that their primary concern in architecture was to work in lower-income minority communities and that this interest and concern was not reflected in the interests or the comprehension of the faculty as much as they had hoped.

What did people do and to whom did they talk when a disturbing incident occurred? Many respondents said they greatly needed the support of their peer group whether it was women or minority, but that they didn't seek this support often enough: "I speak to other students, my friends, my lover. I've never confronted my teachers though I'm getting closer to that now and I do occasionally ask strangers not to call me sweetie or girl." One student reported: "I speak to my friends—in the past I spoke to authorities but became frustrated—they believed these incidents to be 'minor problems' or personality conflicts." [Minority] Several others named specific female faculty or the department's affirmative action officer as a source of help, and one wrote: "There are a number of men in the department who are highly conscious; they are a pleasure."

Unequal Career Development for Faculty

Patterns of ignoring female or minority presence, hostility, condescension, and spotlighting can add up to unequal education for students by undermining their confidence and making them feel less competent than their white male peers. In similar ways, discriminatory attitudes may lead to unequal career development for women and minority faculty. Their reports were perhaps more analytical and less optimistic than those submitted by students.

Although female and minority faculty had many experiences similar to those reported by students and staff, there was less willingness to speak freely among faculty. One minority respondent felt that he would have to write a book if he wrote anything at all. Others thought it easier to focus on their work than to analyze complex interpersonal problems or they didn't want to open a "Pandora's box" of suppressed but emotionally charged issues. There was embarrassment about revealing experiences that people felt were singularly theirs. Some felt they didn't have an adequate typology to describe various experiences, but could relate incidents. It is possible to see all these attitudes as extensions of students' plans for defending their careers—one finds the same problems of invisibility, hostility, and spotlighting; the same attempts to focus or avoid anger; and the same confusion about roles vis-à-vis white males.

Professional Roles—Women in Male-Dominated Groups

Sociologists and psychiatrists who have researched the roles of the one or two females in predominantly male professional groups have illuminated the personality stereotypes that develop to isolate women. Kanter argues that professional men type professional women as mother, dutiful daughter, sex kitten, or iron maiden.[6] "Mother" roles develop when men accept dependence on an older woman, usually for keeping the office "family" together. The "pet" or "dutiful daughter" is forever an obedient protégée, with no chance to grow up. The "seductress" is made a sexual object, constantly flirted with. Any woman, particularly a feminist who resists the preceding three stereotypes becomes an "iron maiden" (or "castrating bitch"), self-confident and assertive about women's rights, etc. Wolman and Frank describe more of the small work-group's dynamic.[7] One professional woman in an otherwise male group tends to become paired as the satellite of a flirtatious or patronizing male group leader, or to become isolated as a "weak" group member, perhaps with a supportive, nonchauvinist male sharing her isolation. They show that, for a woman, becoming "one of the boys" is difficult; becoming group leader is close to impossible. These studies are not limited to the architectural profession, but they provide typologies that fit many work situations and explain why women faculty in particular feel isolated and subjected to different standards of achievement than those applied to white males.

In the architectural school considered here the professional relationships between male faculty and female faculty were cited as presenting difficulties. One woman said:

> I find it difficult to call a male colleague within my field and make a lunch date to discuss a mutual topic of interest. Intellectual curiosity is easily misinterpreted; committee work seems clearly routine, but discussion of ideas for their own sake, more tenuous. At another university, the day I began my first teaching job in the architecture department, I was introduced to a senior professor. I expressed interest in some material he had just published. His response was to suggest we discuss it over lunch. No sooner had we left the department office than he turned to me and propositioned me.

This sort of sexual assault is an extreme version of a more oblique way of making sure a woman's work is not taken seriously:

> I meet with a visiting critic and editor who is publishing an article of mine and wants to discuss further contributions to his journal. It is a business meeting but a senior colleague insists on accompanying us—and then makes sure that the conversation never turns to any substantive issues about work; instead he chats about people that the editor knows, but I do not.

The alternative to the sexual or social ploy may be the cold shoulder:

> The first year I was here, very few male faculty spoke to me. . . .
> It was only after two years that I began to be talked to, invited to lunch very occasionally, and casually joked with by male faculty *about something other than being a woman.*

The invisible female presence may even become institutionalized, as in the case of an incorrect department announcement:

> One part of the department has six regular faculty; three men and three women. Imagine my surprise when I saw an announcement of

our new program which listed ten men and one woman. Two of the female faculty were "forgotten" and seven males from other areas or visitors were added.

Even those male faculty who are able to deal with women on a one-to-one basis may fail in groups:

Male faculty who are friendly and regard me as a peer on a one-to-one basis, are not able to maintain that stance in a group of males. It seems like any group of males has a competitive dynamic, as well as a cliquish one.

Should a woman faculty member persist with an unpopular point of view in a group discussion, males may offer put-downs that reemphasize the female stereotypes they look for, while discounting intellectual content as emotional reaction. Thus:

She's a "nurse" . . . [said of a design teacher with a very serious professional manner, in an attempt to make her seem motherly].

She's just going through her "women's libber" stage [dutiful daughter becoming iron maiden].

She's so difficult, no wonder she's still single [iron maiden; no chance of becoming a seductress].

Not knowing how to relate to women faculty as equals—as women who are not students or secretaries and not mothers, daughters, or lovers, seems to lead many male faculty into even more incidents of hostility and condescension. For example, several female faculty cited committee meetings or other occasions where discriminatory introductions were made:

This is Professor X, this is Professor Y, Professor Z, and this is _____ [first name only; the woman referred to by her first name is also a professor].

Another professor complained that she was not consistently invited to meetings of a faculty group to which she officially belonged. On one occasion a tenured professor asked her advice about ordering the refreshments for these meetings and still did not invite her to attend. When she asked why she was not regularly invited, she was told that it was too far to walk to her office. Also on the subject of names, two female faculty reported a male professor kept confusing their names, joking, "You know, all women look alike to me." Another concludes:

> It is only on the rare occasions when I and my female colleagues surround a single male architect that men have any notion at all of how isolated women professionals are made to feel. The man's reaction to this unusual situation is ofter terror, and then a weak joke: "Is this the ladies club?" or another man's joke, "Is that your harem, Mr. X?"

These expressions, of course, aim to make the group of women professionals just as invisible—as "ladies" or as a "harem"—as any individual woman in a group of men.

Spotlighting

After all these hassles, women are expected to be delighted when someone wants them up front for public relations:

> Until recently a reason frequently given to me for committee appointments was "we need a woman on this committee."

> Two weeks before a regional conference, a program was distributed, which asked me to take part, saying, "These are the speakers we really needed to have. We'd like you to comment on a paper, because we don't have any women."

Spotlighting connected with token committee assignments or work groups may be tied in with hostility and innuendo. One female faculty member reports being telephoned at 2:00 A.M. on a weekday by an abusive faculty member who wanted to discuss a committee meeting; another reported several unexpected midnight calls to discuss work.

In addition to keeping up token representation on committees, minority and women faculty are usually expected to carry the burdens of the department's affirmative action program, appearing at national and regional conferences, initiating department programs, counselling and advising female and minority students. If more white male faculty members were to engage in these activities and especially in recruitment and public relations activities with more enthusiasm, minority and women faculty could have more time out of the spotlight for career development in academic areas.

There are many cases of uneasy group relationships, invisibility, hostility, innuendo, and spotlighting. Keeping up the numbers of women and minority faculty in the department is important to their ability to function. As well as filling a need for more role models for students, additional women and minority faculty would help the existing faculty in those categories to feel less isolated.

Unequal Career Development for Staff

The administrative and secretarial staff in the department reported many incidents concerning their interactions with faculty, students, and the administration. While female students and faculty often wrote about isolation in male peer groups, resulting in hostility and spotlighting, staff experienced a different sort of separateness. They work with predominantly male groups of students and faculty and are expected to conform to stereotypes about "women's" work that are an inverted form of the stereotypes about the "man's" world that women architects encounter. One staff member writes:

> It appears that secretaries have a hard time transcending the role of mechanic (i.e., given a specific duty or order—type a dictated letter, phone so-and-so and tell that person such and such) to [that of] independent thinker and organizer. The word secretary still carries a stigma of noninitiative, a passive role.

The problem is summed up by another who writes:

> In this institution (and no doubt at other large universities as well during these times of low employment levels) many of the [female] "staff" members and other "support personnel" are as highly educated and talented as their superiors. Unfortunately, they rarely have a chance to use their backgrounds and abilities and too easily are stereotyped as "secretaries"—even if that is not their position.

What is expected of a secretary? One respondent commented on illegal hiring practices she had observed, complaining that secretaries may be required to meet certain physical standards set by the boss. Thus someone might request a secretary in a certain age range ("we have a young group here"), someone "attractive," or someone of a certain race. This secretary was also offended by the racist implications when a personnel officer interviewing her described a potential boss, saying "Well, he's black . . . ," and hesitating, which she felt was testing her willingness to work for a black man. Several women complained about nonsecretarial tasks added to their work load, making them "office wives" doing office housework for male bosses, such as having to "make the coffee and heat water for tea no matter how many men and boys take part in the consumption. In some cases she [a secretary] is still expected to make and *serve* it to her boss and his guests."

One of the difficulties of secretarial life may be the vacillation of roles. The secretary may "be constantly interrupted from her (or his) work to do trivial tasks, but she (or he) must not interrupt the boss except in an emergency." She (or he) may be hassled with trivial work that she (or he) feels the boss could perfectly well do himself or herself. She (or he) may be saddled with personal work (at no extra compensation) like making travel arrangements for the boss's family, balancing the boss's checkbook, typing the boss's personal letters, or listening to the boss's marital problems. Even if these activities are performed as personal favors, there is usually little or no personal reciprocity.

In contrast to trivial work and personal work, there is executive work that the secretary may be asked to take on without executive pay. One faculty member was reported to have asked his secretary to grade student work. Other skilled jobs secretaries have been assigned include running conferences, doing graphic design, and reading proofs. All of these jobs rarely lead to planned career development—most often they are extra work at the same pay.

Even if a secretary refuses personal work and executive work as not being part of the job, there is the problem of overwork: "A secretary can expect to be hired to work for one or two people but end up working for more—particularly in cases of new faculty being added to the department with a budget which won't allow for money for a secretary.

Overwork for female administrators can include taking on more and more responsibilities, for more and more people, without the support staff or the salary that a male administrator would receive. One administrator reported that a male doing only one third of her job was paid several thousand dollars more per year, while other males in equivalent jobs enjoyed secretarial assistance and student staff. The case of unequal work for unequal pay leads one to understand why women secretaries resent the entrance of higher-paid, higher-status men with inferior qualifications.

The stresses of overwork may be exacerbated by difficult professional contacts due to hostility, condescension, and sexual innuendo. For example, female staff reported being repeatedly shouted at and sworn at by callers who then behave in an obsequious manner when the boss appears. Personal relationships are also made difficult if a boss expects a secretary to lie to callers—"he (or she) is not here now"—in order to save face or avoid confronting a hostile person. Bosses may also demean their secretaries by referring to them with possessive and diminutive terms such as "my girl" or "the girl" (you never hear "my boy" or even "the boy") that may lead callers to presume upon the boss's patronizing relationship.

Sexual innuendo may become part of such a patronizing relationship. One tenured faculty member was observed being asked by an administrator to attend a committee meeting. He bantered with the female administrator flirtatiously, "Will you be there so we can hold hands?" Gross sexual assault may also threaten the staff:

> One day I was . . . "running an errand" for my boss when a male student in the architecture department, whose name I did not know, ran up behind me and grabbed me between the thighs and turned around and ran off in the opposite direction. When I reported it to two male administrators in the department, one asked if the student was black and when I said "no" he just dropped the subject and walked out of the office and the other said "not one of our students"

and walked away from me. I was able to find this student's department folder with his picture and got his name but felt very humili-
ated about pursuing it. Finally, I reported it to the Campus Patrol so
that it would go on record but they insisted that it must have been
someone from outside the university and suggested I go look at mug
shots at the local police station.

The staff experience is difficult to summarize, since role
definition, office housework, and executive work without executive pay can be related to problems of hierarchy as well as of
sexism and racism. The generally preferential treatment male
staff receive, however, shows that sexism does operate in treatment of female staff. One can ask, "If the staff member or secretary I work with were male, would I treat him any differently?" Problems of long-range career development for staff are
more severe than for students or faculty—others may complain
of not moving up the career ladder, but for staff, beyond a certain point the ladder does not really exist.

Recommendations

How can women and minority students, faculty, and staff
make others sensitive to the difficulties they experience? Perhaps this chapter can illuminate the problems of sexism and
racism and help put them in perspective by showing that incidents of discrimination should not be dismissed as "trivial"
conflicts or as "personality" problems of the victims.

Recommendations for overcoming the unconscious discrimination described in this report include many conscious
steps toward greater equality: hiring and promoting female and
minority faculty and staff; recruiting female and minority students; and making sure that they get adequate scholarship support, their fair share of teaching assistantships in school, and
placement opportunities when they leave. These measures will
contribute toward achieving a department's outward goals.
Examining the curriculum, including the content of courses
and studio design programs, will also help to eliminate intellectual sexism. The work of women and minority architects should
be discussed in courses, and even more important, the needs of

women and minorities as users of the built environment should be carefully examined. The architectural profession has a long history of perpetuating racist stereotypes in the design of segregated facilities for blacks and whites, as well as perpetuating sexist stereotypes in the design of workplaces and dwellings, and this intellectual history will not be easily overcome.

Administrative and curricular vigilance can go a long way towards ending overt discrimination in education, but extirpating unconscious sexism requires even greater effort. Many of the incidents described in this chapter concern "micro-inequalities"— hostile attitudes and unprofessional behavior that clearly tell women and minorities, "you don't belong here," yet are not subject to legal action and are even difficult to pursue as anything more than the victim's "personality problem."[8] For this kind of harassment to end, open discussion of discrimination at the moment it occurs is essential. Verbal confrontation must replace private distress.

While female and minority students, faculty, and staff must learn to support each other by confronting sexism and racism on a daily basis, it is necessary for white males to make just as great an effort. The dean, head of department, or professor who holds a position of power and is alert to the issues described in this chapter can have an enormous influence in creating a social and intellectual climate in which sexism and racism are no longer acceptable. So can the student, staff member, or faculty member who is committed to changing attitudes. So our advice to the reader is to raise your own consciousness; raise your colleagues' consciousness; don't be afraid to apologize (or ask questions) when you think you have offended someone; and don't be afraid to raise the issue when someone has offended you.

Notes

1. Curator of a major museum exhibition of work by women architects, Susana Torre has edited *Women in American Architecture, an Historic and Contemporary Perspective* (New York: Whitney Library of Design,

1977). Richard K. Dozier's discussion of "Black Architectural Experience in America," *AIA Journal* 65 (July 1976):162–164 ff., was accompanied by a traveling exhibition.

2. For an extensive review of the literature on women as designers and users in architecture and urban planning, see Dolores Hayden and Gwendolyn Wright, "Review Essay: Architecture and Urban Planning," *Signs: A Journal of Women in Culture and Society* (summer 1976). For bibliographies of some of the literature on blacks as users, see Lenwood G. Davis, *Black Women in the Cities 1872–1975,* Bibliography no. 751–752, and *The Black Family in Urban Areas,* no. 808–809 (Monticello, Ill.: Council of Planning Librarians, 1975).

3. Robert Rosenthal and Lenore Jacobson, *Pygmalion in the Classroom: Teachers' Expectation and Pupils' Intellectual Development* (New York: Holt, Rinehart & Winston, 1968).

4. Eileen Shapiro, et al., *Obstacles to Equal Education at Harvard Resulting from Sex Discrimination,* a report of the Student Task Force of the Joint Committee on the Status of Women, Harvard Medical School, Harvard School of Dental Medicine, Harvard School of Public Health (October 1974). This describes the administrative and curricula problems women medical students experience.

5. Salary inequities are documented in Judith Edelman, chairperson, AIA Task Force on Women, *Status of Women in the Architectural Profession* (February 1975), reissued in 1977 along with the AIA's hopeless "affirmative action" plan which sets extremely limited goals for redressing these salary inequities. There is a national association of minority architects but no salary surveys are available except Lisa B. Yondrof, "Women and Blacks in Planning," American Society of Planning Officials, Planning Advisory Service *Memo M-10* (Chicago, 1972). See also Ellen Berkeley, "No Jews Need Apply," concerning antisemitism in architects' offices, *Village Voice* (New York) March 22, 1976.

6. Rosabeth Moss Kanter, *Men and Women of the Corporation* (New York: Basic Books, 1977).

7. Carol Wolman, M.D., and Hal Frank, "The Solo Woman in a Professional Peer Group," paper delivered at the annual meeting of the American Psychiatric Association (May 1973). In contrast to the difficulties of becoming "one of the boys" that Wolman and Frank discuss, Margaret Hennig and Anne Jardin, in *The Managerial Woman* (New York: Doubleday Anchor, 1977), give some fascinating advice on how to cope, describing patterns of difference between men and women and recounting case histories of women's successful careers.

8. Mary Rowe, "Saturn's Rings," in *Graduate and Professional Educa-*

tion of Women, Harvard Medical Alumni Bulletin 50, no. 1 (September–October, 1975):14–18; "The Saturn's Rings Phenomenon: Micro-Inequalities and Unequal Opportunity," (1976), working paper. She is also the author of "Go Hire Yourself a Mentor," which outlines ways in which women can actively, rather than passively, seek support.

13

From Kitchen to Storefront:
Women in the Tenant Movement

Ronald Lawson
Stephen Barton
Jenna Weissman Joselit

Introduction

In her history of feminism, *Women, Resistance and Revolution* (1973), Sheila Rowbothom suggested that "the social relations of production" are given the most attention both by society and by its Marxist critics, while those activities that are bound up with the home—what she calls "the social relations of reproduction"—are largely overlooked. Budget matters, childrearing, food shopping, maintenance of the home, and participation in community groups have traditionally been regarded as women's activities; while politics, major decisionmaking, and earning money have been designated "men's work."

This chapter examines the part women have played within the tenant movement—the crusade for the recognition of tenants' rights to security within well-maintained housing at reasonable rents—in New York City from the first major rent strikes in 1904 until the present. Historically, the tenant movement, in terms of its organizers, other members of active cores, and followers, has been largely a movement of women. However, formal leadership has usually been held by men, especially at times when new strategies have been initiated and new structures were emerging.

When we use the term "leader," we are referring to the spokesperson(s) and main decisionmaker(s) for the organization.

The authors wish to thank Joseph Spencer, Jody Dworetzky, and John McLoughlin for their parts in collecting and providing historical data, and Jo Curran for her help in preparing the survey data for analysis.

Often this is a single person bearing a formal title; sometimes the term refers to a group of two or more people. However, rarely do the numbers of "leaders" exceed four or five. By the *active core, activists,* or *secondary leaders* (terms we use interchangeably) we mean the group of people in an organization who together do most of the work—the organizing, publicity, advising of tenants, etc. This group includes the leaders but extends beyond them to include less prominent participants. The size of the active core can vary widely, but in most cases falls between four and fifteen persons.

The tenant movement has evolved a complex structure with three levels of organization (in apartment buildings, neighborhoods, and the city or state as a whole); we refer to these levels as building organizations, neighborhood organizations, and coalitions. As new neighborhood or coalition organizations have appeared, men have been in the forefront. This has occurred despite the presence of a clear majority of women in the ranks of almost all organizations at every structural level. Once the new paths have been pioneered, however, some of these women have assumed leadership positions. This sequence has by now occurred to some extent at all structural levels of the movement, although it is most advanced at lower levels partly because of the different functions and roles of leaders at higher levels. At each level, this evolution has been most likely to occur first in organizations representing tenants of lower socioeconomic status.

The first issue to be considered is the numerical predominance of women in the movement throughout its history: why have they provided a vast majority of the organizers, other active participants, and rank-and-file members?

Involvement in a protest, such as a rent strike over conditions concerning a building, flows directly out of a woman's role as homemaker and budget supervisor and is more common because she spends more time in and around the home and is likely to have developed a friendship network that is locally focused. Any sharp increase in rent or deterioration in services is likely to impinge on a woman more directly than upon a man. She may protest personally to the superintendent or landlord, request help from the authorities, or make an attempt to move elsewhere. She may, perhaps, urge her husband to act for her in any of these cases. If none of these strategies works, she has the option of lapsing into resignation or of becoming involved in a larger protest. If the choice is for joint action with other tenants, she is most likely to be involved personally, not only because the house is seen as primarily her sphere but also because of her involvement in local networks: the common activities of women in their building and neighborhood—watching over children, doing the laundry, neighboring, shopping for food—all tend to create social ties that can provide a basis for mobilization. Men, on the other hand, often lack such local ties, in part because of the split between home and community on the one hand and workplace on the other.

Women are not only more likely to be involved but are also more likely to act as organizers at the local level. The degree of socialization associated with women's roles and their greater stress on expressive behavior develops interpersonal sensitivity that is important to organizing, especially where fellow tenants are fearful and distrustful. Moreover, because of their familiarity with their neighborhoods, women are more likely to know of and to make contact with a neighborhood organization when housing problems arise in their buildings—and it is the person who makes that first contact who is most likely to lead a building organization. Similarly, women's numerical predominance in tenants' efforts to alleviate problems at the building level and their involvement in neighborhood friendship networks lead them to be drawn into efforts to deal with housing problems in other buildings—that is, into neighborhood organizations and, eventually, coalitions.

Despite the fact that they have always been numerically dominant in the tenant movement, women have not tended to take the initiative in forming and leading these higher-level organizations, at least not while the structures and the strategies that they used have been new. This leads us to raise three main questions in this chapter:

1. Why have men tended to occupy leadership positions while higher levels of organizational structure are emerging or new strategies evolving?

2. Under what circumstances have men tended to drop out of these positions once strategies and structures are established?

3. Under what circumstances have women tended to succeed to these leadership positions or to found their own organizations following tried paths?

In order to answer these questions, the following section examines the participation of women in the tenant movement in New York City over a seventy-year period; the next section analyzes the current situation in greater detail; and finally, evidence is brought to bear on the questions raised.

The data for this chapter were collected by the Tenant Movement Study through a combination of three main methods: historical research on the period from 1890 to 1972, extensive field work in tenant organizations at building, neighborhood, and city- and state-wide levels from 1973–1977, and comprehensive surveys of neighborhood and building organizations in 1976–1977.

The First Seventy Years

The first major episode of tenant activism in New York City dates from the spring of 1904. Confronted with increasing rents and decreasing services, residents of the Lower East Side protested in the form of a large-scale rent strike. Contemporary accounts estimate that close to 2,000 families joined the strike. At first, tenants demanded a 25 percent reduction in rent. Failing to have that acceded to, they picketed their buildings, strung signs from slum windows denouncing landlords as "blood suckers" and "parasites," and circulated flyers and posted notices urging would-be residents not to rent space in buildings where landlords had raised rents or evicted strikers.

Newspaper sources covering the "disturbance" found women doing much of the canvassing that led to the initial outbursts of protest. For example, one gave the following assessment after the action had subsided:

A rent strike is not a private matter, it's a communal issue. And women were crucial in it! They began it and by their efforts and enthusiasm spread it. Through their strength even the blackest strike was won. Had it not been for their courage, the rent agitation would never have been possible. (*Jewish Daily Forward*, May 21, 1904.)

However, within a few days of the outbreak of the strike an organization founded by men who were local members of the Socialist Party was established in order to channel tenant indignation, which at that point "had gathered force and spread like an angry wave" (*New York Times*, April 8, 1904). This organization, the New York Rent Protective Association (NYRPA), was conceived of as a labor union for tenants and was intended to aid dispossessed tenants, help form building organizations, and fight landlord-tenant battles in court.

Although this tenants' union was dominated by men, news coverage singled out a woman of nineteen, Bertha Liebson, as one of the more "picturesque" figures of the tenant agitation. Dubbed the "Joan of Arc" of the Lower East Side by the English-language press (*New York Herald*, April 10, 1904; *New York Sun*, April 12, 1904; *New York Times*, April 8, 1904), Bertha Liebson was hailed as the leader of the tenant movement. Not only did she succeed in convincing residents of the area to participate in the tenant protest but she was also in charge of raising funds for the protection and defense of beleaguered tenants and was appointed as the treasurer of the NYRPA. Within a week of holding that position, however, Liebson's tenure was challenged. Claiming that her inexperience and, most importantly, her sex made her unqualified to be treasurer, the leadership of NYRPA removed her from the position. With that, the organization's leadership became an exclusively male preserve.

Small-scale rent strikes continued to occur on the Lower East Side, and in December of 1907 a combination of rent hikes and heavy unemployment helped set off a rent strike involving close to 12,800 tenants that lasted through February 1908. Credit for the swift mobilization of the area's residents was again given to the women of the Lower East Side, or as one contemporary put it: "Woman [sic] . . . plays a predominating part in the war against the East Side landlord." Not only were women leaders of the rent agitation but they were also responsible for achieving its first victory. "Should the tenants continue to secure rent reductions," continued this correspondent, "victory will largely be due to three girls. For they have been largely responsible for starting the movement and since the trouble began have encouraged people by their words of cheer, their advice and their heroic work" (*New York Evening Journal,* January 28, 1908; January 31, 1908).

The three women singled out in this manner were Cecelia Arkin, Florence Margolies, and Pauline Newman. The latter, a politically active woman of eighteen, already familiar to local residents as a former organizer against coal and ice interests and later to become a pioneer in the International Ladies Garment Workers Union (ILGWU), was not only responsible for organizing women tenants and keeping them unified but was also credited with helping to spread the tenant protest uptown. Florence Margolies, a thirty-two-year-old school teacher, did her part in arousing the tenants of the area by writing circulars in Yiddish decrying the rapacity of the landlords. Finally, Cecelia Arkin, a sixteen-year-old stenographer, led and won the first victory against a landlord; due to her impassioned speechmaking and prodding, he capitulated to his tenants' demands and reduced the rent by two dollars. As the leader of the first tenement house to win the antilandlord battle, Arkin became a symbol of tenant power. When asked how she became active in the tenant movement, Arkin replied:

> I simply did what any sensible girl would do. I am not a labor leader or a regular striker and I am also not a troublemaker. I simply joined the strike because I saw it was impossible to exist on the small salary earned these days and then pay large exorbitant rents to the landlords. [*New York Evening Journal,* January 31, 1908]

No sooner had Newman, Margolies, Arkin, and others like them mobilized the community, than the all-male Eighth Assembly District Socialist Party took over the leadership of the movement, forming an umbrella organization attempting to coordinate and speak for the strikers. And again, as in 1904, once the reins were taken by men, women faded from importance.

In subsequent years, tenant activity was relatively rare as the sudden growth of the trade-union movement eclipsed all rival forms of social protest. Not until 1918 was New York to see a repetition of the "tenants rebellion" of 1907–1908. This time, however, the protest was much more widespread.

The first major strike of the next wave of tenant action was in the Bronx in January 1917 and was organized by Theresa Malkiel, a Socialist Party state committee member and member of the Socialist Women's Consumer League. The strike failed, but one year later the Bronx Tenants League was firmly established. While the group seems to have had a high percentage of active women, including the chief organizer, Mary Mardfin, the top positions were held by men. The same was true of the other socialist neighborhood organizations of 1918–1920. For example, the Harlem Tenants League, the East Side Tenants League, and the Brownsville Tenants League all had women active at the grass-roots level—picketing, organizing, and even engaging in occasional violence against landlords—but the leaders were all men, usually lawyers who could represent the rent strikers in court.

In 1919 more conservative "tenant associations," with ties to the Democratic and Republican parties, emerged as rivals to the tenant "leagues" led by socialists. Their initial leaders were almost all men, whose main tactic was to call meetings of sympathizers to endorse requests for legislative action to relieve the rent crisis. After the introduction of rent control in 1920, these associations got a new lease on life; their leaders and activists assisted tenants confused by the complexity of the new law, appeared at hearings when necessary to support the law's extension, and backed up tenant efforts with lobbying activities.

During these years—until 1929, when rent control was allowed to lapse and so removed the *raison d'être* of the associations—women became increasingly more prominent within their leadership ranks. Best known was Agnes Craig, a lawyer who was the key tenant witness and who managed the tenant delegations at the 1923 and 1925 rent-control extension hearings. Many of the associations were by this time led by women, some of whom were also attorneys. In part, this change in the role of women within the associations was a result of men dropping out. One finds frequent statements, especially towards the end of the period, decrying a growing lack of male participation in tenant activity: "the men have fallen down again"; "more men should attend" association meetings (*Bronx Home News,* February 5, 1927). But the greater female role may also be attributed to the fact that women found themselves more comfortable with the advice-giving, settlement-house-like functions the associations performed after 1920, so that they swelled the ranks of the participants; the more confident among them, notably the lawyers, then moved to prominence through lobbying and speaking at public meetings.

Neighborhood tenant organizations reemerged in numbers in the wake of the depression, with a new focus on the decay of housing following a period of high vacancy rates and landlord neglect. Again there were many women among the rank-and-file participants and some among the leaders; this was by now to be expected. But in 1936 when the first regional coalition, the City-Wide Tenants' Council, was created, all the key leaders were men. However, by 1942, when the war removed the male leaders, a woman, Grace Aveles, head of the Chelsea neighborhood organization, was ready to move up from among the group of core activists to become head of the coalition.

Rent controls were reintroduced in 1943 as part of federal wartime price regulations. Three city- or state-wide coalitions emerged from the wartime consumer movement to lobby for the retention of the rent controls after the war; all three were led by men. The more conservative Joint Rent Action Committee (1945-1950) was headed by John S. Lamula, a former Republican assemblyman from the Lower East Side. The Emergency Committee on Rent and Housing, which was more politically aligned with the left, was led by Alfred K. Stern from 1946 to 1948, and its successor, the New York Tenants Council on Rent and Housing (1948-1952), headed by Paul Ross, a former administrative secretary to Mayor William O'Dwyer, and later an American Labor Party candidate for mayor. Nevertheless, male leadership was preeminent only at the top structural level; by and large the core activists were women. In fact, the neighborhood and borough-wide organizations were now headed mostly by women.

The retention of rent control was assured by the passage of

the New York State Rent Control Law in 1950. After this the broad coalitions were dismantled, partly because of the removal of the immediate need for political intervention and partly because of the repression of the McCarthy period, which focused on the leaders of such groups. The result was that the erstwhile male leaders disappeared into the woodwork (Stern, indeed, fled to Prague).

The period that followed was a relatively quiet one for tenant activists; leadership of the movement rested with the borough-wide organizations, which were all led by women: Dr. Helen Harris in the Bronx Council on Rent and Housing; Mildred Wickson in the Brooklyn Tenant, Welfare and Consumer Council; and Estelle Quinn in the Manhattan Council on Rent. They each held these posts for several years.

In the mid-1950s a new type of tenant organization appeared in New York City: the *Save-Our-Homes* committees. These groups arose as a result of the passage of Title One of the Housing Act of 1949, which empowered cities to demolish what it defined as run-down and potentially hazardous neighborhoods. The New York City program, aggressively pushed by Robert Moses, collided with the interests of the residents of those areas, who sought to preserve their homes and neighborhoods against demolition and to avoid the very uncertain prospects of relocation. Women were prominent in neighborhood "Save-Our-Homes" campaigns at both the grass-roots and leadership levels. However, when an effort was started to initiate a city-wide coalition to engage in sustained lobbying against urban renewal, a triumvirate of two men and one woman was chosen as the initial leadership of the Metropolitan Council on Housing.

In the winter of 1963–1964 what was probably the most widely publicized rent strike ever held in the United States broke out in Harlem and spread from there to other areas such as Manhattan's Lower East Side and central Brooklyn. It is still known as the "Jesse Gray rent strike," after the figure who made the speeches and spoke with the media. However, the strike in Harlem was run on a day-by-day basis by two women—Florence Rice and Ann Bradshaw—and women were numerically predominant on the city-wide strike coordinating committee.

Meanwhile, however, the Metropolitan Council on Housing was broadening its interests beyond opposition to urban renewal to the traditional tenant concerns of rents and maintenance and was consolidating its position as a city-wide coalition of tenant organizations. Jane Benedict, from the Yorkville Save-Our-Homes Committee, had been appointed chairperson, replacing the original triumvirate. She has dominated "Met Council" for over nineteen years.

The Tenant Movement Today

Tenant action in New York City has swelled considerably since 1971. Virtually every neighborhood now has at least one tenant organization, and thousands of buildings have organized and gone on rent strikes. The range of tenant strategies has diversified and now includes a real lobbying presence in the state legislature, affirmative-action court cases, the direct expenditure of rent monies on repairs, the management and moderate rehabilitation through "sweat equity" by would-be tenants of totally abandoned buildings, and the fostering of cooperative ownership of their buildings by low-income tenants. The structure of the movement has developed commensurately; there are now one state-wide, four city-wide, and two borough-wide coalitions representing tenants of varying socioeconomic status with different housing problems and stressing somewhat different strategies.

In addition to the seven coalitions, our sample included 123 neighborhood tenant organizations and 108 organized buildings. This represents almost all the community groups active in 1975–1976 whose central purpose was to organize tenants, together with a sample of Office of Economic Opportunity (OEO) funded housing agencies, most of which mainly serviced tenants rather than organizing them. The sample of buildings is broadly representative of the different neighborhoods, but is by no means a random sample of all organized buildings.

When we examine the place of women in the tenant movement today, we find that the historical patterns outlined above continue to hold. The movement is still largely a movement of women in the sense that they make up most of the participants.

Women considerably outnumber men among grass-roots members: 63.4 percent of neighborhood organizations report that the majority of their member/clients (that is, tenants in buildings) are women; only 3.2 percent report that the majority are men. Among core activists, women outnumber men at all levels. However, the situation is different when leaders are considered: the higher the structural level, the more likely leaders are to be males (see Table 13.1).

Significant variations occur within this pattern depending on the socioeconomic status of the tenants involved (see Table 13.2). In general, the higher the income of the tenants being organized/served, the greater the likelihood that leaders are males. Among building organizations, although women are in the majority among both leaders and core activists at all income levels, their predominance decreases as income rises. At the neighborhood level, a small female majority among leaders of

TABLE 13.1 The Sex of Leaders at Different Structural Levels of the Tenant Movement

	Building %	Neighborhood %	Coalition %
Women	50.9	40.7	28.6
Coleaders/Both Sexes	23.1	8.9	–
Men	25.9	50.4	71.4
Total Leaders	108	123	7

TABLE 13.2 The Sex of Leaders of Neighborhood Organizations According to the Average Income of Membership

	Average Income		
	Low (under $8000) %	Moderate ($8000 – 12,500) %	High (over $12,500) %
Women	47.9	26.7	17.4
Coleaders/Both Sexes	11.0	13.3	4.3
Men	41.1	60.0	78.3
Total Organizations	73	15	23

low-income groups is transformed into a clear male preponder-
ance among the heads of middle-income groups.

These general patterns are largely confirmed when the variable of race is introduced (see Table 13.3). We identified an
organization with a particular race if two thirds or more of the
organization's members belonged to it; other organizations
were characterized as of mixed race. At the neighborhood level,
Black, Hispanic, and mixed organizations all have equal numbers of male and female leaders; however, males far outnumber
females among the leaders of White groups. This pattern is
related to the predominance of White groups among middle-
and moderate-income neighborhood organizations, where male
leaders are most common. At the building level, female leadership predominates for each of the racial groups, except for His-
panics, where the leaders are men as often as women. Women
leaders were especially common in Black organizations, where
they formed a majority of the leaders in 55.6 percent of cases,
with another 33.3 percent evenly divided. These variations
would probably be predicted from cultural differences.

Nevertheless, the patterns do not simply indicate that the
most prominent leaders within the tenant movement are men,
nor do they support the generalization that this is a movement
of women led by men. Some women have achieved considerable
prominence within the movement. For example, Jane Benedict's
long rule over the Metropolitan Council on Housing and her
numerous appearances on television and radio as the fiery and
outspoken champion of tenant rights have made her the best-
known tenant leader in New York City today. Again, in 1974,

TABLE 13.3   The Sex of Leaders of Neighborhood Organizations
According to the Race of Membership

	White %	Black %	Race Hispanic %	Mixed %
Women	21.9	48.0	45.5	40.6
Coleaders/Both Sexes	6.3	4.0	9.1	15.6
Men	71.9	48.0	45.5	43.8
Total Organizations	32	25	22	32

Marie Runyon, a past president of the Columbia Tenants' Union, succeeded Jesse Gray to the New York State Assembly. The general patterns suggested earlier in this section must therefore be modified by another issue that cuts across them: men tend to lead when new paths are being pioneered, but women often follow these same paths to prominence once they are established. It is possible to find considerable evidence supporting this contention in the contemporary tenant movement to place beside that adduced from the movement's history.

Males are likely to play a more dominant part when higher level organizations initiate change. In the case of prominent leaders at the coalition level, all examples of leadership succession involving a change in sex have been from male to female. It was noted previously that in the case of the Metropolitan Council, the oldest of the currently existing coalitions, the original triumvirate of two men and a woman was early replaced by a lone woman. In 1976 Margaret McNeil succeeded to the presidency of the Association of Neighborhood Housing Developers (although the structure of that coalition provides for a sharing of power between the president and the director— a post held continuously by a male). We consider it very likely that women from the active cores of several other coalitions would replace the present male leaders should the incumbents resign. Similarly, when leadership changes occur in neighborhood organizations they have tended to be from male to female, and the data show that this trend is also present among the secondary leadership.

The same pattern—males leading in new directions and females taking over once the directions become established— is very clear when particular strategies are examined. A number of neighborhood organizations have recently been developing a new array of strategies to save or reclaim buildings from abandonment, such as moderate rehabilitation, sweat-equity rehabilitation, and the forming of low-income cooperatives. These groups deal with very poor tenants where the majority of neighborhood organizations are woman-led; but sixteen of the twenty organizations now using these strategies are led by men. Again a group of organizations in the Bronx has been developing an approach where they seek to build community power, Alinsky-style, by attacking a range of issues so that housing becomes for them the central but not the only problem. In 1976 all eight of these organizations were led by men; however, a woman has recently succeeded to the directorship of the oldest and most successful of them. Yet another example is provided by fourteen middle-income groups based in large housing developments, with from 2,000 to 60,000 tenants under one landlord. These developments had never been organized until recently, but the sudden threat of forced condominium conversion or massive rent increases brought them into the movement. Twelve of the fourteen groups are led by men. Each of these innovative organizations has been developing new approaches to the legislature, housing bureaucracies, and institutions such as banks.

On the other hand, women are in the majority among the neighborhood organizations following the more traditional strategies—fostering rent strikes, opposing demolition of buildings for redevelopment and institutional expansion (the successors to those who fought urban renewal in the 1950s and 1960s), and mainly or solely servicing individual tenants. However, the neighborhood organizations that encourage tenants who are being stonewalled by landlords to strike and spend their rent monies directly on fuel and/or repairs have equal numbers of men and women leaders, despite the fact that rent strikes are still considered to be somewhat daring.

There are, therefore, signs that the newer strategies are beginning to be accepted as part of the arsenal of women leaders, and many of these neighborhood organizations have a female majority among their activist cores. Several women leaders are also successfully helping tenants manage their buildings under the City's Receivership Program. The recent election of Margaret McNeil as President of the Association of Neighborhood Housing Developers, which provides crucial technical assistance to groups engaged in fostering tenant management, low-income cooperatives, and tenant-controlled rehabilitation, seems, then, to have important symbolic significance.

Conclusion

The ranks of the tenant movement have been, and are, composed largely of women. Our analysis has traced this to the split between home and community on the one hand—the traditional sphere of the woman—and the workplace, the sphere of the man, on the other. We have also linked the fact that women have made up the bulk of the organizers, especially among the poorer, more fearful tenants, where the importance of the social-emotional role of the leader is an important element in people mobilization.

However, leadership positions have usually been filled by men, especially when higher-level structures or new strategies (which involved dealing with politicians and bureaucrats) have been emerging. Why has this been so? Functional roles are more important to such strategic undertakings and males have been better prepared to fill those roles, both as a result of their early and continuing socialization and because the structure of other institutions has placed them in positions where they gain the skills and confidence to lead when opportunities arise. Much of the time leadership goes to those who seize initiative, as is illustrated by the examples of the socialists in 1904 and 1907, the men with political ties who established the tenant associations in 1919, and those who headed the city-wide coalitions after World War II. A more recent example is Robert Schur, who in 1975 moved from a post as an administrator within the City Housing and Development Administration to become director of the Association of Neighborhood Housing Developers. Men are more likely than women to see taking such leadership positions as a step towards their career goals. Paul Ross later ran for mayor, and Jesse Gray ran for several offices before being elected to the State Assembly as the "Harlem Rent Strike Leader" nine years after the event. Today two other assemblymen continue to lead the neighborhood organizations that are their main political bases, two others hold well-paying appointed positions while also controlling their local organizations, and several others clearly aspire to similar advancements.

We have accumulated some evidence, however, that bureau-

cracies have specifically demanded to deal with male leaders:
for example, some judges have attempted to insist that tenants
be represented by lawyers (more likely to be male) rather than
by women organizers. There have also been cases where women
seem to have assumed that a male would be taken more seriously
by authorities or that they themselves would not be adequate,
and so have put up a man to front for them. And there was at
least one case of overt discrimination among tenants on the
basis of sex—Bertha Liebson in 1904. Nevertheless, most of the
evidence shows that self-appointed leaders—usually males—
take the initiative to found a higher level organization and then
pull in activists—often women—as the organizational core.

With time many of the original male leaders retire from their
posts. Some may be described as having vaulted upwards successfully from their tenant coalition or neighborhood bases to
political or administrative careers, after which they cut the
formal ties to these organizations. Some, such as Stern during
the McCarthy period, have fled before repression (women in
the tenant movement at that time apparently did not hold
sufficiently prominent positions to attract such unwelcome
scrutiny). Others have been removed by such outside forces
as the draft or the split in the Socialist Party in 1920. However,
the majority have found the personal costs of tenant activism
unmatched by the rewards and have retired to private lives or
moved on to other issues. It is pertinent to point out here that
where movements have been enlarged and institutionalized to
the point that they offer highly rewarding careers, men have
often stayed in leadership for as long as possible, as is illustrated
by the experiences of such unions as the ILGWU and the Amal-
gamated Clothing Workers, despite their predominantly female
memberships. Male leaders have, in the past, been especially
likely to drop out of the tenant movement during waning
periods, since these posts then appeared less likely to provide
avenues to political influence or a means of personal career
advancement.

Over the years women have gradually moved up the ranks of
the movement as a whole, taking over the leadership positions
from men. This process has accelerated since the growth of the
modern Women's Movement, which has made it easier for

women to enter male-dominated areas. The current leadership data confirm this, and women are moving into leadership positions in the tenant movement more rapidly than in the past. Nevertheless, our analysis serves to stress the split between home and community on one hand and workplace on the other, and the relative importance of social-emotional and functional roles for people mobilization. One result of these structural and interactional factors has been that women have tended to be the organizers and followers and men the leaders of the tenant movement. Nevertheless, women have successfully learned the necessary skills and broken through the structural barriers to become leaders in their own right, and one can only hope that organization members will come to recognize and use the social skills that women have brought to bear in organizing tenants at the grass-roots level.

Reference

Sheila Rowbotham. *Women, Resistance and Revolution: A History of Women and the Revolution in the Modern World.* New York: Pantheon, 1973.

14
Women at City Hall

Richard W. Butler
Susan Phillips

There is a relative lack of empirical studies documenting the specific ways women influence and shape the environments in which they live. This chapter discusses the concerns women have about the quality of life in urban environments, and the role women play in the decisionmaking process in one Canadian city: London, Ontario.[1] It is based on research conducted during 1975 for one of a series of studies commissioned by the Ministry of State for Urban Affairs as its contribution to the Canadian government's program for International Women's Year (MSUA, 1975).

The study was concerned with identifying and analyzing the desires and goals of women and women's organizations in the urban sphere, and in documenting the degree to which these goals were being achieved in practice. An assessment was made of the actual influence and role that women had in controlling and shaping the urban environment in London through their membership in city government committees or other agencies with responsibilities for improving the quality of the city's environment.

It was found that while women's organizations do take positions on a wide range of urban issues, they have not focused their efforts on the particular problem areas affecting women in the city. Indeed most women's organizations are not intended to play an active role in influencing policy decisions. This is reflected in their relatively insignificant role in London as a pressure group that raises women's issues before city government bodies and particularly in the lack of women members (whether elected or appointed) on committees and other bodies.

Data used in this chapter came from a review of existing published information (including reports and briefs relating to the general quality of life in London and women's problems and concerns in particular, and from academic research, local newspaper coverage, and the 1974 minutes of all public bodies). Interviews with women's organizations and specific individuals identified during the course of the study also supplied information. The interviews focused on the nature of the organizations, their structure and membership, the activities they engaged in, the quality of life concerns with which they were involved, and their views on women's involvement and representation on decisionmaking bodies.

The review of existing reports, academic studies, and newspaper coverage of women and their concerns and activities revealed an extensive coverage of many urban issues during the previous three years. But day care was the only issue covered that was directly identified with women's concerns and involvement. However, it would appear from the newspaper coverage that the growth of women's awareness and involvement in the affairs of the city had increased markedly during the period of 1973 to 1975. This was borne out by the establishment of the Woman's Resource Centre in 1973 and of Womanpower (a counselling and placement organization) in 1974, and also by the greater visibility of the London Council of Women (an umbrella organization of some fifty women's organizations in London) and the election in 1973 of a noted supporter of women's rights as the first female mayor of London.

It is difficult to assess the response of the women's organizations contacted in the study in relation to the raising of urban issues of particular concern to women. There is clearly concern with a wide range of general urban issues, but the specific focus tends to be on the quality of urban services, the availability of housing and employment, and on securing personal safety. Definition of women's problems was not well developed, particularly in political terms. In fact, many organizations indicated that they were not prepared or allowed (either by their own constitutions or by those of their parent organizations) to become actively involved in political activity or urban decision-making. However, organizations that had been formed specifically to become involved in the decisionmaking process were more active in the political arena and identified a wider range of concerns than those that did not participate in this way.

Three categories of organization, comprising a quarter of those interviewed, identified the widest range of concerns: they were associated with education, women's issues, and the environment. They involve many of the most politically active organizations, including the London Council of Women, which is the only women's organization given formal representation on certain committees of City Hall.

Interviews conducted with individual women, many of whom were members of the organizations interviewed, provide a more direct sense of the concerns of women in London regarding their urban environment. The most frequently mentioned concern involved the general character and form of the city. But there was some confusion in objectives: London's growth and expansion should be limited, but the clustering of high-rise developments or low-income housing projects could lead to "ghetto living" for certain segments of the population and low densities should be retained!

The general trend of opinion is clearer in relation to planning issues. There was a particular emphasis on keeping the core "alive" and maintaining its present functions. The preservation of historical and architectural sites, supplying small neighborhood parks and playgrounds, retaining core-area schools, and encouraging a variety of business types, were all suggested as ways to enable a healthy mix of people to continue to live around the city center. The issue of closing central elementary schools with low enrollments was felt to have far-reaching implications for the planning and development of the affected neighborhoods. The outward migration of young families, the transition to a more homogeneous population composition, new core functions replacing the old residential functions, and the general stagnation of the city center were viewed as undesirable possibilities.

Several criticisms were directed at the apparent lack of overall city planning and the ease with which zoning codes could be changed in London. The result could be a depletion of open space, the introduction of incompatible land uses, undesirable population densities, and profit to a few at the expense of the many. The preservation of open spaces, conservation of the floodplain, emphasis on natural amenities, pollution control, and urban aesthetics were all strong positive themes identified. Housing type, availability, and price were also mentioned as problems.

Of great concern in London was the apparent lack of social planning, which was considered as high a priority as the provision of physical necessities. Improved public transport, enrichment opportunities for adults and children, social gathering spaces for people, recreation, health care, and other social services were noted as major areas of concern. Suggestions were directed at improved social planning, including the decentralization of social services, the encouragement of grass-roots organizations within the neighborhoods and communities for the planning of their particular social needs, municipal day-care centers, and the creation of more opportunities for leisure-time pursuits within the community for both adults and children. Improved information services within the city with the capacity to channel people to the appropriate service, and increased coordination and cooperation among different levels of government as well as between government and private enterprise were also necessary. It was remarked that society in general and government social services in particular are organized and capable of dealing only with effects rather than causes; few are able to take preventative action.

Some criticisms of the education program in London were aimed at the inequities within the system based on socioeconomic differences in the city. This was felt to have had a profound influence on the children's future employment opportunities. Several people also stated an active interest in the area of safety and security for children and students: driver education, bicycle and motorcycle safety, crosswalks, the development of bike paths, babysitting courses, and the Block Parent Plan. It was also felt that more employment and further educational opportunities should be available to women. This would require counselling, retraining, and adult educational services so that women would have equal opportunity when reentering the work force. The need for fluency in English for new Canadians in London to ease problems of integration into Canadian and local society was also noted, and educational and orientation programs were suggested.

In general, the concerns identified by the individuals interviewed supported and expanded many of the areas of concern identified by the women's organizations, with a greater emphasis on the need for overall planning and development of a higher quality urban environment and the ways of achieving this goal.

Information indicating the relative strength of women's concerns was sought in the minutes of public decisionmaking bodies in the form of references to submissions made by women and women's organizations. Accordingly, the 1974 minutes of meetings of ten public bodies were examined in order to identify items relevant to the study: the City Council; the four Standing Committees of Council; the Planning Board; the Public Utilities Commission (dealing with parks, recreation, electrical power, and water); the Board of Education; the Separate School Board; and the London Transportation Commission.

The low level of political action among women is reflected by the fact that of these bodies, only the Board of Education received direct input regarding the status of women, employment opportunities for women, and the promotion of women in the teaching profession. This input came in the form of letters and briefs from the Status of Women Council, Womanpower, and the London Women Teacher's Association of Ontario. The latter group had three of their recommendations accepted: suggestions relating to equal opportunities for women, access to job descriptions, and the establishment of a committee to study the status and promotion of women in the London school system. The Womanpower submission was related to equal accessibility of social facilities for all students. For the rest, direct representation by women was sparse and related mainly to specific local issues without direct reference to the concerns of women. However, submissions from women regarding the frequency and coverage of London Transportation Commission services obviously have a strong indirect relationship to women's needs.

In general, the concerns raised at meetings of the public bodies reflect the patterns discussed earlier, with educational matters causing the greatest concern. A survey of minutes does not reveal issues that individuals and organizations took to their local elected representatives, that were discussed at committee meetings, or that possibly resulted in action. It does, however, indicate some problems that individuals and organizations thought to be of sufficient magnitude to raise at appropriate meetings.

There is, therefore, some clear general agreement about the concerns women in London have about the quality of life in the city. The chief areas of concern include education, health care and services, social services and planning, environmental planning, housing, and employment. Many of these concerns were also identified in the other eight Canadian cities studied, which would suggest that whatever the differences in specific local problems, women in urban centers share the same general problems and concerns wherever they live in Canada. Since these areas of concern involve many aspects of urban life and the planning of the urban environment, they suggest the potentially major roles that women could play, were they to become heavily involved in the decisionmaking process. The similarity of the concerns across Canada, however, perhaps indicates a failure in many cases to have these issues discussed adequately by the agencies responsible. The relative absence of references to women's concerns and the lack of direct representation at official bodies in London also suggest that this may be the case.

Women's Roles in Decisionmaking in London

Given the above definition of women's areas of concern, it is necessary to examine the formal role that women play in shaping the urban environment in which they live and about which they obviously care. Women have traditionally taken a much smaller role than men in the decisionmaking process at every level of society, and the urban environment is no exception to this pattern. The minor role of women was noted as one of the major concerns of women in most of the nine MSUA studies, and it was felt to work to the detriment of urban planning and the urban environment (MSUA, 1975). As these traditional roles are changing, women are now participating to a greater extent in other aspects of society, particularly at the urban level, but they still have a considerable way to go before a level beyond that of token representation is reached.

There are two ways in which women, or any specific group of individuals, can become involved in the decisionmaking process: one is by attempting individually to influence the opinions of decisionmakers and their actions, and the other is by becoming part of the process as a member of an organization or in elected or appointed positions. In London an individual may apply to become a City Council appointee to a number of the committees involved in the decisionmaking process or he or she may run for election for a variety of positions (mayor, member of the Board of Control, alderman, Public Utilities commissioner, or trustee of the Board of Education and Separate School Boards). At present, political parties have not been directly involved in elections, although the political affiliations of several of the elected representatives are often discussed in the media. Similarly, no elected representative, at least in the recent past, has campaigned as a representative of any specific interest or pressure group. Endorsement by various groups such as the Chamber of Commerce and professional and labor organizations is not uncommon, however.

If one intends to influence the decisionmaking structure without becoming a member of it, a number of avenues are open, ranging from attending meetings and writing letters to active lobbying and taking legal action to force or prevent action on specific issues. It is clear from the increasing number of women who are becoming involved in the decisionmaking process, particularly at the urban level, that fewer are now prepared to accept a passive role.

This chapter is primarily concerned with decisionmaking at the urban level, and it is therefore focused on city government and not on the roles of the regional, provincial, or federal authorities. In fact, London and its surrounding region has no female elected representative at the provincial or federal levels.

The political organization in London consists of the mayor; a four-member Board of Control elected on a city-wide basis;

and a nineteen-member City Council, comprising the mayor, members of the Board of Control, and fourteen aldermen—two elected from each of seven wards. In 1975 women held three of the nineteen elected positions (filling the posts of mayor and two aldermen). The other elected positions in the city are four members of the Public Utilities Commission, twelve members of the Board of Education, and sixteen members of the Separate School Board. In 1975, as in previous years, there were no women on the Public Utilities Commission, which in London has responsibility for the operation of parks and recreational facilities in the city as well as the more traditional responsibilities of electrical power and water supply. Women held five positions on the Board of Education and three on the Separate School Board. This higher proportion of women members on the education boards as compared to the City Council perhaps reflects the traditional interest of women in education—a fact emphasized in the earlier discussion.

The poor representation of women on City Council reflects the fact that only six women ran for election in December 1974. In fact, women had a slightly better record of success at the municipal elections in 1974 than men (50 percent compared to 43 percent), but this was accounted for in part by the fact that the three successful female candidates were all incumbents, which tends to be an advantage in local elections.

The composition of City Council determines the makeup of the standing committees of council: Land Use and Development; Social and Community Services; Streets, Traffic, and Transportation; and Environment and Protection Services. With only two women aldermen, two of the four committees inevitably had no female representation (with the exception of the mayor, who is an ex officio member of all committees). This factor also influences the sex of the city representatives on a number of other committees to which the City Council appoints its representatives.

The nonelected agencies fall into three broad groups: those whose membership includes elected representatives; those whose membership includes City Hall nonelected appointees (i.e., staff of City Hall departments); and those whose membership includes members of the general public appointed by City

Council from a list of individuals who applied to be considered for such positions.

Women were represented in seven out of the sixteen City Council–appointed committees in 1975 (exclusive of the mayor); they filled 6 percent of the total number of positions on the committees. One committee had a woman chairman and in general women sat on committees concerned with social, cultural, and local concerns, rather than with technical, financial, or special city-wide services. Of the thirteen committees, boards, and commissions with nonelected city appointees, three had women members who accounted for 2 percent of the total membership. These bodies are primarily concerned with the management of public utilities and facilities, but they also include the London Chamber of Commerce, which had no woman member appointed by City Hall in 1975. No women sat on any of the seven administrative committees associated with such areas as parking, sanitation, and landfill. Citizens at large are not permitted to sit on any of these committees. The positions are only open to elected officials, city employees, or appointees from other official and related organizations and agencies.

Following a November 1974 advertisement, an increased number of applications for civic appointments seemed to indicate a growing public involvement in local politics; more than seventy citizens applied for the twenty-eight available appointments, although surprisingly none of the applicants were women. This situation was somewhat misleading since women have traditionally applied for these positions in earlier years. However, since applicants and appointments go hand in hand, no woman became a city appointee to the various committees in 1975.

Finally, with reference to women's representation on committees, boards, and commissions with citizens' appointments, exclusive of the mayor, nine of the fifteen bodies had female appointees in 1975. However, female representation on these bodies accounted for only 6 percent of total membership, and again only one women's organization (London Council of Women) has been formally recognized and represented—on the City Management Committee.

Table 14.1 summarizes women's representation on the principal decisionmaking agencies in the city of London when they are grouped according to the concerns identified by women. In none of these bodies were women in the majority, in no case did women reach equality of representation with men, and in only two cases did women chair a committee. Clearly, therefore, although women are represented on many of the decisionmaking agencies, their numbers never reflect their position as the majority of the population. It is important therefore to ascertain if women's views and concerns are made known to the decisionmaking agencies, especially those without female representation; how those concerns are viewed and treated; and what the attitudes of agency members are towards greater participation by women and better representation of their views. To this end, representatives of ten agencies that had little or no female representation were interviewed.[2] These agencies were selected as being of particular relevance in view of the major concerns expressed by women.

It was found that while concerns identified by women did come before the decisionmaking agencies on a small number of occasions, such concerns did not represent a major element

TABLE 14.1   Women's Representation on City of London Committees
According to Areas of Concern

	Total Committees	Committees With Women's Representation 1975
Education	5	5
Arts & Culture	4	4
Day Care/Child Care	2	2
Employment Opportunities	2	2
Social Services/Social Problems	6	5
Housing	7	5
Health Care	3	2
Community Matters	2	1
School Closures	2	1
Planning/City Growth/Development	11	5
Natural Environment	8	2
Safety/Security/Law	4	1
Parks/Recreation	3	1
Urban Services	7	1

of their work. This presumably confirmed to the satisfaction of almost all of the male representatives on these bodies that there was no need for greater representation of women's views, since it was not felt that they differed significantly from those of men. This is clearly not a satisfactory position from the point of view of the resolution of many of women's problems and concerns. A greater representation of women on these agencies would certainly ensure that these issues were at least discussed.

The opinions of the women representatives of agencies with little or no female membership were quite different from those expressed by the male members of the agencies. Both of the women aldermen felt that women's representation at the de-cisionmaking level was inadequate because so few women run for public office. It was agreed that women work too much in the background, and that their lack of participation at the de-cisionmaking level may be attributed in part to their financial status. One recommended solution was to increase women's involvement in decisionmaking at the local level by providing "grass-roots" opportunities within the neighborhood or com-munity.

Another woman on both the City of London Safety Sub-Committee and the Committee of Adjustment also felt that women were not adequately involved at decisionmaking levels and attributed this to the fact that too few women entered politics, although this was currently changing. It was again felt that women did not participate because they did not have the time or money to do so. Others criticized women for not taking an active role in municipal affairs and for not running for politi-cal office, both of which were attributed to apathy and lack of self-confidence.

The only divergent opinion among the women interviewed who had connections at city hall came from a representative of Pollution Probe (an active environmental pressure group) who was also a member of the Citizen's Waste Advisory Com-mittee. She did not perceive any variation of opinions between men and women with regard to their views on the environment and therefore felt that the male-female ratio in existence at the decisionmaking levels in areas concerning the environment was unimportant.

It was apparent from the responses of female staff members at city hall that they, too, were sensitive to the issues and concerns raised by the women's organizations and the individual women who were interviewed. The majority of women on the city hall staff wanted to see more female participation at the decisionmaking level. They particularly referred to the fact that women's groups that do become politically active make valuable contributions for the women of London. In contrast, the male staff on public committees, boards, and commissions did not perceive a significant difference between the views of men and women and so did not see the need for more female representation.

Conclusions

The concerns that have been identified and the relatively low level of participation in decisionmaking indicate clearly that women have a great deal of ground to make up if they wish to reshape the environment to better suit their needs and desires. Changes in economic patterns and living styles in Canadian cities have contributed to a much greater acceptance of the idea that women want to participate actively in shaping the environment in which they live. Women and women's organizations are taking more stands on issues critical to them, including the ones identified in this chapter, not only in order to achieve their own goals and independence, but also to improve the overall quality of life of the urban areas in which 80 percent of Canada's population now live.

There is undoubtedly a great necessity for women's needs and desires to be researched in more detail and to be made known to planners and decisionmakers. Much of this research and publicity will inevitably have to be undertaken by women themselves, or at the very least encouraged and instigated by women. A major conclusion of the MSUA study was that there must be much more citizen involvement in planning, allowing all individuals and groups (and especially women) to make effective input into the planning, and hence the decisionmaking, process.

There are many factors inhibiting greater involvement by

women in this process, and they can only be discussed briefly here. The traditional roles assigned to women effectively limit the opportunities for women's involvement in any outside activity. Responsibilities relating to the family and to children in particular are often cited as reasons for lack of involvement. The provision of adequate and suitable day-care facilities for children to free women of some of these responsibilities and to allow them the chance to take advantage of educational, employment, and political opportunities is probably the major need. Counselling, education, and retraining programs for women will also be necessary to give many of them the skills and knowledge to make the greater contributions they are capable of.

Efforts to ensure that women's concerns will be more strongly represented in local government are complicated by a number of factors, particularly in relation to the reluctance of many women's groups to become involved in political affairs. This is especially true in London where several influential groups have not taken a stand on women's views or represented them in the decisionmaking process. The fact that many organizations have few links or channels of communication with others hinders the flow of information and ideas and often slows action or results in divided and unsynchronized efforts. This lack of co-ordination between groups can also result in duplication of effort and waste of resources, as has often happened in London in the past. The stereotyping of many active women's organizations as "feminist" and "liberationist" has also undoubtedly reduced support from more conservative but active and successful women.

Certain basic improvements in the situation are required before many of the above problems can be overcome. Dissemination of information concerning city government, women's organizations and projects, and reference materials is clearly needed. A central reference facility, easily accessible, would be a realistic solution, accompanied by a general information-oriented newsletter or other publication. Greater efforts need to be made to persuade women to run for public office and to apply for citizen appointments. Impetus could come from women's organizations; other local interest groups could also provide a base from which women could gain experience and be further encouraged to become part of the city's decision-making process. This integration could be assisted if formal recognition and greater representation were given to women's organizations on more city committees and boards.

Until the current low level of participation can be raised to equal the high level of interest and concern expressed by women in the urban environment, women's views will not be expressed as clearly or as strongly as they might, and action will be slow in coming.

Notes

1. London, Ontario, is Canada's tenth largest city, with a population of almost 244,000, situated midway between Toronto and Windsor-Detroit. This university city has relatively little heavy industrial development and emphasizes retail, insurance, and auxiliary services for the large rural hinterland of southwestern Ontario.

2. Interviewed were the Streets, Traffic and Transportation Committee; London-Middlesex District Health Unit; Public Utilities Commission; Joint Committee to Study Student Pedestrian Safety; Technical Advisory Committee for the London Urban Transportation Committee; Planning Board; London Transportation Commission; Committee for the Development and Use of Community Facilities; Boulevard Parking Sub-Committee; and the Conservation and Valley Advisory Committee.

References

Anonymous, *People's Needs Index.* London, 1974.

Butler, R. W., and S. E. Phillips, *Women's Concerns About the Quality of Life in London, Ontario.* London: Department of Geography, University of Western Ontario, 1975.

City of London. *Municipal Year Book.* London, 1975.

Family and Children's Services of London and Middlesex. *Social Profiles of the Twenty-One Planning Districts in the City of London.* 1972.

Ministry of State for Urban Affairs (MSUA). *Metropolitan Canada, Women's Views of Urban Problems.* Ottawa: MSUA, 1975.

Part 4

Women as Environmental Activists

Introduction

Rebecca Peterson

Part 4 contains chapters illustrating situations where women have played central roles in the creation of new environments designed for use by women. As we suggested in the general introduction, it is difficult to assemble examples of work of this kind since the women who are developing innovative environments seldom have the time to write about the process. The chapters in this section represent a substantial shift in focus from those in Part 3. There, the focus was on institutional barriers to change; the focus here is on cases where women's needs for new environments have been identified, with women as active participants in that process, and where change has actually occurred.

Sheila de Bretteville's chapter reviews four years of the development of the Los Angeles Woman's Building, a public space created to house woman's culture. The chapter traces historical precedents in the feminist wave of the late nineteenth and early twentieth centuries and compares them to the spaces of the 1960s and 1970s feminist movement. The Women's Building has already weathered a major change of physical space, since the original space was sold and the facilities had to be relocated. De Bretteville compares the advantages and disadvantages of the original space and the present space, as well as making projections about possible future needs for housing the groups that are identified with the building. The number and variety of groups that occupy or have occupied space in the building has created special management problems. Her chapter addresses the symbolic requirements of the building as well as the strictly spatial needs identified by these groups. As with most innovative women's groups, the Woman's Building faces continual funding crises. The other chapters in Part 4 clearly reinforce the theme of women's lack of financial resources.

Anne Cools' chapter also addresses the issue of funding for an innovative women's environment. Cools describes Women in Transition, a female-conceptualized and administered environment for women in marital transition. The clientele of this woman-created space face the disruption of a marriage, a shift from dependent to sole-support parent, and many other problems. Many times this includes violence in the home environment and with immigrant women, language problems and problems of isolation from their community. Cools describes how Women in Transition differs radically from the "normal" response of social services created by general welfare policy and procedures. The innovative aspects of Women in Transition include participation of residents in administering the environment, control by women staff and administration, concern with counselling as well as meeting basic needs for shelter, and direct responsiveness to the special needs of women.

The women who leave an environment such as Women in Transition must then find suitable housing to meet their needs as heads of single-parent households. Mary Soper's contribution presents a design for single-parent housing that was developed by a women's group that participated in the planning of Le Breton Flats, an urban development project in Ottawa, Canada. This design includes a two-stage housing model incorporating a transitional complex and long-term housing solutions for single parents. The design included units for single young and elderly people who might have needs for interaction with single parents. The chapter describes and evaluates the planning process and the outcome, which included finally economic constraints that prevented the actual building of the complex!

We do not want to underestimate the contribution that these kinds of innovations are making toward changing women's role in creating environments, but some things in these chapters are obvious. First of all, they all refer to innovations in small-scale environments. This is illustrative of the tendency for women to operate easily at the small scale. There are some in-

instances where women are moving into change efforts at the wider urban scale; however, it seems that the next step that women are trying to take is to link promising small-scale changes like the ones discussed here with the changes that are required in environmental decisionmaking institutions like those that were discussed in Part 3. It is this linking of innovations at the middle level of societal change that holds the most promise and the greatest challenge for women who are working toward the transformation of our environments and the creation of new space for women.

15

The Los Angeles Woman's Building:
A Public Center for Woman's Culture

Sheila Levrant de Bretteville

The Woman's Building in Los Angeles is a setting for the discovery, creation, and presentation of woman's culture. Its existence expresses a mutually supportive relationship with a participating public. The visual and physical forms of the building and the activities it houses are tangible evidence of a community informed by women's history and are appropriate to their contemporary needs and desires for the future.

As an alternative physical context, the Woman's Building is strategically placed between the private house, in which woman's culture was confined and isolated, and the professional system that devalues and renders it dysfunctional. As a public center, the Woman's Building extends woman's culture, sharing it with a large constituency. Its existence and persistence validate women's actions in the world from a base of mutual support and communitarian values.

This chapter considers the four years of the Woman's Building's existence, during which it has generated a wide variety of private and collective enterprises: woman's art, woman's words, woman's music, and woman's social forms. The chapter deals particularly with the role of the physical environments in which the Woman's Building has been housed: first in a two-story, unused art school building and then in a three-story warehouse. During this time the Woman's Building has been the locus of national conferences, local workshops, and classes attended by people from throughout the United States and abroad, joyous celebrations, organizations of protest, accidental and planned conversations, and occasional and continued involvement by individuals and groups. This chapter further considers the process that set up and maintained the women's environment encompassing these activities, the possibilities for its survival, and its future role.

Some Precedents

The first wave of active feminism in the late nineteenth and early twentieth centuries provided several precedents for the Woman's Building's goals, activities, and physical presence, as well as its name. In the space between domestic and business life many nineteenth-century women's groups extended the cooperative, caring, and socially responsible modes that were limited and isolated within the private home and provided themselves with alternative physical environments to house their shared activities. Despite the differences in political orientation, the collective kitchens of the Cooperative Housekeeping Movement, the urban Settlement Houses and Women's Clubs, as well as the Woman's Building at the 1893 Columbian Exposition in Chicago, are nineteenth-century structures that the Los Angeles Woman's Building can claim as its historical roots.[1]

The second wave of feminism in the 1960s and 1970s has gathered women together again to focus upon many of the same needs for discovering and sharing personal, professional, and political experience and information. Essentially three types of physical space have been utilized for this feminist activity: living rooms, kitchens, and studios in private residences; storefronts and offices in commercial buildings; and classrooms and studios in educational institutions. The attributes of many of these physical structures within which the provisional and isolated activities have taken place often contradicted newly discovered feminist attitudes.

Few women's groups in Los Angeles were neighborhood based; many were composed of women who came from all over the city to weekly meetings held in each other's homes. The private home or studio provided a setting for consciousness raising that aided the bonding process, and the intimate connection women found in these small groups was enhanced by the personal as well as the shared cultural attributes of private space. But when some groups became committed to working together, providing services and information as self-supporting, rather than after-hours activities, they found a need for different kinds of public rather than private space.

Identification of Need and Search Process

The Feminist Studio Workshop was among those growing nodes of feminist activity that moved from borrowed space to a space of its own. In the winter of 1973, Arlene Raven (an art historian), Judy Chicago (an artist), and I (a designer) formed an educational nonprofit corporation—Feminist Studio Workshop Inc. The purpose was to create an independent environment in which women in the arts could work with us, combining an exploration of themselves as women in society and the production of expressive forms that could be created from this process. We had previously initiated and nurtured the Feminist Art Program in the School of Art and the Women's Design Program in the School of Design at the California Institute of the Arts and had become acutely aware of the ways in which this male, hierarchical organizational setting affected the value and content of the work.

The first expression of our alternative environment was a brochure that announced the creation of a new working context: the Feminist Studio Workshop (FSW). The name and the brochure gave form to our values and goals before we had actually begun to determine the physical expression of the FSW in terms of place.[2] Our model was to create a studio/gallery, insular during the personal exploratory process, but opened periodically to the public for exhibitions, performances, lectures, and discussions.

When thirty-two women arrived from all over the United States to become the first members of the Feminist Studio Workshop, we met in a private space (my home) while we negotiated with the California Institute of the Arts to lease the vacant Chouinard Art School building at Grandview. We proposed to Cal Arts that they lease it to us since we had the commitment of five existing women's groups and businesses and had

encouraged the creation of three more who had chosen appropriate spaces and rents. The commitment of these groups made
the acquisition of the building possible despite the absence of
any initial capital from the Feminist Studio Workshop. The
possibility of a larger feminist and physical context for our
workshop, the growth of the women artists' movement, as well
as the growing number of women's groups offering services to
the public effectively changed the prospective use of the building from a focus on individual artists to use by a larger community.[3]

Physical Environment of the Grandview Site

The goals of the Woman's Building had been to provide an
environment that would allow the potential mixing of users in
different spaces, foster communications between various
women's groups and their constituencies, and provide a sense
of the abundance and vitality of women's collective work.

The grand opening in November 1973 brought together
4,000 people; each group had attracted its own constituency
who intermingled in the courtyard and on the stairways, and
squeezed through corridors to see what was going on elsewhere
in the building. The Woman's Building had effectively brought
together members of the art community, the feminist community, and old students who had used the building during its
Chouinard life. Friends, family, associates, and acquaintances
of all who participated, as well as those who had heard about it
through the media, were effectively brought together in a way
that only the sharing of physical space can accomplish. A review in the *Los Angeles Times* (May 3, 1974) announced
"contemporary art continues lively in the cheerful, active
ambience of the Woman's Building . . . exhibitions are squirreled
into every corner." The building gave breadth to our image and
ambition, extending and often overextending our energies.

The physical design of the first Los Angeles Woman's Building tended to encourage all possibilities, as well as to reinforce
our difficulties. The building's space was organized into two
stories of discreet units entered off a hallway that lined a courtyard. The spaces with windows and doors onto the courtyard

allowed users to know of other activities, and opened the possibility of mixing. On the other hand, features of the building
encouraged privatization and the isolation of groups from one
another. The entrance corridor hid the existence of the shared
space—the courtyard—further limiting the understanding of
the overall organization of space, and contributing to the diminution of the sense of a series of parts contributing to a larger
whole.

We had formed the Woman's Building by joining together
with other groups of women performing services in diverse parts
of Los Angeles. Within each of these smaller groups, decisionmaking and the taking of responsibility for work was equalized.
We wanted to see ourselves as a collective of organized women
trying not to repeat the alienating hierarchical organizational
structures of the various institutions within which we had spent
our working lives. Looking for a nonhierarchical large-group
model, we chose the town-meeting format for the airing of ideas,
goals, and grievances. It was our hope that this large-group context could accommodate the need for program development
and enactment and that the equal sharing of joint work could
be decided and dispensed in this way.

Although the legal responsibility for the building was that of
the Feminist Studio Workshop Inc., upon the appropriation of
the Chouinard building we created a tenants union named the
Board of Lady Managers, after the governing body of the 1893
Woman's Building. However, it was clear from early on that the
amount of participation in decisionmaking varied greatly. The
groups in the building generally planned activities that took
place only within their own space. Most residents had difficulty
realizing that "The Woman's Building" *was* its participant group
and that there was no one else to take care of the social, economic, and physical context.

In the first year at the Woman's Building feelings of trust and
an awareness of the potential of our community were created.
Cleaning the building, readying the walls for exhibitions, concerts, performances, and autograph parties built a participating
public who became progressively more accustomed to coming
to the Woman's Building. In particular, the Feminist Studio
Workshop women grew in pride and strength seeing projects

actualized in this new alternative context at a scale more common to nineteenth-century feminist activity.

By the fall of 1973, the FSW had changed. Some groups and individuals left. Judy Chicago withdrew to do her own work, starting a large art project in her home/studio. Arlene Raven and I placed more of our creative and professional energy into the Woman's Building although we continued to give lectures and to contribute to feminist art programs in other institutions outside Los Angeles. Also during this period, a nucleus of people who became the collective teaching staff of FSW began to coalesce. We left Cal Arts, bringing colleagues with us: Deena Metzger (a poet and novelist); Ruth Iskin (an art historian); Suzanne Lacey (a performance artist); and Helen Alm Roth (a printer and graphic artist). This group of feminist artists and teachers have remained the collective teaching staff of FSW.

The second year at the Grandview site was an extraordinarily expansive year. We initiated an extension program of classes and workshops involving new students and teachers, and as part of the spring break, a series of national conferences in design, writing, performance, and film video were held. It was the students and staff of the FSW who most often took the leadership and gave form to these and other expressions of the Woman's Building. When a tenant group left and while another was being found, the creative and committed energy of FSW members filled the gap.

The experience of this women's community as a context for work enhanced the creative energies of most members of the FSW. We began to share what we were doing by giving lectures, organizing exhibitions, and running educational workshops. Within the Woman's Building and in educational and professional institutions throughout the United States we made the attitudes, processes, and work of the Woman's Building known.

This public description and analysis of our work resulted in a better understanding and communication of woman's culture. Our tone was "conversational" (Deena Metzger), the function of our art was "to raise consciousness, invite dialogue, and transform culture" (Arlene Raven). I called our process "the

gentle art of mutual aid," a phrase taken from an early article
on female involvement in urban reforms.[4]

Development of Strains

Over time, there was a growing demand for use of the Woman's
Building both by local people and by touring shows. Due to
heightened consciousness, increased need and sense of cooperation, and the publicity given to the Woman's Building, local
people, as well as those visiting Los Angeles, began to contact
the Woman's Building to schedule performances. Attendance
at the monthly exhibitions, as well as at the lectures, rallies,
dances, and autograph parties provided a regular indication of
the continued involvement of a growing participatory community.

As demands on the Woman's Building increased, strains also
began to be felt. Growing demands for the use of the building
began to tax our administrative capacity, and the increasing
use of the building for social functions like dances raised questions about the educational and feminist goals of the organization. Attempts to share leadership among groups involved in the
operation of the building had not been entirely successful and
had created problems of cohesion. At the same time, turnover
among tenants required vast amounts of energy to find replace-
ments and integrate them into the community. However, by
far the greatest strains were created by poverty; despite a large
building and an extensive program, the Woman's Building was
largely sustained on feminist energy and had no continuing
sources of funding. The imminent sale of the building intensified some of the problems.

Taking our activities out of one building and moving them to
another forced us to confront the problems created by our high-
risk entrepreneurial style, which was based on vision, graphic
expression, physical manifestation, and public participation.
If we were to continue, we needed a thorough understanding
of our economic position, greater sharing of the responsibilities
(and ambiguities) of leadership, and increased public involvement in our activities.

During the eight months of searching for a new home, the physical and economic situation at the Woman's Building remained ambiguous. Several component groups dissolved or withdrew, stating reasons ranging from an inability to attract customers due to our location (the Grandview site was in a busy working-class neighborhood on the east side of town) to political, professional, or personal differences within the particular group. While we had originally been able to pay the monthly rent out of the cumulative sum paid by the residents, the loss of groups made it necessary to search more actively for individuals and groups who wished to perform, read, rally, or celebrate.

In an effort to continue to exist within these contradictions, we incorporated into the search the requirements of all the groups and individuals that had participated in the first two years of the Woman's Building. Most women assumed that we would find a building with all of the advantages and none of the disadvantages of the first and with all the newly articulated needs fulfilled. However, our work and optimistic visions were identified with the first spatial environment we had renovated and used for two years. Few women were able to envision the Woman's Building program housed in other spaces.

The spatial requirements we defined reflected our experience at the Grandview site. We wanted comparable square footage, spaces that could accommodate the types of activities we had developed. We needed public performance space, since it had been the major source of rental fees for concerts, performances, and dances at the Grandview site, despite the lack of professional lighting, seating, and sound equipment. The commercial operations within the Woman's Building—Sisterhood Bookstore, Womantours Travel Agency—needed easy street access, preferably on the first floor. The Woman's Graphic Center also needed space on the ground floor to accommodate heavy presses and paper stock. Office space was required for the administrative functions of the building, as well as for the resident professional services provided by individual therapists and attorneys who wished to continue to locate their offices in the Woman's Building. Appropriate spaces for a cafe, exhibitions, and classes were also needed.

The symbolic requirements had become clearer also. Our space could not be private if we were to be seen as an effective participant in the public sphere. The building would have to be a discernible unit, not embedded in other structures that could limit the value or scope of our work. If those female attributes—designated in and generally relegated to the home, such as caring and mutually supportive relationships—were to be valued as appropriate to professional work, then we could not tuck the space away again in a residential neighborhood. It would have to be accessible to as broad a public as could be found in a city in which neighborhoods tend to be homogeneous by race, economic status, and often political and professional affiliation.

We looked at automobile showrooms and body shops, churches, fire stations, and small factories. We found absolutely nothing we could afford until June 1974, the deadline for our departure from the Grandview site, when a building was found that fulfilled more than a couple of our requirements, while adapting to our economic constraints. Despite its limitations, we responded to this building's potential and as officers of Women's Community Inc., Arlene Raven and I signed a five-year lease agreeing to pay $1,000 a month in rent.

The Spring Street Building

The difficulties associated with the move threatened to destroy our young institution, and while the Spring Street building offered a home and some possibilities, it also had several severe drawbacks. The main positive characteristic was cost—we were getting 18,000 square feet of space for 5.5 cents a square foot, when previously we had seen no building for under 11.0 cents a square foot. (At the Grandview site we had paid only 3.5 cents a square foot!)

The Spring Street building was a three-story red brick structure, easily discernible as a unit. It had originally been designed as the administrative offices of the Standard Oil Company of California in the 1920s, and had been converted into a warehouse in the forties. Virtually all of the marble had been ripped off the floors and the internal walls had been removed. The central core had originally been illuminated by natural light from a skylight in the center of the roof, but the skylight had since been filled in.

We had, therefore, three floors of undifferentiated space—except for regular steel and wood columns and wooden floors. The ten-foot ceilings, an elevator, and particularly the natural light that flooded the space from the many large windows on two sides of the building fulfilled some practical and inspirational needs. So, the actual building drew few negative responses, although the facade was somewhat formidable, and there was no easy open-air access.[5]

The location of the building, however, brought mostly negative comment. Although we were to be between diverse ethnic groups, creating the possibility of new participants from groups not previously involved in building activities, the immediate neighborhood was industrial. There were active areas nearby—the old city center, Chinatown, Little Tokyo, and a Mexican-American community—but our street was generally unfrequented, and the unfamiliarity of the site promised to make the building difficult to find. The seeming isolation could be misconstrued to mean that contact and interrelationships were not wanted, cutting the community in the building off from continued relationships with a large participating public and threatening the business aspects of the building.

The Creation of the New Building

In four months over 2,500 people helped to prepare the physical space for our use and to repair the emotional disorientation caused by the difficulties in finding and accepting our new home. To rebuild our community and restore our optimistic spirit, the design and reconstruction process had to be as inclusive as possible. When the third session of the Feminist Workshop Studio began in October 1975, its members had learned that barriers and growth are part of the process of creating a community through building its space. This shared participation in the process of cleaning, scraping, patching, sawing, hammering, and painting had recreated and enlarged our community. It is perhaps through this mass participation in the creation of the building that we have most completely actualized our intentions of bringing together people from all areas of the city, as well as people of all ages, classes, races, and ethnic origins. Each built a personal connection through seeing the impact of her work on the quality and use of the space, as well as by participating in the community of workers (see Figures 15.1 and 15.2).

Most of the space was prepared for multiple use by a variety of undetermined individuals and groups who could appropriate it for a specific period, maintaining their connection with the building, but not permanently owning the space. This was perhaps a more precarious model, demanding a more extensive outreach by our scant administrative staff, but it took account of the difficulties we had experienced when residents left or groups dissolved, and it had the potential for increasing the number of creators of events. Groups housed elsewhere would be able to participate in program development by planning events to take place in the building. We could define the types of activities in terms of physical requirements, such as number of possible participants, amount of noise, need for natural light, and so on. Few of our actual needs were so specific as

FIGURE 15.1 Three women doing renovations on the Los Angeles Woman's Building. (Maria Karras)

FIGURE 15.2 Sheila de Bretteville (right) works on drywalling at the Los
Angeles Woman's Building. (Maria Karras)

to limit the use of space to one group; for example, the psychologists and lawyers sublet their offices for night classes.

Those businesses that remained with the building throughout the transition period were extraordinarily patient, but they
now needed to move in and start earning money. The revenue-
producing spaces—the offices and store, as well as the performance space—had to be readied immediately. Needs for
privacy and security had been aroused by fears of the new
neighborhood and lack of experience with an open-plan design
or the process of defining one's space according to personal
values and needs. So spaces defined in response to individual
needs were more closed off from the public areas than they
might have been had there been more time for interaction,
discussion, and experience with open spaces in the new setting.

However, to accomplish our goals the design emphasized
open forms and generous circulation spaces as the settings for
conversation, protest, and celebration. Again, there was a
utopian model: spaces were provided in which to meander and
to encourage personal, professional, and cultural interaction

within which the attraction of new work and people might be encouraged.

The area along the periphery was to be an indoor street, bringing the public space inside and diminishing, perhaps, the separation between "inside" and "outside" that tradition and the building's formidable facade set up. Initial demands by individuals for "my" window, rather than any ideas about general office landscaping, provided the need for a solution that would make natural light part of the shared public environment. All new walls facing the windowed exterior walls were kept to eight-foot high partitions. Efforts were made to encourage windows in some of these walls to reinforce the street associations and to make it even more possible to know what was going on inside. It was hoped that keeping the density at the center of the building would facilitate perception of the larger physical unit and encourage exploration of its parts.

The first floor was the most defined by the specific needs of the tenants and by code requirements. The desire for openness and visibility was balanced by the need to provide security for tenants on the street level. The indoor street was created outside the more specific spaces within the eight-foot high partitions facing the exterior windowed walls. Originally we had hoped to enclose the bookstore with only a protective sliding grate that would be pulled back during business hours, but the bookstore seemed too vulnerable, and a solid wall was built instead. The space adjacent to the bookstore was rented for gallery space. It has sliding glass doors that make the exhibited work visible even when the gallery is closed.

On the second floor a full-height wall wraps around to define a gallery that includes a more private and protected internal space at the central core and a wide gallery hall that connects the two stairways. This gallery area is an enlargement of the already generous circulation spaces that have been designated gallery space, so that art work can be experienced on the way to and from anywhere else on the floor. Along the backbone wall facing the windowed exterior walls we constructed two small spaces (for 50 to 100 people) for classes and meetings, thinking of them as the first of a series of spaces to be built on this "quiet" floor. It now seems unlikely that we will build these other spaces, for we have become accustomed to the variety of events that can take place in the open space.

The third floor was left completely open, with no interruptions in the 6,000 square feet of skylit space. This level houses a cafe and a performance area. An inviting space for seated conversation and nourishment was created in the far corner, and by adding a windowed wall and glazed front doors, the space will become more like a restaurant in a public piazza, and will be separated from the sounds and activities coming from the adjacent large public space where theatrical performances are often scheduled.

The names of the spaces in the Woman's Building have been intentionally chosen to affect the way in which they are seen and used. Calling the circulation spaces on the second floor "Street Gallery" helped users to see this space as an indoor street, as well as encouraging performance and art work to be placed here. Naming the enlarged circulation space "Environmental Gallery" evoked inventive walk-through installations.

During our two years at the Grandview site the building had overlapped many of the activities of other women's centers. Providing services and a meeting place meant that we needed to make our specific orientation clearer, so we enlarged our self-definition and stressed our desire for inclusive participation. Knowing that people coming to the Woman's Building were unsure of what it was they were visiting, we made an explicit welcoming area, in which each visitor would be warmly greeted. Behind her the wall opens out and in large clear letters we state "The Woman's Building, a public center for woman's culture, welcomes you."

Future Fantasies: Expansion of the Woman's Building

A painful and productive tension exists between space built with ideal goals and the actual human processes and needs expressed by the users of the place. As the creators of the space are also included among the users, there is perhaps more potential for a synthesis between the material aspects of the Woman's Building and the organization within it.

The involvement of new people and audiences in the work

of the Woman's Building is itself expressive of the vitality of the Woman's Building and enough to encourage me to share some future fantasies. Just as the institution needs to keep reaching out and extending itself, so the physical space of the Woman's Building requires some extension.

With the growth of the Woman's Building it may become possible to build a roof garden that might extend the potential of the cafe to open-air eating and enjoyment of the view of Elysian Park, the trains, and Los Angeles—the city in which we work. Behind the Woman's Building on Spring Street, between it and the railroad tracks, is a plot of land at present used for junked cars: perhaps we could acquire it and cultivate a garden of flowers, fruits, and vegetables. Given our proximity to the railway we could bring a caboose from the track alongside the building to act as a place for children to play and work while their friends and parents were at the Woman's Building. Since this would exhaust our limited parking area, and because we need more parking space during large openings and performances, we might obtain the parking lot next door on a permanent basis.

We may bring more electricity into the building and up to the roof to light the building up at night, and also light the parking areas. We could fly balloons, kites, and in many inventive, non-energy-wasting ways reach out into the physical environment around our building and make our existence known. At present, our physical environment ends at the exterior walls, while the women within have created numerous outreach programs in other institutions around the country. We have not as yet put a large sign on the Woman's Building exterior—perhaps an expression of our self-confidence in affecting interior space, but not the external dominant culture. This internalized emphasis is contradictory to our purpose, and some of these fantasies are important steps in institutional self-actualization.

In 1980 our lease on the Spring Street site is up and we will have the choice of renewing the lease, getting a new building, or having a crisis similar to that of spring 1974. If we are in a similar economic position as at present, renewing the lease would be advantageous, saving the institution from the trauma of a second move. Also, I expect some of the more modest physical improvements will have been accomplished, making the present building more usable.

The possible revitalization of the downtown area may bring more people to our part of town, particularly if we can set up a minibus service from the nearby tourist and ethnic areas to the Woman's Building. By having a planning committee start at once, we might find a building that we could buy or get another for little or no rent through some municipal program— as yet undiscovered. But a crisis could easily develop, particularly if through an overextension of staff we continue to deal with problems on a day-to-day basis without any long-term planning.

The size of our institution in terms of the number of events and classes, as well as the ambitious goals we have for ourselves are backed up by personal commitment and energy, but little money. This poverty has an errosive effect that we try to counteract by broadening involvement. It is the people who are at the building daily and those who handle the books who know best our precarious financial position. It has been suggested that we hold only those functions that pay for themselves, but then we would not be fulfilling the real purpose of the Woman's Building. The accomplishment evident in the building's physical environment expresses the dignity and presence not associated with our inability to take care of ourselves without help.

Accomplishments of the Woman's Building

The accomplishments of the Woman's Building have been various; symbolically, it has expressed the vitality of feminism and served as a model for others; physically, it has united diverse aspects of the feminist community and provided opportunities for communication and a nucleus for organizing around specific issues.

A major strength of the Woman's Building as an actual environment is its symbol-making function. The sheer existence and persistence of an environment created for women by women is expressive of the vitality of the second wave of feminism. For women in other areas of the world, as well as for those who can visit and work at the building, it is an inspirational model. The Woman's Building has brought into focus the precarious existence of independent thought and action in daily public life. Understanding the Woman's Building as a cultural sign reaffirms an important function of the material world: that it can be given meaning and can nourish people in relation to the significance they have assigned it.

The larger physical environment of the Woman's Building—in comparison with the private home, studio, office, or storefront—has acted as a vehicle for physically uniting diverse elements of the women's community, bringing them together at the same time in the same place. In the mid-1970s fragmentation of women's interests have made this progressively more difficult, though recent threats to the ERA, gay rights, and racial integration may provide a new wave of combined activity. But generally there has been some focusing again on the differences between women as a result of socioeconomic class, sexual preference, profession, and life-style. This fragmentation and reghettoization cannot be halted by the sheer physical presence of the Woman's Building, but our very existence, stated goals, and inclusive accomplishments imply an alternative.

Despite the avowed intentions of the Woman's Building to involve a broad spectrum of women and the existence of an outreach program aimed at ethnic and disadvantaged women, the largest constituency consists of women in their early twenties to late thirties who are essentially homosocial and homosexual. In order to accept the Woman's Building as their place, all women have to see their own experience represented at the Woman's Building and be able to see others like themselves. To this end, members of the Feminist Studio Workshop have created numerous in-house, as well as outreach, programs that provide various groups with a familiar context in the hope of wider participation by members of diverse ethnic, economic, and political groups.

The orientation, accomplishments, and difficulties of this Woman's Building can provide a useful model for women elsewhere who might wish to create a new independent cultural and feminist institution. As the goal of this institution is to project women's culture into the public sphere, the more women can group together to locate and create this culture, the more likely we are to have a positive effect on society at large.

Notes

The Woman's Building and this chapter about its physical life could not exist without "the gentle art of mutual aid." In particular, I am grateful to Dolores Hayden for having suggested that a record of the Woman's Building be included in this volume, and for providing me with criticism and comfort while I put some of the work that has been such a major part of my life into words.

1. For more information on nineteenth-century activities, see Dolores Hayden, "Redesigning the Domestic Workplace," *Chrysalis* 1 (1977): 19–29.

2. For a discussion of feminist form language as expressed in built and graphic work, see S. L. de Bretteville, "A Reevaluation of the Design Arts from the Perspective of the Woman Designer," *Arts in Society* (spring/summer 1974):115–124.

3. For a discussion of the growth and accomplishments of the Los Angeles women artists' movement see Faith Widing, *By Our Own Hands* (Los Angeles: Double X, 1977).

4. Caroline Hunt, "Women's Public Work for the Home: An Ethical Substitute for Cooperative Housekeeping," *The Journal of Home Economics* 1, no. 3 (1909):574–576.

5. There were additional problems that threatened the use of this building that were encountered while getting building permits. Fees, requirements, and new laws are applied when a building's designated use is changed. Building, fire, and electrical inspectors have certified that the building is up to code for a manufacturing company, the registered designated use that we have continued. Since it is impossible to change it to "public" without getting a variance, future ownership seems to be ruled out.

16

Emergency Shelter: The Development of an Innovative Women's Environment

Anne Cools

This chapter recounts the outcome of a specific attempt to translate the working idea of a female environment into an area of vital social service need for women. Women in Transition is an innovative social service aimed at alleviating a most neglected area of social need. Women in Transition was specifically set up to house women and their children who have been forced to suddenly depart their homes and who must confront marital breakdown and single-support parenthood against the backdrop of immediate homelessness. In this context, Women in Transition is grounded in an understanding of the fact that married women frequently possess no personal income and are thus totally dependent on their husbands for financial support. In addition, all societal practices, customs, and laws presuppose such financial support to be the responsibility of the husband. This financial dependence poses problems enough while domestic relations remain harmonious. When they deteriorate and the marital situation sours, the matter of financial dependence becomes an insurmountable problem. When the marriage breakdown is accompanied by domestic violence and physical brutality on the part of the husband, the condition becomes pathological. Wife battery, threats, and the kidnapping of children are all too common incivilities accompanying marital breakdown. For the women involved this is a terrifying experience—no place to turn to, no money, no alternatives, much agony, and frightened children to support.

This is the primary area of need to which our services are directed. We are also concerned with the temporary housing needs of single-support mothers—another overlooked area of need that can involve (1) mothers and their children who suddenly find themselves homeless due to fire, eviction, etc., (2) mothers who have been released from total-care institutions (hospitals, psychiatric units, prisons, etc.) and who are about to be reunited with their children, (3) mothers and their children who have been abroad for some years and who wish to return to Canada, and (4) mothers moving from another province. There is no doubt that single-support mothers frequently need emergency and temporary accommodation and very often have no friends or relatives to call upon.

Women in Transition, like so many current Canadian innovative services, was initiated through a federal government Local Initiatives Program (LIP) grant. A group of young Toronto women opened our residence in February 1974, and following a rushed and disorganized inception, the community at large demonstrated a tremendous response to this kind of service. Clients came thick and fast; the demands for our services were overwhelming, so that when the LIP funds terminated in the fall of 1974 the staff agreed to continue to work on a full-time basis without pay while efforts were made to secure permanent support for the organization's continued operation and to change its status from that of a "project" to an established "agency."

With time we stabilized our operations, obtaining funds from the United Community Fund and increasing our allocations from Metro Social Services. In June 1975, we relocated from the initial rather dilapidated quarters to our present premises in the same inner-city neighborhood. The new house, which is rented from the property department of Metro Toronto, permitted us to increase our resident capacity, to improve the physical condition of our household, and to widen the range of services we are able to provide.

It has already been explained that women most often come to us in a distraught state. Their loneliness in these circumstances is beyond measure, and it is reinforced by their ignorance of their rights and of the services available to them in society at large. Quite often they are incapable of identifying their problems or of articulating their needs. Our services are designed to assist each particular woman in her own personal crisis. When categorized in social terms this implies the provision of food, shelter, counselling, referrals, day care, crisis intervention, and a variety of support services. We deliver these services in a highly individualized form, and most important of all, it is done in an atmosphere that is supportive, informal, and continuous. In a wider sense, the main service that we provide is to help close the gaps between existing social-service agencies. Since they are not at all integrated, our presence demands different forms of coordination in relation to individual residents. In this respect we are so innovative that nowhere is our role described in the funding criteria, in either the public or private sector.

We generally admit only women with children. We do admit an occasional woman without children who has child-related problems, such as being thrown out of her marital home and forced to leave the children behind. The essential criteria for admission is need, which is assessed in relation to the individual woman's situation. About one in five of the women entering Women in Transition comes as a result of some personal initiative—word of mouth, seeing our name in the telephone book— but the vast majority come as a result of a referral from some social agency (like the Children's Aid Society or Family Services), from other emergency houses, or through the police, Family Court, or other public agencies.

A resident's length of stay is a function of her individual circumstances. However, for "maritals" the maximum length of stay is four to six weeks and for "housings," two weeks. We try to make these decisions with a high degree of flexibility, discretion, and integrity. Women are allowed to stay a little longer if they are responding to the situation and look like they are pulling their lives together. The more they respond, the more we can do. The shelter provided is the base-line service; the real intent is to encourage the inhabitants to learn how to cope. Some women actually manage to reconstruct themselves during their stay; but six weeks is a very short period of time.

At present, Women in Transition operates on a very small scale. This scale element is crucial. Ultimately the only way any kind of institution can survive financially is to increase the scale of its operation—in our case to increase the number of residents housed. Our maximum is sixteen to eighteen persons, and it takes $17 a day to keep a person at Women in Transition. If by increasing the number of residents that figure can be reduced, the possibility of stability and permanence would be increased. Still, thirty people would be a maximum, since the whole direction of Women in Transition is associated with the humanity of its environment and with the transfer of that feeling to the residents so that there is concern among them for each other. Ideally, the house community is formed by a series of families functioning together as a single family.

Our residents come from all socioeconomic backgrounds. Contrary to general public opinion, wife battery seems to afflict all levels of society. However, the majority of our residents come from the lower middle class. They come from all parts of Toronto, with a few from other provinces and small towns in Ontario. Data collected at Women in Transition over the past year show that the typical resident is Canadian and in her mid-twenties. She comes to us as a result of marital crisis, accompanied by two children, having been referred to Women in Transition by personal contacts, social welfare agencies, or voluntary organizations. She is normally unemployed and may not have worked for over a year. Her previous employment will have been in labor or clerical occupations. Her present financial support will either be coming from her husband/partner's job or from some form of welfare payments. When she is admitted to Women in Transition she will often be penniless and very unlikely to have more than $25 in her purse. Her husband is probably also unemployed; his usual occupation will be in the labor or trades categories. Her relationship with her husband will have lasted several years, and previous separations are likely to have taken place. Almost all women entering due to marital crisis will have suffered battery and physical abuse from their husbands/partners.

We are dealing mainly with women who married young and never really interacted with the world: women who went from their mother's arms to their husband's arms. Under such circumstances, marriage sets up promises that it cannot always deliver. Our residents are women who have accepted those promises so completely that they have no independence in any area. Some do not know their way around the city or how to use public transportation. They have been quite isolated, almost imprisoned in their homes, having very little contact with the outside world or with persons other than their immediate nuclear family.

This sense of isolation is especially present among immigrant women who are cut off from even their women friends after they have left their husbands—cut adrift. Immigrant women make up one in three of the residents of the house. There is need for special services for these women, since at present their particular problems are not handled by the regular immigrant agencies. In this respect, our mandate is very open; unlike some other institutions, which operate under limiting legislation, our purpose is to assist women in marital crisis in a total sense.

While Women in Transition is administered by its staff, the residents play a crucial role. This is demonstrated in the organization and presentation of meals. Menu planning and the purchase of food are performed by the staff; the preparation of meals and the cooking are conducted by the residents in carefully organized rotations. Since our budget does not permit funds for hiring personnel for cleaning and cooking, our residents carry the responsibility for their own maintenance. We have observed that this responsibility is therapeutic for the residents, and in addition it alleviates feelings of charity.

After a six-week stay at Women in Transition, approximately a quarter of the women go back to their husbands, but most continue to live alone with their children and move into small apartments, attend job-retraining courses, and organize day-care services. For some, we know from the beginning they cannot be helped. There is always a tendency to invest energy in those who show signs of helping themselves, but who helps the real losers? They are up against a terrible problem; they have left their husbands and are cut adrift with no one to talk to. With these women we try to apply a humane approach, judging each on her own merits. The results are demonstrated by the fact that in 1977 around 70 percent of the residents were assessed by the staff to have related well to the community life of Women in Transition.

The maintenance and survival of this kind of operation involves the challenging of general welfare policy and procedures. But we have to continue to raise money to survive; every time we develop an association with a funding organization we have to develop the process from scratch. In addition we have to liaise with the local community and establish many other contacts, as well as run the house. We have not inherited a stable situation, but we continually have to try to stabilize our internal operations.

We have seven staff members who operate throughout the day on three shifts. Tasks are organized by attaching particular responsibilities to different shifts. If you want to build a framework that can outlast the presence of the current staff, you have to back off the belief held by many women's organizations that they should operate as a loose collective. We have to define and identify particular tasks and attach them to a particular shift so that if any one of the staff leaves, the person coming in can be trained into the process. This leads to specializing responsibilities—food purchasing, menus, linen, organization of staff development sessions, data collection, appliance maintenance, and so on. We had no models to follow, no consultants or experts in the field to tell us how to do these things. However, staff relations are harmonious, a necessary condition in such a totally comprehensive and intimate work situation. Limited funds prohibit the payment of the kinds of salaries professionally trained personnel demand. This seems to be characteristic of innovative services—the implication being that it is not trained personnel who innovate in social services.

First and foremost, Women in Transition is a female-conceptualized and -administered environment. It is run by women—they are in charge—and for me that is crucial, for the people we serve it is even more crucial. We have to confront daily the realization that most women are not challenging their oppression. Women who have even a semblance of awareness of the problem cannot comprehend the extent of the dependence, lack of skills, and emotional substance that we have to take as a given at Women in Transition.

This is the key issue, and it is most manifest in the male children, who begin by asking "who runs this house?" Then they refer to me as "that man," because I seem to have the power! For the women who come to Women in Transition, seeing other women with authority telling them "you can do it" is very helpful. They are facing the reality of being a woman in a new role as single parent. In this situation they will be discriminated against from the beginning (for example, in trying to find a place to live and finding how few landlords will accept women tenants). Working in an environment that is under women's control also has its effects on the staff. They are used to being in jobs where they have little responsibility in terms of the overall institution. The staff at Women in Transition have to confront that responsibility. They say "tell me what to do," but it is crucial that they learn to "do it" themselves and not wait to take orders.

The great problem in operating Women in Transition is money. Consistent funding comes from two sources: the municipality (Metro Social Services), through the General Welfare Assistance Act, which entitles everyone to food and shelter at the rate of $13 per day per person (however, they are not interested in funding our counselling services); and the United Way Appeal Fund, in which Women in Transition has recently been awarded membership. These sources provide the core funding; capital expenditure has to come from different sources. For things like equipment and furniture we have to raise funds independently from corporations and foundations. The survival of an innovative service is intertwined with dedication, commitment, and the endurance and energy of those involved in it. Places like Women in Transition survive because people put their blood and energy behind it.

Women in Transition is described in the social service system as an "innovative" agency. The term suggests initiative, creativity, and novelty. What then, are the innovative qualities about Women in Transition? Perhaps the primary fact is that it is directly addressed to the needs of women who must confront the trauma of marital breakdown, family violence, and single-support parenthood—alone and penniless. This is innovative because the social-service system has never been particularly concerned with the special needs of women; as a matter of fact, social services, like most other institutions, have often scoffed at the emotional desperation of women.

The second innovative aspect of Women in Transition's service is its explicit concern with the dependency of women. As a service, it insists on utilizing the energies of the clients themselves. In this regard, the notion is one of self-help and self-actualization. These notions are closely related to those of Maria Montessori. Her ideas of "altering the fields of learning" and "calling out the potential" of people have strongly influenced my approach to Women in Transition.

A third form of innovation associated with Women in Transition is demonstrated by its form of counselling. This is direct and open, insisting that the clients confront the nature of their situation. It is built around access to the staff twenty-four hours a day. In addition, since Women in Transition is a residential service, counselling can take place in an environment in which the woman feels comfortable. When we say that there should be feminist counselling, we are saying that there should be honesty, integrity, and compassion—values that often seem absent in society at large.

A final aspect of the innovative quality of Women in Transition is the fact that administration is carried out by a female staff; the authority is female, and female characteristics are exalted. I am dedicated to the belief that women have the potential to do things, but that it is necessary to unlock that potential. I am very concerned with the submissive nature of the female learning process. At Women in Transition, learning takes place outside the male control system, and here often for the first time the residents share their desperation, frustration, and fears with other women. It is the beginning of learning how to deal with them. It becomes increasingly evident that the potential of women is being unlocked, and in the same way that the innovative social service must penetrate the social-service system, so must female environments penetrate the urban environment—for its own good.

17

Housing for Single-Parent Families: A Women's Design

Mary Soper

The project described here represents a small but significant innovation in planning for women's housing needs. It demonstrates that women's own experiences and energies can be mobilized to define their special needs—in this case, the needs of women who are sole-support mothers. It further demonstrates that women with no professional design experience but with some access to outside experts can come up with a sophisticated design proposal for a housing complex supportive of the life-style of single-parent families.

This chapter outlines an experiment, supported by a federal government agency, to involve women in the planning of a federal demonstration housing project in Ottawa, Canada. It discusses the evaluation of women's environmental needs that was undertaken, and then describes, from concept to actual design, the development of a housing complex designed to suit a particular life-style group dominated by women. Finally, there is an evaluation of the project two years after the experiment began.

Background

In Canada, the National Capital Commission (NCC) is the federal body responsible for planning the National Capital Region, Ottawa-Hull. Recognizing the importance of the ideas represented by International Women's Year (1975), women employees for the NCC proposed several projects related to women and their environments in the National Capital Region.

A National Workshop on the "Concerns of Women in Shaping the Urban Environment" was initiated by the NCC and held in Ottawa in October 1975.[1] The workshop initiating committee expressed concern for involving women in planning and focusing on women as a distinct user group. The basis for discussions at the workshop was to be a collection of papers from across Canada describing various professional, political, and community workers' views on planning for and by women. The NCC hoped to contribute by reporting on an experiment in which women would be encouraged to participate in a planning process. The opportunity for this arose when the planning for a federal demonstration housing project in Ottawa began in May 1975.

The project, known as LeBreton Flats, was initiated jointly by NCC and the federal housing authority—Central Mortgage and Housing Corporation (CMHC). The project site was 400 acres of parkland in downtown Ottawa, situated less than a mile west of Parliament Hill, between older Ottawa neighborhoods and the Ottawa River. Previously the location of an older French neighborhood, the site had been cleared early in the 1960s for renewal, but it was never redeveloped. The broad objectives for the housing project were to develop housing that would suit a wide range of income and age groups, fit well with the surrounding established neighborhoods, and stay within existing housing regulations. The planning team for the project included officials from NCC, CMHC, Ottawa, Ottawa regional government, and the federal Department of Public Works, together with architectural, transportation, social planning, and marketing consultants. A citizens' committee consisting of representatives of neighboring community associations, special interest citizen groups, and other interested individuals was set up as an advisory body to the planning team.

The NCC Women's Workshop coordinators established the Women's Resource Group (WRG) to participate on the citizens' committee as an experiment to be discussed at the fall workshop. The WRG was to focus specifically on environmental needs of women, encourage the contribution of women's viewpoints to planning, and experiment with various participation approaches to achieve these goals. The members of the group were to be volunteers from the communities neighboring on LeBreton Flats. The author, employed by NCC, was assigned to the WRG for three months to initiate, monitor, and report on the experiences of the group. The report, which included recommendations to the NCC for the future of the WRG and its relevance for further encouragement of a special women's involvement in NCC planning, was prepared as a discussion paper for the National Workshop.[2]

Evaluation of Women's Housing Needs

Because time and resource constraints prohibited an investigation of the needs of women in all possible life-style alternatives, priority was assigned to groups most disadvantaged in the present housing market and to those life-style groups not served by present housing environments. Due to the large numbers of disadvantaged households in neighborhoods surrounding LeBreton, the WRG felt it was important to concentrate on the needs of those who wish to stay in a downtown location such as that offered by LeBreton Flats. For many households without a car, reliance on public transit increases the attraction of a central location close to job markets and a wide range of services. Further, low rents characteristic of older areas are the only option for the poorest households.

The group addressed the following questions: Do current living environments meet the needs of women's present life-styles? And if not, how can they be altered to do so? Social-service groups serving neighborhoods surrounding the project site were contacted.[3] Members of the service groups, along with other volunteers from the community, identified groups of women requiring special planning in terms of housing and specific issues and objectives for the planning team to address.

In the course of the discussions, the social-service groups voiced the following concerns about women's housing needs:

- the inadequacies of housing for single-parent families whose numbers are increasing every year and who dominate welfare case loads;
- the need for social acceptance of the single-parent family

as a legitimate life-style and the need for housing to suit
that life-style;

- the importance of the effects of physical and organizational environments (particularly housing) on life-styles;
- the possibility of using housing to improve the presently
unhealthy living environments of single-parent families;
- the need for women's analysis of their own life-styles based
on direct experience.

They concluded that, in the private market, a large number of
women are handicapped either by lack of mobility or by low
income and thus have little choice in housing. Women living
in public housing stressed that, despite a generally good physical
standard of publicly built or assisted housing, the women who
live there feel it fails to suit their needs in many basic ways.

The number of households headed by women has increased
dramatically in the past ten years. In Canada, the proportion
of households with female heads rose to 16.5 percent in 1971
from the 13 percent of 1961. If we look only at families with
one parent in 1971, we find that 80 percent have a female head.[4]
Since these households headed by women have, on the average,
lower incomes, fewer cars (if any), pay lower rents, and generally
have fewer household amenities,[5] it is apparent that families
headed by women may have special needs for urban services
that are not being met. Social-service groups are not able to
deal with their most basic problem—unemployment—since they
primarily offer counselling services. They have observed women
in crisis situations coping with the breakup of a marriage and
the consequent problems of adjusting to the limited housing
opportunities available to them at affordable rents. The list
of problems is endless: the boredom of no adult contact for
mothers at home with children; the usual lack of a car and its
mobility and convenience; the insecurity of renting and the lack
of control over their environment; the diverting of food money
to supplement rent payments; the unfavorable attitude of many
city areas toward single-parent families; lack of day care (thus
preventing mothers from seeking employment); insufficient
financial support for training in a job skill; the absence of a
father figure for the children; the necessity for many children

to play in hallways of apartment buildings; and so on. In general the women they see are lonely, dependent on welfare, feel they are treated as second-class citizens, and are not organized to voice their concerns.

In public housing projects, however, where the proportion of single-parent families is high within a small geographic area, many of these women have organized themselves in a fight for their survival and that of their children. The mutual support, characteristic of the community orientation in public housing, often enables these families to control, at least partially, their immediate environment. Their concern with the social viability of housing—meaning communities of similar families—often puts them at odds with planners who are seen as offering a catalogue of alternatives based on economic decisions and a policy of integration.

Meeting together through the Ottawa Tenants' Council, which represents public housing residents, a group of women developed a concept of their own way of life and needs as single parents and of what was lacking in the environment of the public housing project to meet these needs. Aline Akeson, a leader of this group, identified the goal of transferring the concept into a physical design that could be incorporated into the LeBreton Flats project. Because of this already existing initiative, the Women's Resource Group of the National Capital Commission decided to document the development of this concept of single-parent family housing and the success of its application to LeBreton Flats.

A Design for Single-Parent Family Housing

The women developed a concept of their own way of life as single parents, based on their housing needs at each stage in their transition from being members of a two-parent family to becoming the head of a single-parent family. The two phases of this process are reflected in their separate architectural solutions: the crisis and readjustment phase and the period of reassimilation into the community.

Translated into a physical design, the first phase would call for a Transitional Complex. Its components would include an "interval house" section having places for women to stay at the time of marriage breakup, offering physical protection, strong psychological and organizational support, and a place for mother and children to stay together. Also in the complex would be a women's center with facilities and staff to teach women and men about their potential role in society through films, discussions, and counselling, educating them in practical areas to increase their independence and decrease their vulnerability to sales ads and poor service. A crisis housing provision for "burnt out" families would also be included. In essence, a Transitional Complex would provide living accommodation for single-parent families during the process of learning new survival skills in the transformation of their lives from dependence to freedom.

As Anne Cools has indicated, in most Canadian cities only scattered efforts are made to aid women and children in crisis situations. Interval houses operate in older neighborhoods, surviving on shaky and insufficient financial support, working on the basis of self-help or "kitchen-table" counselling, and the demands on their services are overwhelming. These women saw the Transitional Complex as an environment that would be deliberately planned to be supportive and nurturant during a time of great trauma for the family unit.

Families ready for reassimilation into the community after a brief respite in an Interval House receive little support. Present public housing, with inadequate facilities and an institutional, ghettoized image, provides only the bare minimum—shelter. The object in the second phase is to provide an environment that would be supportive of single-parent families (whether the parent was male or female) "who have adjusted to their new independence." This environment would allow parents to practice learned skills and be independent with a renewed self-respect; provide reinforcement of societal acceptance of the single-parent family; and relate to the individual and not to a sex-stereotyped role. Due to the greater proportion of female-headed, single-parent families, this would probably be a female-dominated environment, but would in no way exclude males. In fact, males would be a necessary and integral part of the housing environment.

The concept of an improved life-style for single-parent

families included the development of a child-oriented atmosphere. The proposal addressed children's needs in a housing environment through a good mix of ages and life-styles in close proximity, a reduction in mundane work to free parents' time, a desirable balance between privacy and communal living, allowance for changes in life-styles through the years, and easy access to services for all members of households.

Although the environment was to be designed to support single-parent households, the women were conscious of the dangers of creating a ghetto. Thus, they decided that the complex should provide housing for some single people and elderly households since these groups might be complementary to single parents and provide other role models for the children.

This concept suggested a group of units of different types around a common area designed for specific uses. Some separation of family types was desirable to reduce potential conflicts between household types, while at the same time providing opportunities for contact. The solution was to separate types of households by level and location in the complex—with family households at the ground level giving easy access to play areas, elderly also near ground level but slightly separated from family units for quiet, and singles at higher levels. Shared entranceways, stairways, and facilities were designed to bring residents together in common areas.

The services of an architect were made available by the Social Planning Council Housing Committee to assist in translating the concept for single-parent family accommodation into a physical design. The complex developed in conjunction with architect Bill Latimer has space for thirty-two households including units for single-parent families, singles, and elderly, about half of them with ground access and parking at their private entrances (see Figures 17.1 and 17.2). The front of the building is street-oriented with facilities for other parking and service vehicles, while the back opens onto a recreation area and pedestrian walkway link to other complexes. Basement areas offer storage, cold-cellar, and workshop areas for residents.

In the complex, unit design is considered as important as the relationship between units. For example, bathroom facilities must be designed to aid a mother in washing her child's hair—

326

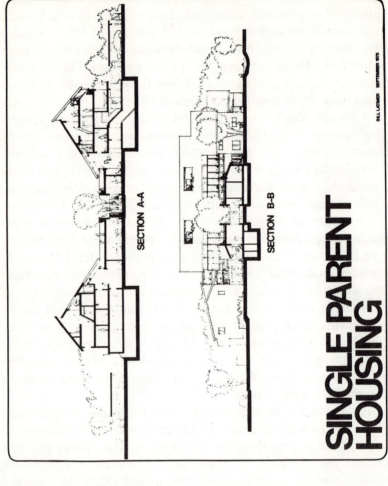

FIGURE 17.1 Single-parent housing designed by the Women's Resource Group (WRG) set up by the National Capital Commission, Ottawa, in association with Bill Latimer. These cross sections show the scale of the structures proposed, the location of the central space for shared facilities, and the distinctive living spaces for different household types located on each level. (By permission of the architect)

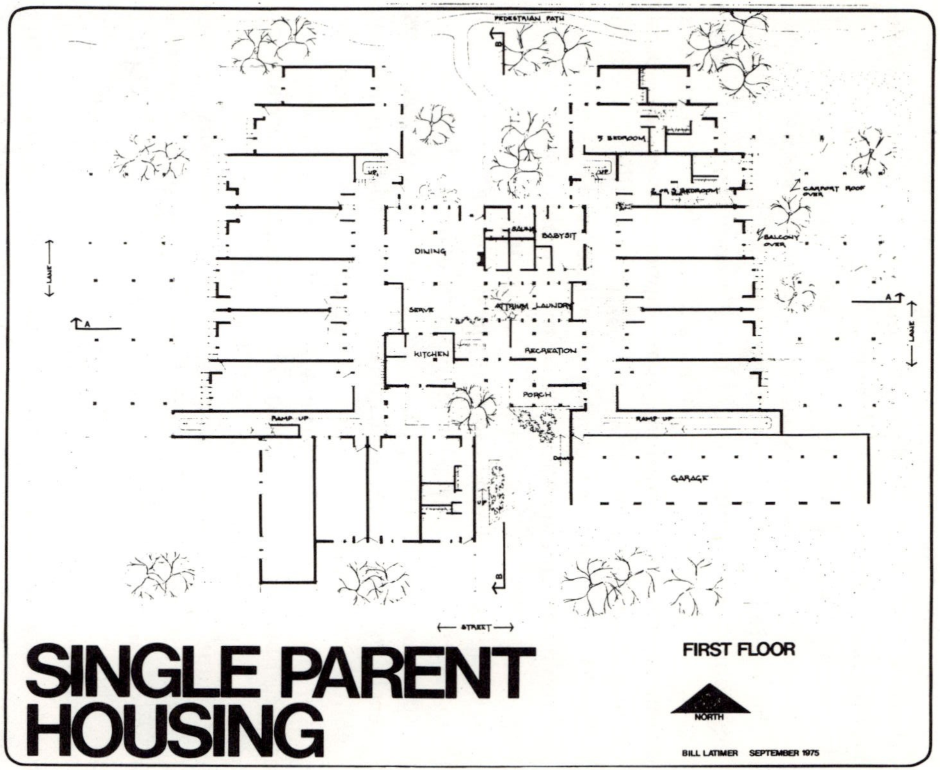

FIGURE 17.2 Single-parent housing designed by the WRG, Ottawa. The first floor plan shows the grouping of living aspects around centrally located communal facilities. (By permission of the architect)

a very frequent task. Also, in providing for the needs of single mothers or fathers, a bed-as-alcove room might be more suitable than the traditional master bedroom.

In the proposal, it was recognized that the management of the complex would be a crucial factor in its success. In particular, the operation of joint facilities such as day care, shared eating rooms, and laundry could provide employment for residents whose low-income position and families demanded a location nearby. In addition, many opportunities for social exchange could be available to adults traditionally isolated in the home. The degree of control each household would have over its own unit and the operation of the complex would greatly influence resident satisfaction with the housing.

The complex was planned so that physical design, technology, and management of shared facilities could be used to reduce time spent on menial tasks, fill in social and psychological gaps of present environments, and allow residents the opportunity to contribute usefully to their community. By relating the needs of different household types, mutual advantages would be possible. For example, a shared small cafeteria-café could supplement private kitchens—an asset for working mothers, those living alone, and elderly couples. A shared laundry would eliminate the necessity for each household to own expensive appliances and would reduce the problems of a mother coping with laundry and children simultaneously. Working and nonworking parents could benefit from neighboring singles, young or old, whose formal babysitting or casual surveillance of outdoor play spaces would lessen the pressure on each parent to continuously watch her children. Communal bathing facilities and saunas were seen as a way to promote socializing among households, expose children to a wider range of parent figures, and enable children to develop sensible images of the body. The designers also recognized that good design and management of the building's air circulation system would save the mother's personal energy by reducing unnecessary housework.

There are a number of features about the proposal that make it a unique and creative response to the housing needs of single-parent families: the encouragement of mutual support as provided by the inclusion of many similar families; the integration of elderly and single persons who have similar needs for shared facilities; the small scale of the project in contrast to traditional private and public developments; the variety of unit designs responding to specific life-styles; the development of the concept by those most familiar with the life-styles; attempts to support a life-style not yet fully accepted despite its growing numbers; the emphasis on social viability; the opportunity for residents to control more than immediate environments through management of common facilities; and the focus on a low-income group recognizing its domination by women.

Participation by Women

The experience of the WRG prompts some comments about the value of focusing on women as users and involving them as planners of housing environments. From this experience, recommendations can be made about involving women in planning their environments.

A poor understanding of present life-styles by designers, politicians, and developers has led to the current situation in which housing fails to suit a growing proportion of households. There is a lack of housing appropriate to those not fitting the middle-class, two-parent family model. Women head the largest proportion of these atypical households (including the poor, the one-parent family, the elderly, and the single) and they are in the best position to clearly identify the problem, its scope, and solution.

In the development of the design proposal, women who worked or lived with problems of unsuitable housing provided a valuable analysis of their own needs. They showed that one might greatly improve housing environments by first looking beyond the design of the unit to the interactions between residents and their relationships with the rest of the community. The crucial next step was bringing these people together with designers who could translate their ideas into physical design.

Often the most disadvantaged groups, having the least means to participate in the planning of their dwellings, suffer most from the misinterpretation of their life-styles by others. Low income, low mobility, and lack of day care prevent their involvement unless monetary compensation is available. Mothers who single-handedly manage a job and family rarely have time to attend regular discussions or pursue housing officials. At some point even those women who have participated actively in community associations must return to more pressing obligations at home.[6]

Other sources of experience, information, and motivation in the community are the people who work in social-service associations. From extensive observations and the personal experience of their members or clients, they have developed insights into the breadth and severity of the problems of different households. They also have the organizational techniques necessary to bring women into a participation process. It was this mechanism that helped to bring forward the concepts of single-parent families as developed by the public housing women and observed by the WRG. Unfortunately, not all types of women are served by such groups.

The WRG considered alternative models of organization for the involvement of many types of women in planning LeBreton. To reach out to women who could describe, analyze, and develop a concept of housing suited to their needs would be too large a job for volunteers. Without a financial commitment from a sponsoring agency it was impossible to set up a viable network of committed volunteers. At the least financial support was required for a paid organizer to coordinate wide-ranging participation. The continuity and resources of a paid organizer are necessary, particularly when the target group is handicapped by lack of financial support or mobility. Technical expertise is also essential if the analysis of problems is to be developed to the level of physical design. The group must work closely with the designer/planner at every stage to ensure that ideas are interpreted effectively and appropriate trade-offs made.

The full-time, paid position of citizen participation coordinator in the LeBreton project appeared to be a successful example of the sort of position considered a necessary basis for the WRG. The coordinator was to initiate a citizens' committee using her resources as a bilingual member of the community and to encourage individuals or groups who had an interest in the development of the project or its management. As the liaison between the planning team and the citizens' committee, she worked closely with both groups. Technical and financial resources provided by the employer and the planning team allowed for representation of those who could not participate directly. However, the citizens were well aware of the potential loyalty problems in the coordinator's position. In addition, public housing women expressed the necessity, in most cases, for their groups to be in opposition to (not cooperating with) the planning team in order to ensure effective participation in the planning process. This was at odds with the planning team's view of the role of a citizens' committee.

Conclusions

The WRG no longer exists, despite continuation of planning for the LeBreton Flats housing project. No NCC money or other backing was given to continue the group beyond the initial three months. Several women who worked with the group are still active on the citizens' committee but without a specific program of contacting community women. However, the Ottawa Tenants' Council is continuing its interest in the project and is conducting a study of the needs of public housing residents. Although many participants of the WRG were frustrated with what often seemed to be their lack of influence on the planning of LeBreton Flats, they experienced many realities of the planning process.

The plan for a complex proposed by the tenants' group was rejected by the planning team as being too expensive. A year-and-a-half of persistent and repeated exposure of the proposal on radio and television, to the Central Mortgage and Housing Corporation (the federal agency responsible for housing), and to Ontario Housing officials (the agency responsible for public housing) has produced little result. Meanwhile, some of the public housing tenants who worked on the proposal are forming a nonprofit corporation. Plans are underway to set up an advisory board to begin the project. The board would gradually be replaced by future residents as they become involved in the planning. An ongoing study would be conducted to observe the progress of children in the new environment. As yet the proposal needs many details of management and financing, but when the time comes to begin the building of LeBreton, the group hopes to be ready.

It is difficult to judge such a project on a traditional unit-cost basis as it includes more than just dwelling units. Above all, it may hold social advantages that are not always quantifiable but that are critically important in the lives of the single-parent families. The women's viewpoint served to bring into focus a prevalent female-dominated life-style, the needs of which are not being met by present housing. Crucial to meeting these needs is participation in the planning and design of housing by those who live and understand those life-styles.

Notes

1. N. Griffiths, *Report of the National Workshop on the Concerns of Women in Shaping the Urban Environment* (Ottawa: National Capital Commission, 1975).

2. M. F. Soper, "Report of the Women's Resource Group for LeBreton Flats," a paper prepared for the NCC National Workshop on the Concerns of Women in Shaping the Urban Environment (Ottawa, 1975).

3. These included Community Service Centre, Women's Resource Centre, Ottawa Tenants' Council, Social Planning Council, and day-care groups.

4. See Statistics Canada, *Census of Canada, 1971,* Catalogue 93–718, vol. II, pt. 2, Families, Table 51; *1966,* Catalogue 93–612, vol. 2, Households and Families, Table 79; *1961,* Catalogue 93–516, vol. II, pt. 1, Families, Table 73.

5. See, for example, Statistics Canada, *Census of Canada,* Catalogue 95–745; Table 2, Housing and Labour Force Characteristics by Census Tract for Ottawa-Hull, 1971; and Table 3, Income Distribution by Census tract for Ottawa-Hull, 1971.

6. See Novia Carter, *Volunteers: The Untapped Potential* (Ottawa: Canadian Council on Social Development, 1975).